MONTRÉAL

Forthcoming titles include

Malta • Tenerife • Thai Beaches and Islands
US Rockies • Vancouver

Forthcoming reference guides include

Personal Computers • Videogaming • Web Directory

Rough Guides online

www.roughguides.com

Rough Guide Credits

Text editor: Stephen Timblin
Series editor: Mark Ellingham
Production: Helen Prior and Michelle Draycott
Cartography: Melissa Baker
Proofreading: Russell Walton

Publishing Information

This first edition published July 2001
by Rough Guides Ltd,
62–70 Shorts Gardens, London WC2H 9AH

Distributed by the Penguin Group:
Penguin Books Ltd, 27 Wrights Lane, London W8 5TZ
Penguin Putnam, Inc. 375 Hudson Street, New York 10014, USA
Penguin Books Australia Ltd, 487 Maroondah Highway,
PO Box 257, Ringwood, Victoria 3134, Australia
Penguin Books Canada Ltd, 10 Alcorn Avenue,
Toronto, Ontario, Canada M4V 1E4
Penguin Books (NZ) Ltd,
182–190 Wairau Road, Auckland 10, New Zealand

Typeset in Bembo and Helvetica to an original design by Henry Iles.
Printed in Spain by Graphy Cems.

© Arabella Bowen and John Shandy Watson, 352p includes index
A catalogue record for this book is available from the British Library.

ISBN 1-85828-704-9

THE ROUGH GUIDE TO

MONTRÉAL

by Arabella Bowen
and John Shandy Watson

ROUGH
GUIDES

We set out to do something different when the first Rough Guide was published in 1982. Mark Ellingham, just out of university, was travelling in Greece. He brought along the popular guides of the day, but found they were all lacking in some way. They were either strong on ruins and museums but went on for pages without mentioning a beach or taverna. Or they were so conscious of the need to save money that they lost sight of Greece's cultural and historical significance. Also, none of the books told him anything about Greece's contemporary life – its politics, its culture, its people, and how they lived.

So with no job in prospect, Mark decided to write his own guidebook, one which aimed to provide practical information that was second to none, detailing the best beaches and the hottest clubs and restaurants, while also giving hard-hitting accounts of every sight, both famous and obscure, and providing up-to-the-minute information on contemporary culture. It was a guide that encouraged independent travellers to find the best of Greece, and was a great success, getting shortlisted for the Thomas Cook travel guide award, and encouraging Mark, along with three friends, to expand the series.

The Rough Guide list grew rapidly and the letters flooded in, indicating a much broader readership than had been anticipated, but one which uniformly appreciated the Rough Guide mix of practical detail and humour, irreverence and enthusiasm. Things haven't changed. The same four friends who began the series are still the caretakers of the Rough Guide mission today: to provide the most reliable, up-to-date and entertaining information to independent-minded travellers of all ages, on all budgets.

We now publish more than 150 titles and have offices in London and New York. The travel guides are written and researched by a dedicated team of more than 100 authors, based in Britain, Europe, the USA and Australia. We have also created a unique series of phrasebooks to accompany the travel series, along with an acclaimed series of music guides, and a best-selling pocket guide to the Internet and World Wide Web. We also publish comprehensive travel information on our Web site: www.roughguides.com

Help us update

We've gone to a lot of trouble to ensure that this Rough Guide to Montréal is as up-to-date and accurate as possible. However, things do change and any suggestions, comments or corrections are much appreciated, and we'll send a copy of the next edition (or any other Rough Guide if you prefer) for the best letters.

Please mark letters "Rough Guide Montréal Update" and send to:

Rough Guides, 62–70 Shorts Gardens, London WC2H 9AH, or
Rough Guides, 4th Floor, 345 Hudson St, New York NY, 10014.

Or send email to: mail@roughguides.co.uk
Online updates about this book can be found on
Rough Guides' Web site (see opposite)

The authors

Arabella Bowen moved to Montréal from her native Toronto in the mid-1990s to indulge her addiction to French language and culture. Settling in the Plateau before it was trendy, she went on to write a weekly column for the *Montreal Gazette*, freelance for a host of local and national print media, and contribute to the *Rough Guide to Canada*.

John Shandy Watson was born and raised in Canada and fell in love with Montréal while studying at McGill and Concordia universities. After stints in Berlin, Vienna and Vancouver, he landed in London where he now works as a freelance writer and editor. He has written a number of online city guides and contributed to the *Rough Guide to Canada*.

Acknowledgements

Arabella: Many thanks to Jean-François Perrier of Tourisme Montréal for opening doors, Heritage Montreal's extensive archives and Robert Klein's assistance and good humour in navigating them, and Fiona Malins for her enthusiastic and informative tour of the Golden Square Mile. Thanks too, go to Natasha, M-J, John, Stéfany, Denis, Mark and Dermod for their help and support. Very special thanks to the Rough Guide team, particularly my diligent and detailed editor Stephen Timblin, who saw the project through, and my partner, John Shandy Watson, for inviting me along on the ride.

John: A big thank you to Roselyne Hébert at Tourisme Québec, Jean-François Perrier at Tourisme Montréal and Dinu Bumbaru at Héritage Montréal, as well as Thu-Hoa Bui at Musée du Québec and Richard Séguin, Carole Turmel and François Leduc at Greater Québec Area Tourism and Convention Bureau. Thanks also to Richard Burnett, Thierry Giasson, Brett Shymanski, Kai Wood Mah, Patrick Vallée, Cory Garfinkel, Gaëtan Charlebois, Ahmar Husain and especially Darren Henriet, Angela Songui and Stephanie Halley for specific advice and whole-hearted support in Montréal; Pierre-Yves Legault and Robert Stewart in Québec City; Neil Chadwick, Nonke Beyer and Sophie Howard for taking care of me in London; and Mom and Dad. Heaps of thanks to Stephen Timblin and Andrew Rosenberg for turning our rambling sentences into punchy prose, to Don Bapst for guiding us through the early stages, to Melissa Baker for the terrific maps and to Arabella for being there throughout.

CONTENTS

Introduction   x

The Guide   1

1   Introducing the City   3

2   Viex-Montréal and the Vieux-Port   18

3   Downtown Montréal   37

4   Golden Square Mile   55

5   Mont Royal and the Plateau   67

6   Parc Olympique and Jardin Botanique   80

7   Parc Jean-Drapeau   91

8   Westmount and the Lachine Canal   98

Listings   107

9   Accommodation   109

10 Eating 125

11 Drinking 156

12 Nightlife 169

13 Performing arts and film 181

14 Shopping 194

15 Gay and Lesbian Montréal 214

16 Sports and outdoor activities 221

17 Kids' Montréal 229

18 Festivals 235

19 City directory 242

Out of the City 247

20 Québec City 249

21 Les Laurentides 278

22 Les Cantons-de-l'Est 287

Contexts 295

A brief history of Montréal 297

Books 308

French language and glossary 313

Index 318

MAP LIST

Québec City   257

Color maps at back of book

1 Southwest Québec

2 Montréal

3 Downtown and the Golden Square Mile

4 Vieux-Montréal

5 Mont Royal and the Plateau

6 Montréal Métro

Introduction

Montréal is by far Canada's most cosmopolitan city. Toronto may have the country's economic power and Vancouver its most majestic scenery, but the centuries-old marriage of English and French cultures that defines Montréal has given the city an allure and dynamic unique to North America – a captivating atmosphere that is admittedly hard to describe. Its ethnic make-up is in truth fairly diverse, what with plenty of Italians, Greeks, Eastern Europeans, Jews, Chinese and Portuguese putting down roots in various neighbourhoods over the last century. But ever since the French first flew the flag here back in the 1600s, the struggle for the city's soul has centred on – and largely set apart – its English and French factions.

As such Montréal has always been a pivotal player in the politics of Québec **separatism**, the tension between the two main linguistic groups having reached a searing low in the late 1960s, when the Front de Libération du Québec waged a terrorist campaign on the city as the province was undergoing a "francization" that would affect Montréal most of all. In the wake of legislation that enshrined French-language dominance in Québec, English-Quebecers fled in droves, tipping the nation's economic supremacy from Montréal to Toronto. After decades of linguistic dispute, though, a truce appears to have at last settled in, and nowadays it's hard to believe that only a few years ago a narrowly failed 1995 referendum on separation transformed the city into a pitched battlefield over linguistic and territorial rights. It seems virtually everyone can speak French, while the younger generation of Francophones also speak *l'anglais* – certainly a blessing for English-speaking visitors who should have no problem finding someone who speaks the language. The truce has also gone hand in hand with the city's economic resurgence, which sees Montréal at the fore of Canada's high-tech industry.

The duality of Montréal's social mix is also reflected in its urban make-up. Sandwiched between the banks of the **St Lawrence River** and the forested, trail-laced rise of **Mont Royal**, the heart of the city is an engaging melange of Old and New World aesthetics. Busy **downtown**, with its wide boulevards lined by sleek office towers and rambling shopping malls, is emblematic of a typical North American metropolis, while just to its south, **Vieux-Montréal** preserves the city's unmistakable French heritage in its layout of narrow, cobblestone streets and town squares anchored by the radiant **Basilique Notre-Dame**. Balancing these are traces of the city's greatest international moment, **Expo '67**, echoes of which remain on **Parc Jean-Drapeau**, the islands across from Vieux-Montréal that hosted the successful World Fair. A few kilometres east stands perhaps the city's greatest folly, the **Stade Olympique** built for the 1976 Olympics, its leaning tower overshadowing the expansive **Jardin Botanique**, second only to London's Kew Gardens.

Specific sights aside, it's the street-level vibe that makes Montréal such a great place to visit. Like the homegrown **Cirque du Soleil**, Montréal has a ceaseless – and contagious – energy that infuses its **café** and **lounge** culture, its exciting into-the-wee-hour **nightlife**, and the boisterous summer **festivals** that put everyone in a party mood.

Nowhere captures this free-spirited ethos better than **Plateau Mont-Royal**, the trendiest neighbourhood in town and effective meeting point of Montréal's founding and immigrant cultures. Here, the best restaurants, bars and clubs hum and groove along **boulevard St-Laurent**, the symbolic divide between the city's French and English communities, under the watchful gaze of the city's most prominent landmark, the **cross** atop Mont Royal that recalls Montréal's initial founding as a Catholic colony.

In some contrast, **Québec City**, around 250km east, seems immune to outside forces, its walled old town steadfastly embodying the province's French fact. Perched atop a promontory with a commanding view of the St Lawrence and laced with winding, cobblestone streets flanked by seventeenth- and eighteenth-century stone houses, it ranks as Québec's most romantic and beautifully situated city. Closer to Montréal, two other enchanting regions – the **Eastern Townships** (Les Cantons-de-l'Est) and the **Laurentian mountains** (Les Laurentides) – provide excellent getaways, along with top-notch skiing, away from the teeming city centre.

When to visit

Montréal's **climate** is one of extremes – bone chilling winter temperatures morph into sweaty summer highs with barely an iota of spring to ease the transition. Though tourist authorities are fond of minimizing the true extent of the city's winters, the season is in fact bitterly cold; temperatures often fall well below the zero mark and snowfalls don't dust the city – they bury it. Though a boon for avid skiers and snowboarders, the period between November and late April can be positively grim for everyone else. That said, if you're here during a cold snap, spending the afternoon tucked inside a cosy café is a wonderful antidote.

The transition from winter to summer passes almost unnoticed, and locals quickly replace their complaints about the cold to gripes about the humidity. The population seems to double come summer as the city's residents come out of hibernation; still, despite the heat and the crowds, late June through to early August is one of the best times to visit, thanks in part to a rotating cast of wild festivals. Likewise, Montréal can be simply glorious during the autumn months. Though it's cooler in the evenings, the days remain quite warm and, best of all, the changing leaves set the city ablaze with bursts of yellows, oranges and reds. Indeed, the season is perfect for hikers as the provincial parks resonate with colour, though traipsing up Mont Royal is just as splendid.

	C°		F°		RAINFALL	
	AVERAGE DAILY		AVERAGE DAILY		AVERAGE MONTHLY	
	MAX	MIN	MAX	MIN	MM	IN
Jan	-6	-15	22	5	63.3	2.5
Feb	-4	-14	24	8	56.4	2.2
March	2	-7	36	20	67.6	2.7
April	11	1	51	33	74.8	2.9
May	19	7	65	45	68.3	2.7
June	23	13	74	54	82.5	3.3
July	26	15	79	60	85.6	3.4
Aug	25	14	76	57	100.3	4.0
Sept	20	9	68	49	86.5	3.4
Oct	13	4	55	38	75.4	3.0
Nov	5	-2	41	28	93.4	3.7
Dec	-3	-11	27	12	85.6	3.4

THE GUIDE

1	Introducing the city	3
2	Vieux-Montréal and the Vieux-Port	18
3	Downtown Montréal	37
4	Golden Square Mile	55
5	Mont Royal and the Plateau	67
6	Parc Olympique and Jardin Botanique	80
7	Parc Jean-Drapeau	91
8	Westmount and the Lachine Canal	98

Introducing the city

The roughly triangular Île de Montréal, surrounded by the St Lawrence River to the south and east and the Rivière des Prairies to the northwest, is dominated by Mont Royal – known by everyone as the mountain. The city of Montréal wraps around this large hill, extending out to the island's edges. Fortunately for visitors, most attractions, restaurants and the city's lively nightlife scene are in the fairly compact area to the south and east of the mountain and easily explored on foot. Even the more distant attractions are accessible by a short bus or Métro journey.

Invariably, most first-time visitors head straight for **Vieux-Montréal**, the oldest part of the city, with the continent's finest collection of seventeenth- to nineteenth-century buildings lining the cobblestone streets between rue St-Antoine and rue de la Commune, bordering the St Lawrence River. Sights are clustered around a number of public spaces, and **Place d'Armes** dominated by the **Basilique Notre-Dame**, is the best place to start from. In the neighbouring streets are historic museums as well as the delicately steepled **Chapelle Notre-Dame-de-Bon-Secours** and the silver-domed **Marché Bonsecours**, one of the city's best known landmarks. Back to the southwest, excellent archeology and history museums give a good introduction to Montréal's three-and-a-half centuries of history, while running along the length of Vieux-Montréal, the reclaimed land of the **Vieux-Port** is lined with promenades, parks and a number of harbourfront attractions.

Between Vieux-Montréal and the mountain, you'll find Montréal's modern **downtown**, centred on the east–west artery **rue Ste-Catherine**, filled with a collection of department stores, hotels, restaurants and cinemas. On boulevard René-Lévesque, one block south, the cross-shaped **Place Ville Marie** towers over the city, sitting atop the shopping mall that began the **Underground City**'s network of pedestrian tunnels linking the Métro system to shopping centres, offices and cultural institutions. The foremost example of the latter is the complex of theatres that, along with the **Musée d'Art Contemporain de Montréal**, comprises **Place des Arts**, half a dozen blocks east of Place Ville Marie. The southern and eastern edges of downtown are marked respectively by the small yet bustling **Chinatown** and the bars and cafés of the **Quartier Latin**. A similar vibrant energy infuses the **Village**, the openly gay and lesbian district further east along rue Ste-Catherine.

The area code for the island of Montréal is ☎514.

The west end of downtown overlaps the **Golden Square Mile**, which clings to the southern slope of the mountain and is the historic enclave of Montréal's wealthy Anglophone elite. Their contributions include a number of sumptuous mansions and such public institutions as **McGill University** and the **Musée des Beaux-Arts** facing onto rue Sherbrooke, the premier address for upscale galleries and boutiques. By contrast, the **Plateau Mont-Royal** district on the mountain's eastern flank is more down-to-earth, with largely Francophone neighbourhoods to the east of chic **rue St-Denis**, and a panoply of ethnic businesses and trendy restaurants on and around **boulevard St-Laurent**, known as "The Main". Rising above downtown but best accessed from the Plateau, **Mont Royal** is the city's largest park, wound about with trails and terrific views over the city. The **Oratoire St-Joseph** and its massive dome tower above the western flank of the mountain, while to the north, the vast cemeteries give way to tony, Francophone **Outremont** and the Greek and Jewish communities of **Mile End**.

Some of Montréal's chief tourist attractions are a bit far from the centre, but remain easily accessed via the Métro. In the city's east end, the **Stade Olympique**, with its unique inclined tower, lies between the **Biodôme**, with four ecosystems under one roof, and the enormous **Jardin Botanique**. To the south, in the middle of the St Lawrence opposite the Vieux-Port, visitors and locals alike head to **Parc Jean–Drapeau**, consisting of **Île Ste-Hélène** and man-made **Île Notre-Dame,** for its green spaces, amusement park, casino and Grand Prix racing track. West of downtown is the staid Anglophone enclave of **Westmount**, while south of that and strung along the Lachine Canal are a few workaday communities, the most intriguing of which are **Pointe St-Charles**, **St-Henri** and, at the canal's end, **Lachine**.

For an introduction to Québec City, including details on arrival and getting around, see pp.249–253 in Chapter 20, "Québec City".

Arrival

With direct international **flights** from across Canada and the US, as well as many European cities, Montréal is an easy city to get to. A number of rail lines also converge on the city, bringing VIA Rail **trains** from the rest of Canada and Amtrak trains from the US. Orléans Express **buses** link the city with other Québec destinations, while a variety of companies handle trans-border routes. Both train and bus stations are right downtown and well integrated into the city's efficient public-transport system. Numerous **autoroutes** provide a relatively quick way to reach downtown, though access to the island via the Lafontaine tunnel and many bridges can create traffic bottlenecks at rush hour.

BY AIR

All flights on major airlines and some charter flights to the city touch down at **Aéroport de Montréal-Dorval** (☎394-7377 or 1-800/465-1213, ⓦ*www.admtl.com*), 25km west of downtown. The airport's layout is simple, with the domestic and international wings connected by a large concourse on the upstairs Departures level and separated by a long corridor on the ground-floor Arrivals, where currency exchange and car-rental desks are available outside the baggage-claim areas. ATMs are dotted throughout.

The cheapest way to get downtown is by **local bus**, a complicated journey you don't want to think about unless on an extremely tight budget. From outside the terminal catch #204 (2 hourly; Mon–Fri 6.15am–10.30pm, Sat 6.15am–12.30am, Sun 9.30am–12.30am; $2) to the Dorval bus and train station due south of the airport (check that the bus is going directly to the station – if it's on the outward trip from the station you'll get a lengthy tour of the suburbs). From there, switch to either one of the infrequent commuter trains downtown or bus #211 (or Métrobus #190 or #221 during rush hour) to Métro Lionel-Groulx, from where you can catch the orange or green line downtown. In theory, you can do the trip in an hour, but count on it taking at least ninety minutes. Instead, most visitors opt for the straightforward and luggage-friendly **Aérobus shuttle** (☎931-9002; 2–3 hourly, daily 7am–1am; tickets from the information counter in domestic Arrivals or the booth just outside the terminal between the domestic and international Arrivals), which drops passengers off at the downtown Aérobus Station (adjacent to the main rail station) and main bus station in 35 to 45 minutes. Included in the $11 fare ($19.75 return) are free minibuses that connect the Aérobus Station with 40 hotels in downtown, Vieux-Montréal and the Quartier Latin.

Taxis queue up outside Arrivals and will take you anywhere within the wider downtown area (from Vieux-Montréal to around avenue des Pins, between Atwater and Papineau) for a flat rate of $28; other destinations are metered.

A $10 Airport Improvement Fee is payable by cash or credit card for all departures from Dorval.

If you're travelling by charter flight, you may have the misfortune of arriving at **Aéroport de Montréal-Mirabel**, 53km north of the city. Originally designed to handle the city's international traffic, the lack of co-operation between the federal and provincial governments left the airport without the rail link that would have made it viable and it was eventually abandoned by the major carriers. The **Aérobus shuttle** ($18 single, $25 return) runs on an irregular schedule timed to most flights; otherwise a **taxi** will set you back about $70.

ARRIVAL: BY AIR

BY TRAIN

Montréal is one of the main passenger **rail** hubs in Canada, with **VIA Rail** trains (☎989-2626 or 1-888/842-7245, ⓦ*www.viarail.ca*) arriving from Toronto, Ottawa, Québec City and the Maritimes, as well as **Amtrak** trains (☎1-800/835-8725, ⓦ*www.amtrak.com*) from New York City and Washington DC. The main terminus is **Gare Centrale**, in the heart of downtown and linked to Métro Bonaventure and other Métro stations via the Underground City. Trains arriving from the west also stop at Dorval station.

BY BUS

One of the main modes of travel within the province of Québec is by **bus**, with **Orléans Express** handling services to Montréal from Québec City and the Gaspé area and a number of different carriers handling travel from other provinces and the US. The main terminus, **Station Centrale d'Autobus Montréal**, lies just east of the Quartier Latin at 505 boul de Maisonneuve E (☎842-2281), and connects directly with Métro Berri-UQAM. Buses from Québec City also stop at the Longueuil terminus on the South Shore, at the end of the yellow Métro line.

Allô-Stop provides a ridesharing service with
links to Montréal from other cities in Québec –
see Chapter 19, "City directory".

BY CAR

If you're coming to Montréal by **car**, you'll approach the city on one of the numerous *autoroutes* (motorways or expressways) that, outside of rush hours, provide speedy access into town. From the Ontario border, **Hwy 40** (stretches of which are known as the Route Trans-Canadienne and the Autoroute Métropolitaine) crosses the island through the city's northern suburbs, while **Hwy 20** more closely follows the southern shore, passing Dorval airport before turning into **Hwy 720** (Autoroute Ville-Marie) as it approaches downtown. From Québec City, 250km to the northeast, hwys 20 and 40 run along the south and north sides of the river, respectively. The former crosses to the island on the Pont Champlain, from where **Hwy 10** (Autoroute Bonaventure) leads directly downtown and **Hwy 15** splits off into the trench-like Autoroute Décarie, intersecting with Hwy 40 before passing north towards Mirabel and the Laurentian ski resorts. From the US, Interstate-87 from New York State continues across the border as Hwy 15, while I-89 and I-91 join up with Hwy 10 (Autoroute des Cantons de l'Est), both coinciding with Hwy 20 on the Pont Champlain crossing. The city's bridges are notorious bottlenecks, and it's worth listening to the radio traffic reports to see if Pont Victoria or Pont Jacques-Cartier may be less time-consuming options. In any event, care should be taken in planning out your route as signage is in French and often gives inadequate warning of an impending exit.

Information

The main tourist information office is the downtown **Centre Infotouriste** located in the Dominion Square Building facing Square Dorchester (daily: June to early Sept 7am–8pm; early Sept to May 9am–6pm; ☎873-2015 or

MONTRÉAL ON THE INTERNET

The Internet provides an excellent way of finding out every-thing from what's happening in Montréal's rapidly changing nightlife scene to the latest blockbuster exhibitions at the city's museums – if the homepage is in French, you can usually click through to an English version. We've listed Web sites through-out the guide, but below you'll find a few of the more helpful and interesting general sites on offer.

Direction Gay Québec ⓦ*www.directiongayquebec.com*
Divided into ladies and men's rooms, the city's best general gay site for English content has travel info and event listings supplementing news and features from the province and Canada as a whole.

Heavyweight Art Installation ⓦ*www.hvw8.com*
Site featuring the works of a popular Montréal urban art collec-tive, Heavyweight, which hold frequent public-art happenings produced at and inspired by live club events.

Montréal CAM ⓦ*www.montrealcam.com*
If you can't wait to see Montréal, check out this site for live Web-cam images taken from around the city.

Montrealplus ⓦ*www.english.montrealplus.ca*
This site features reviews on everything from local shops and

1-877/266-5687, ⓦ*www.bonjourquebec.com*). Run by Tourisme Québec, it has loads of brochures and informa-tion on Montréal sights (including free maps and the useful *Montréal Official Tourist Guide* booklet), and those of the rest of the province, making it an excellent stop if you're plan-ning to do some travelling outside the city. In addition, there's an accommodation service and a counter where pri-

galleries to the best bars, restaurants and clubs, along with a handy mapping device that locates venues for you.

MoreMontreal.com   Ⓦ *www.moremontreal.com*
Directory-style site with hundreds of links organized by category, along with a quick menu of popular Web sites and an opinionated e-guide to the city.

Place des Arts   Ⓦ *www.PdArts.com*
Montréal's primo cultural venue has a calendar of events and online booking here. Click on "Info Arts" for links to Québec-based performers' and companies' sites as well as festivals and venues.

StateThis!   Ⓦ *www.statethis.com*
Hip lifestyle Webzine with quarterly reports on the music, film and fashion scenes in Montréal.

Tourisme Montréal   Ⓦ *www.tourism-montreal.org*
The city tourist office's official site, with listings of sights, hotels, restaurants, entertainment and events.

Tourisme Québec   Ⓦ *www.bonjourquebec.com*
The official site of the province's tourist board is useful if you're intending to explore outside the city, with information on cities across the province and links to regional tourist-board sites.

vate companies offer currency exchange, car rental and city tours – most bus tours depart from directly in front of the office.

The city-run tourist office, the **Bureau d'information touristique de Vieux-Montréal**, is on the corner of Place Jacques-Cartier at 174 rue Notre-Dame E (mid-March to mid-June & early Sept to mid-Oct daily

9am–5pm; mid-June to early Sept daily 9am–7pm; mid-Oct to mid-March Thurs–Sun 9am–5pm; ⓦ*www.tourism-montreal.org*).

THE MEDIA

The city's main English daily, *The Montreal Gazette* (57¢ weekdays, $1.75 Saturday; ⓦ*www.montrealgazette.com*), has been keeping locals abreast of all the latest news for over two centuries and contains fairly comprehensive entertainment listings; watch out for special supplements tied to the starts of major festivals. Still, the best place to find out what's happening entertainment-wise are the free alternative weeklies – the two tabloid-size English papers, *Hour* (ⓦ*www.afterhour.com*) and the *Montreal Mirror* (ⓦ*www.montrealmirror.com*) are virtually indistinguishable in content from one another and you can pick them up all over town. Their French counterparts are *ici* and *Voir*, the most respected of the lot.

Despite the primacy of French in the city, there are three local English-language TV stations: CBC on channel 6, CFCF (CTV) on channel 12 and CKMI (Global) on channel 46. The main French channels are Radio-Canada (2), TVA (10), Télé-Québec (17) and Télévision Quatre-Saisons (35). On the radio, CBC One (88.5 FM) is the national broadcaster's flagship station, with programming focusing on news and commentary, while CBC Two (93.5) plays classical music. For rock, stick to the FM dial: CHOM (97.7 FM) and MIX 96 (96.9) are the best of a mediocre lot. Talk-radio stations are on AM frequencies – try CJAD (800 AM) to hear what has the local "angryphones" up in arms this week. Student-run CKUT (90.3 FM) has a hit-or-miss schedule of music and spoken word covering all genres.

PASSES

If you're planning to see a lot of museums while in Montréal, it's worth picking up a **Carte Musées Montréal** (Montréal Museums Pass), which gives you access to some 25 attractions, including the Musée des Beaux-Arts, the "Centre Canadien d'Architecture" and the Musée d'Archéologie, for $20. It's valid for two out of three consecutive days and you can buy it at any of the participating museums or either of the tourist information centres listed on pp.9 and 11. However, the main attractions east of downtown aren't included. Instead, you can see the Biodôme and Jardin Botanique with the **Nature Package** for $15.25, while the $22.50 **Get an Eyeful** pass adds on a trip up the Stade Olympique's tower.

Getting around

If you're not planning to stray too far from the city centre, you can easily get around in Montréal without a car. Certainly in Vieux-Montréal with its narrow streets and nightmarish parking, **walking** is your best bet. And although **public transport** is available only on the fringes of Vieux-Montréal, the Métro and buses offer a frequent and fairly speedy way for seeing the rest of the city. The system is run by the **STCUM** (Société de transport de la Communauté urbaine de Montréal; ☎288-6287, Ⓦ*www.stcum.qc.ca*), whose Web site and phone line can provide you with detailed journey information. Free maps of the Métro and bus network are also available at most stations – if they've run out, drop by the system's main information desk at Métro Berri-UQAM, opposite the turnstiles nearest to the Station Centrale d'Autobus exit. Another option is to rent a **bicycle** – a great way to get a feel for the city's many neighbourhoods, as well as to check out the industrial landscapes along the Lachine Canal.

For information on cycling and where to rent bicycles, see Chapter 16, "Sports and outdoor activities".

TOURS

There's a wide range of options for organized sightseeing in Montréal. For information on bus tours and cruises on the St Lawrence, the easiest thing is to compare what's on offer at the Centre Infotouriste (see p.9). More interesting, though, are the possibilities outlined below.

Walking tours

Guidatour

(☏844-4021 or 1-800/363-4021, ⓦwww.guidatour.qc.ca). Tours of Vieux-Montréal depart at 11am and 1.30pm from the front of Basilique Notre-Dame from late June to September. The ninety-minute tours focus on the history and architecture of the area and cost $11.50.

Heritage Montréal

(☏286-2662, ⓦwww.heritagemontreal.qc.ca). The non-profit preservation group runs an excellent series of two-hour "Architectours", with historians covering the architectural legacy and history of city neighbourhoods. Tickets are $8.

Mobile literary workshops

(☏345-2629 ext 3017, ⓦwww.jewishpubliclibrary.org). On summer Sundays, local English teacher Stan Asher leads

THE MÉTRO

The clean and quiet (the trains run on rubber tires) **Métro system** has four lines that are colour-coded and identified by the terminus in each direction. The most heavily used lines both pass through downtown – the **green line** snakes along from west to east, heading out past the Stade Olympique, while the **orange line** makes a large "U", with the arms heading north from downtown on either side

evocative literary rambles, full of anecdotes and quotations from the works of Montréal writers such as Mordecai Richler and A.M. Klein. A donation of a non-perishable kosher food item is all it costs.

Old Montréal Ghost Trail

(☎863-0303, Ⓦ*www.phvm.qc.ca*). Costumed actors pop up as ghosts of famous Montrealers on these summer tours (Wed–Sun 8.30pm; $12); tickets from the kiosk at the foot of Quai Jacques-Cartier.

Other tours
Amphi-Bus

(☎849-5181, Ⓦ*www.amphibustours.qc.ca*). From May to October, you can see Vieux-Montréal by land and by water from a totally customized military landing craft. The 1hr tour costs $18; pick up tickets from the corner of boulevard St-Laurent and rue de la Commune.

Maison des Cyclistes

(☎521-8356, Ⓦ*www.velo.qc.ca*). The cycling advocacy group based opposite Parc Lafontaine at 1251 rue Rachel E offers three-hour tours of the Plateau ($25; $15 with your own wheels) and further afield.

THE MÉTRO

See colour map 6 for a plan of the Métro system.
----

of the mountain. The east–west **blue line** runs north of the mountain, intersecting with the orange line at Snowdon and Jean-Talon stations. The **yellow line** only has three stops, but is the best way to get to Parc Jean-Drapeau – you can transfer from the orange or green lines at Berri-UQAM station. Service starts at 5.30am daily on all lines. The last trains on the blue line are at 11pm; the others stop running at 12.30am, 1am on Saturday.

Single tickets cost $2 but are a bit of a rip-off when compared to buying a *carnet* (book of six tickets) for $8.25, which you can get at retail outlets such as pharmacies and *dépanneurs* (corner shops) throughout the city as well as the stations themselves. Just after passing through the turnstiles, be sure to take a transfer from one of the inconspicuous machines if you intend to continue your journey by bus. If you're planning to make more extensive use of the Métro and bus system, it's worth investing in a **Tourist Card** – the one-day pass is $7 from downtown stations (but is only available at Métro Berri-UQAM from Nov–March). If you want any longer than that, the **CAM Hebdo** (a weekly commuter pass) is $12.50, giving you more days for less money than the three-day tourist card at $14.

BUSES

The city's fleet of **buses** supplements the Métro system, filling in the gaps between the lines and fanning out into the suburbs. Prices are the same as for the Métro (exact fare required if paying by cash rather than a ticket) and if you want to transfer from one bus to another or on to the Métro, ask the driver for *une correspondance* when you pay your fare. Bus stops indicate which Métro station the bus is heading towards and many also have a unique telephone number you can call for the schedule for that particular stop. Night services run on a limited number of routes after midnight.

TAXIS

Taxis are pretty easy to find downtown and on the main roads everywhere, and can also be found at taxi ranks near the larger hotels and transport termini. The largest and most reliable of the city's taxi firms are Taxi Diamond (℡273-6331) and Taxi Co-op (℡725-9885). **Fares** start at $2.80 and the meter clocks another $1.13 for each kilometre travelled; a fifteen percent tip is standard. Trips between downtown and the airport are a fixed $28, not including tip.

Vieux-Montréal and the Vieux-Port

The clichés that abound about **Vieux-Montréal** (Old Montréal) are, for the most part, true. Walking the neighbourhood's cobblestone streets lined with seventeenth-century buildings is every bit like exploring an old French village, and an extremely well-kept one at that. While cars rumbling down the narrow lanes may momentarily break the reverie, the sight of Victorian lampposts and the sound of horse-drawn calèches echoing off the stone buildings can easily transport you back to a bygone era.

Braced by rue Saint-Antoine to the north, rue Berri to the east, rue McGill to the west and the St Lawrence to the south, Vieux-Montréal was Canada's financial and commercial hub up until the early twentieth century. Largely left to decay after business moved to the present downtown, the decision to hold Expo '67 on the islands facing Vieux-Montréal (see Chapter 7, "Parc Jean-Drapeau") helped bring people back into the neighbourhood, kick-starting the long process of refurbishment that continues to this day.

Vieux-Montréal is relatively compact and therefore best visited on foot. You could easily spend a day just strolling the streets, starting with **rue St-Sulpice**, which runs alongside the **Basilique Notre-Dame**, and ending with **rue St-Paul**, arguably the old town's most attractive thoroughfare. But there's plenty to do indoors as well, and two museums in particular should not be missed. On the eastern side of Vieux-Montréal stands the **Musée de l'Archéologie**, located on the precise spot of Montréal's founding in 1642 and full of centuries-old artefacts excavated from the soil beneath. The **Musée du Château Ramezay**, at the opposite end of the neighbourhood, showcases hundreds of well-worn articles dating from the city's fur-trading days through to its financial zenith.

The area covered in this chapter is shown in detail on colour map 4.

Given that Vieux-Montréal was the birthplace of the city's institution as a Catholic mission, it should come as no surprise that two of Montréal's most important churches are also located here. The intimate **Chapelle Notre-Dame-de-Bon-Secours** faces onto the Vieux-Port and the St Lawrence, while the aforementioned Basilique Notre-Dame, site of the country's most impressive state funerals and marriages, looks north to **Place d'Armes**, the old heart of the city.

After the heady history of Vieux-Montréal, the **Vieux-Port** (Old Port), wedged between rue de la Commune and the St Lawrence, makes a great place to chill out, its pedestrian-only parkland offering plenty of places to sit and watch the spectacle pass by.

The city-run tourist office is located on the northwest corner of Place Jacques-Cartier; see p.11 for details. Vieux-Montréal's Web site is Ⓦ*www.vieux.montreal.qc.ca*.

PLACE D'ARMES

Map 4, D3. Métro Place-d'Armes.

Begin your explorations at **Place d'Armes**, the square that was once the financial centre of the city but which now banks mostly on tourism thanks to its location directly in front of Basilique Notre-Dame. In the colony's early days, the square served as both a cemetery and a common battlefield – the most legendary confrontation saw an unarmed Paul de Chomedey take on an armed Iroquois chief in 1644 and emerge victorious. A century later, French regiments surrendered their arms here in 1760, after the British captured the city.

- -
**Horse-drawn calèches can be hired at
Place d'Armes for $30/30 minutes and $60/hour.**
- -

The square's centrepiece is a century-old **fountain** commemorating the founding of Montréal capped by a strident flag-bearing statue of de Chomedey. Among the figures circling the base designed by Quebec sculptor Louis-Philippe Hébert is Pilote, the dog whose barking allegedly warned de Chomedey and his troops of the impending 1644 Iroquois attack.

There's not much else to the square itself – most of the interest is in the surrounding buildings, such as the domed shrine of the **Banque de Montréal**, located on the north side at 119 rue St-Jacques ouest. Founded in 1817 by local Scottish merchants, it served the entire nation until the Bank of Canada was created in the 1930s, and is credited with initiating rue St-Jacques' development as the Wall Street of Canada. One of the most glorious buildings in the area, the bank is outwardly modelled on the Pantheon in Rome and has interior chambers that reek of opulence with deluxe marble counters, green syenite columns and gleaming bronze fittings. Off to the left of the main entrance, a small **Numismatic Museum** (Mon–Fri 10am–4pm; free) displays old account books, banknotes, coins and photographs of the colony's early days.

The east side of the square is equally imposing, starting with the red-sandstone building on the northeast corner built in 1888 for the **New York Life Insurance Company**. At eight storeys high, it was the city's first sky-scraper, though you won't be able to check the view – access is limited to the dimly lit lobby, whose ceiling is stamped with handsome copper mouldings. Next door, at no. 507, the 23-storey Art Deco **Aldred Building** is the city's finest example of the ziggurat style made famous by the Empire State Building. The set-back roof answered a 1929 city ordinance mandating that structures over ten storeys design their building profiles to maximize the amount of sunlight let onto nearby streets.

The ugly black monolith housing the **Banque Nationale** on the west side of the square would be nothing more than an eyesore but for its symbolic importance. Towering over its neighbours, the 1967 building is sup-posed to represent the power of the Francophone business class over their former oppressors, the Church and the English.

BASILIQUE NOTRE-DAME

Map 4, D3 & D4. 110 rue Notre-Dame O, daily 7am–8pm; $2.
Métro Place-d'Armes.

Facing Place d'Armes is the twin-towered, Gothic-revival **Basilique Notre-Dame**, cathedral of the Catholic faithful since 1829 – the largest religious building in North America at the time. It made such an impression on its architect, a Protestant Irish-American named James O'Donnell, that he converted to Catholicism six months before its inauguration. He died a year later and is buried in a rather inauspicious (and inaccessible) grave in the church basement.

The basilica is often compared to Notre-Dame-de-Paris, but more closely resembles Westminster Abbey thanks to its severe towers, named La Persévérance and La Tempérance. Persévérance, the westernmost of the two, holds the twelve ton Jean-Baptiste bell affectionately called *le Gros Bourdon* (the big bell), which required twelve bell-ringers to get it moving before electricity was installed. Though rarely rung nowadays – the former Prime Minister Pierre Elliott Trudeau's state funeral in 2000 was a notable exception – its low rumbling peals could be heard as far as 25km away in the days before urban development blocked the sound.

The lushness of the vast interior comes as a surprise after the stern exterior. It positively explodes with colour as the wooden mouldings above the 3500-seat vault are painted in dense blues, reds, golds and greens. The vibrant blue ribs adorned with hundreds of gold-leaf stars give the impression of sitting under a midnight sky, while light from three rose windows in the ceiling combine with flickering votive candle flames to create a sense of intense warmth and intimacy.

To get the most out of your visit to the Basilica, take one of the free guided tours that start every twenty minutes from the reception desk near the entrance.

About halfway toward the altar, you'll find an ornately decorated staircase leading up to the pulpit; the base is guarded by Louis-Philippe Hébert's exceptional woodcarvings of the prophets. The soaring altar is a masterpiece of detailing by French sculptor Henri Bouriché, whose exquisite sculptures of biblical figures themed on the Eucharist have Christ's Crucifixion as the focal point.

Behind the altar lies the bright and modern **Chapelle**

BASILIQUE NOTRE-DAME

Sacré-Coeur, fondly referred to as the Wedding Chapel – up to five weddings a day are held here on summer weekends. Against the back wall, an enormous 16m-high bronze altarpiece depicts man's progression from birth to heaven, the gates of which are represented by the sweeping wings of a dove over Christ's head.

Séminaire de St-Sulpice

Map 4, C3 & D3. 116 rue Notre-Dame O. Métro Place-d'Armes.
Adjoined to the presbytery on the western side of the basilica is the city's oldest building, the mock-medieval **Séminaire de St-Sulpice**, whose main doorway is topped by North America's oldest public clock, installed in 1701. The central part of the building dates from 1685 and was built as the headquarters of the Paris-based order of Sulpician priests that instigated Montréal's establishment as a religious colony and ruled the city for two centuries. There is no public access to the building: 25 Sulpicians still live there today and maintain the basilica.

RUE ST-SULPICE, RUE LE ROYER AND THE PALAIS DE JUSTICE

Map 4, D4–F3. Métro Place-d'Armes.
From the basilica, head south along **rue St-Sulpice**, a street rife with history. Many of the continent's first explorers lived in houses here, and while some are still private residences – those that aren't have been converted into shops – they are embellished with easily identifiable historical plaques. The man after which Duluth, Minnesota is named, Daniel Greysolon du Luth, lodged in the corner building at 88 rue Notre-Dame in 1675, while the Le Moyne brothers, founders of the American cities Biloxi,

Mobile and New Orleans, as well as the state of Louisiana, were born and raised at 404 rue St-Sulpice. Pierre Gaulthier de Varennes, known for charting South Dakota, the Rockies and Wyoming, is thought to have resided on the site of the basilica itself.

About halfway down the street on the east side is **rue le Royer**, an austere courtyard lined with late-nineteenth-century warehouses that recall Montréal's past as a major shipping port. Walking to the courtyard's far end will bring you to boulevard St-Laurent, from which it's a short block north to the intersection of rue Notre-Dame, presided over by the mammoth **Palais de Justice**, the courthouse that handles all legal cases today. Two different courthouses on the same street once did legal duty, the first being the **Old Courthouse**, at 155 rue Notre-Dame est, which was built by the British in 1856, and designed to look like a Greek temple. The third storey and incongruous white dome were added 35 years later. Across the street at 100 rue Notre-Dame est is the other courthouse, the colonnade-fronted **Édifice Ernest-Cormier**, which held criminal trials after the courts were separated in 1926. Massive bronze doors embossed with the symbols of justice guard the entrance, while inside the lofty grand hall you may hear strains of music as the building now houses a dramatic arts and music conservatory.

PLACE JACQUES-CARTIER

Map 4, G3 & G4. Métro Champ-de-Mars.

The main activity on rue Notre-Dame est is found further east, around the cobblestoned **Place Jacques-Cartier**, which served as the city's public market from 1804 to 1960. The only echo of its former use is the lone flower stall at the square's north end, and most of the action now is in the form of buskers and artists hustling for change from the crowds that swarm to the square's bustling restaurants and terrace-fronted cafés.

The **Nelson Monument** at the north end of the square features a likeness of Admiral Nelson atop a drab column one-third the height of its better-known London counterpart. The statue's interest lies less in its composition than in the controversy that continues to dog it. Funded by a group of Montréal Anglophones delighted at Nelson's defeat of the French at Trafalgar in 1805, it later became a source of sovereignist ire, reminding some of British colonialism. A faction plotted to blow it up as early as 1890, and grumbling continued in the 1970s, when the surrounding taverns were hotbeds of sovereignist activity. Debate renewed as recently as 1997, when the city proposed moving it to a far away Anglophone neighbourhood. Public opposition allowed Nelson to keep his spot, although he still came down from his perch for two years for cleaning. The statue there now is actually a reproduction of the original; it turned out Nelson was so weather-ravaged he had to be replaced.

CHAMP DE MARS AND HÔTEL DE VILLE

Map 4, F2 & G2. Métro Champ-de-Mars.

Facing Place Jacques-Cartier on the north side of rue Notre-Dame, the intimate **Place Vauquelin** features French Quebecers' answer to the Nelson Monument: a statue of French naval commander Jean Vauquelin. Once the site of the city jail, Place Vauquelin has been a public space since 1858 and is outfitted with a pretty fountain surrounded by park benches.

At the square's north end, a set of stairs lead down to the **Champ de Mars**, a grassy expanse named for the god of war, though the only action it ever experienced consisted of military drills. By the 1820s, the park became a public

A FORTIFIED CITY

Even though Vieux-Montréal was a walled fortress for over a century, all that remains of the **fortifications** that once surrounded it are stretches in the Champs-de-Mars and an extensive chunk inside the Musée d'Archéologie et d'Histoire. The first wall, a 2800m-long row of cedar posts, was erected in 1687 to protect against Iroquois attack. The structure got more use as firewood, and by 1713 it was deemed an insufficient barrier against the city's new enemy: the British. Construction on new walls began soon after, and by 1744 the city was wrapped in a stone cocoon that measured more than 4m high in places. Those thirty-odd years of labour proved unnecessary though – the war they were built to defend against was fought in Québec City in 1759. When the British took over the colony, they dropped Montréal as the military centre and focused on fortifying the capital. In 1796, a public petition requested that the walls, by then unkempt and blocking the town's expansion, be demolished. The public's will was approved in 1801, and the walls came down with an act advancing the city's "Salubrity, Convenience and Embellishment" – official-speak for urban development.

promenade that Montrealers took to in their finest Sunday dress and, ironically, the city's favoured spot for public hangings. Though converted into a car park in the early twentieth century, the green space you see today was returned in honour of the city's 350th anniversary, when remains of the **stone fortifications** that once surrounded the city were also excavated (see box above) – you can see them cutting through the grass.

Hôtel de Ville

Map 4, G2 & G3. 275 rue Notre-Dame E. Mon–Fri 10am–4pm; free. Métro Champ-de-Mars.

East of Place Vauquelin, the second-floor balcony of the immense **Hôtel de Ville** was chosen by French President General de Gaulle for his incendiary rallying cry, "Vive le Québec libre!" during his state visit to Expo '67. His words left the city's Anglophones reeling at the thought that Québec was on its way to independent status and infused Francophones with a political fervour that peaked with the 1970 October Crisis (see Contexts, p.305). Notably, French presidents have stayed mum – publicly anyway – as to their views on Quebec's independence since then.

The building itself is quite opulent for a city hall with its mansard roof and turreted entranceway, and the interior is just as impressive after renovations following a serious fire in 1922 were undertaken in the Beaux-Arts style. These produced the grand two-storey-high Hall of Honour adorned with bronze balustrades and pilasters, and overhung with an immense bronze chandelier. If the municipal government isn't in session, take a peek into the council chambers where five stained-glass windows depict Montréal at the beginning of the twentieth century in mauve-tinted hues.

MUSÉE DU CHÂTEAU RAMEZAY AND AROUND

Map 4, G3. 280 rue Notre-Dame E. June–Sept daily 10am–6pm; Oct–May Tues–Sun 10am–4.30pm; $6; ⓦ *www.chateauramezay. qc.ca*. Métro Champ-de-Mars.

Built in 1705 for the eleventh governor of Montréal, Claude de Ramezay, the history of the **Château Ramezay**, the low, fieldstone manor house opposite the Hôtel de Ville, is as interesting as the articles now on display in its many chambers. It served as the North American headquarters of the Compagnie des Indes Occidental, a fur-trading company, before passing into the hands of the British after the conquest in 1760. Fifteen year later, Benjamin Franklin and his cohorts set up shop here during the fleeting American invasion and attempted to persuade the young colony to join the United States.

Since 1895, the Ramezay has served as a historical **museum**, and its lack of pretension is tremendously appealing. The collection of artefacts from the eighteenth and nineteenth centuries on display have a genuinely used feel about them – leather firemen's hats are creased from wear, a stretched beaver hide is circled with tree branches instead of manufactured pine braces, and a metal safe from the Banque de Montréal has dents in its sides. But even if these don't interest you, the Ramezay's reconstruction of the *Grande Salle* of the Compagnie des Indes Occidental is worth the entrance fee alone. The two-room salon has walls of rich mahogany imported from Nantes, France, lavishly textured with rose trellises, cherubs and musical instruments. It's the work of Louis XIV and Louis XV's principal architect, Germain Boffrand, and the Ramezay honours the salon's musical theme by putting on 45-minute concerts here the last Sunday of the month (call ☏861-3708 for information; free with museum admission).

Lieu Historique Sir-George-Étienne-Cartier

Map 4, I3. 458 rue Notre-Dame E. May–Sept daily 10am–6pm; Oct–April Wed–Sun 10am–5pm; $3.25; Ⓦ*www.parkscanada.wc.ca/cartier*. Métro Champ-de-Mars.

Further east along rue Notre-Dame, the **Lieu Historique Sir-George-Étienne-Cartier** comprises two adjoining houses that were inhabited by the Cartier family from 1848 to 1871. Sir George-Étienne Cartier was one of the fathers of Confederation, persuading the French-Canadians to join the Dominion of Canada. Today, leaders of Québec nationalism decry Cartier as a collaborator, and the displays in the east house diplomatically skirt over the issue of whether he was right or wrong and instead emphasize his role in the construction of Canada's railways. Such conservatism is carried out in a decidedly bizarre fashion however: Muppet-like figures represent the founding fathers on the main floor, while eight white-painted papier-mâché models of Cartier himself sit around a glass-domed, round table upstairs. The rooms in the west house re-create the period when Sir George lived here, though in no less hokey a manner: original domestic objects are tied around a dinner theme and recordings of conversations between fictitious house staff start playing once you walk into the rooms.

RUE ST-PAUL AND AROUND

Map 4, I3–A5. Métro Champ-de-Mars to Square-Victoria.
One block south of the Cartier museum is one of the city's most attractive thoroughfares, **rue St-Paul**, which runs parallel to rue Notre-Dame the length of Vieux-Montréal. The nineteenth-century commercial buildings and Victorian lampposts that line the street look much the same today as they did when Charles Dickens stayed at the **Rasco Hotel** (now an office building) at nos. 281-295 in 1842. The storefront windows house upscale art galleries, antique stores and clothing boutiques, with some tacky souvenir shops thrown in, but if you walk around to the back of the buildings on rue de la Commune, you'll note that several resemble warehouses from the rear. It's an architectural trompe l'oeil that reflects the habits of the time, when goods were delivered to the back and sold in the front.

The street's most attractive building is the three-storey **Maison du Calvet**, at 409 rue St-Paul est, built in 1725 for the American Revolution supporter Pierre du Calvet. The house, now part of an inn, is the city's finest example of French domestic architecture, retaining two of the style's most distinctive characteristics: exterior stone walls that extend past the rooftop and "S"-shaped irons inset into the walls. The walls were built higher to prevent blazes from spreading between houses, and the irons are anchors – they connect to rods that hold the opposing fieldstone walls in place.

For a review of the *Pierre du Calvet* inn, see p.112.

Kitty-corner to the Maison du Calvet, the splendid silver-domed **Marché Bonsecours** at 350 rue Saint-Paul E, is Vieux-Montréal's quintessential shopping symbol. Erected in 1846 as an interior counterpart to Place Jacques-Cartier's outdoor market, its upper floor served stints as United Canada's House of Parliament and Montréal's City Hall in the 1800s, while the produce stalls bustled on the ground floor until 1964. After being taken over entirely by municipal offices, it was restored to its former duty as a market place in 1992 and now houses designer boutiques and commercial art galleries. They're OK for a browse but the price tags are outrageous.

Chapelle Notre-Dame-de-Bon-Secours

Map 4, H3 & I3. 400 rue Saint-Paul E. Métro Champ-de-Mars.
Facing Maison du Calvet is the delicate and profusely steepled **Chapelle Notre-Dame-de-Bon-Secours**, its fieldstone walls supporting six copper-and-stone spires of various heights. The location earned it the nickname of the Sailors' Church, and mariners would endow it with model ships as thanks for having safely reached the shore – many of these are still on display. The chapel served as

Montréal's first church under the leadership of Sœur Marguerite Bourgeoys, who became Canada's first saint in 1982. The structure you see today, though, postdates her by some seventy years as it was rebuilt in 1771 following a serious fire.

Adjacent to the chapel, a **museum** (May–Oct Tues–Sun 10am–5pm; Nov to mid-Jan & mid-March to April 11am–3.30pm; $5) devoted to Bourgeoy's life adds a touching note; one small room is filled with 58 handcrafted miniature doll scenes tracing her life from birth to death. One hundred narrow stairs behind the museum entrance lead to a small "aerial chapel", which gives excellent views over the port and the crammed network of streets around the church.

POINTE-À-CALLIÈRE AND AROUND

Map 4, C5 & D5. Métro Square-Victoria.

Montréal is one of those rare cities that can pinpoint the exact location on which it was founded: **Pointe-à-Callière** a triangular spit of land that juts out into rue de la Commune at the western edge of Vieux-Montréal. But while the founding's location is clear, the precise date of the event is slightly murky – the only thing for sure is that it happened mid-May, 1642.

Musée d'Archéologie et d'Histoire de Montréal

Map 4, D5. 350 Place Royale. Late June to early Sept Mon–Fri 10am–6pm, Sat and Sun 11am–6pm; early Sept to late June Tues–Fri 10am–5pm, Sat & Sun 11am– 5pm; $9.50; ⓦ*www.musee-pointe-a-calliere.qc.ca.* Métro Square-Victoria.

The splendid **Musée d'Archéologie et d'Histoire de Montréal** rises up from the point of Paul de

Chomedey's landing, looking much like a ship that's run ashore. Inside the modern limestone structure, the boat motif carries on with finishing touches like portholes that are inset in the entrance floor, and industrial stairwells connecting the building's four levels. The name of the edifice equally captures its shipping theme – it's known as the Éperon (cutwater).

The Éperon is connected by underground passageway to the Old Customs House, a Neoclassical building from the 1830s situated on the rue St-Paul side of Place Royale, just northeast of the museum. The passageway between the two is where you'll find the museum's stellar collection of archeological finds excavated from the soil surrounding the buildings between 1983 and 1992. Temporary exhibits are also hosted on the first floors of the Éperon and Customs House.

By far the best way to experience the museum is on one of the free hour-long guided tours that begin at the ground-floor ticket desk (July to early Sept daily 2pm; early Sept to June Sat & Sun 2pm).

Before heading into the basement, start your tour with the fifteen-minute-long multimedia history presentation in the Éperon's main-floor theatre. Once downstairs, the most riveting find is a Catholic cemetery dating from 1648 – the city's first – discovered here in 1989. Some 38 bodies were buried beneath the floor, although only seven of the empty gravesites have been unearthed, visible through glass windows – the one skeleton not washed away by centuries of floods has been removed. Further along, a walkway takes you over an eighteenth-century water main and sewage system lined with cobblestones – during the spring thaw, the sewer still gets filled. Beyond that, an exhibition chamber contains five intricate scale models of the surrounding area from different time periods. These are set under glass below the floor and illustrate the days when only natives roamed the grassy shores through to the late 1800s under British rule. Nearby, you can take the stairs up to the Old Customs House, home of the museum's boutique.

Centre d'Histoire de Montréal and around

Map 4, B5. 335 Place d'Youville. Mid-May to mid-Sept daily 10am–5pm; mid-Sept to mid-May Tues–Sun 10am–5pm; $4.50; Ⓦ*www.ville.montreal.qc.ca/chm*. Métro Square-Victoria.

Directly west of the archeology museum is **Place d'Youville**, a narrow public square anchored by the **Centre d'Histoire de Montréal** museum, a converted red-brick fire station focusing on the city's social history. Inside, dioramas depict Montréal's days as an Iroquois settlement to its present expansions – fine for a sketchy overview but not terribly engaging. There's also a collection of retro magazines, department-store boxes and old street signs that provide a sufficiently amusing diversion.

South of Place d'Youville, at 138 rue St-Pierre, the **Hôpital Général des Soeurs-Grises** cared for the colony's sick, old and orphaned children, though all that remains of the original H-shaped structure is the stone chapel and west wing. Next door, the **Musée Marc-Aurèle Fortin**, at no. 118 (Tues–Sun 11am–5pm; $4), is a small gallery dedicated to a prolific Québécois landscape painter who considered himself the first to found a "Canadian school" that wasn't influenced by Europeans. Judging by the mundane works inside, he probably could have used the help.

VIEUX-PORT

Map 4, B7–I4. Métro Square-Victoria to Champ-de-Mars.

Lying between Vieux-Montréal and the St Lawrence, the **Vieux-Port** (Old Port) was once the most important port in Canada, its location at the head of the Lachine Canal that connected ships with the Great Lakes assuring its maritime dominance. The construction of the St Lawrence Seaway in 1959 that allowed ships to bypass the Canal altogether ended the port's glory days and it was left to deteriorate for three decades. Refurbishment came about in the early 1990s, in honour of the city's 350th birthday, and the parkland that was created turned the port into one of Montréal's most idyllic playgrounds. The area is graced with superb biking, cross-country skiing and rollerblading paths that offer spectacular vistas onto the waterfront to the south and the warehouses lining rue de la Commune to the north.

A small booth on Quai Jacques-Cartier below Jacques-Cartier has information on portside activities (June to mid-Oct daily 8am–8pm); you can also visit Ⓦ www.oldportofmontreal.com.

Traces still remain of the port's former shipping duty in the ghostly junkyard remnants of grain elevator **Silo no. 2**, at the port's eastern end, and the **Tour de l'Horloge**, a watchtower completed in 1922. But these are largely overlooked by those in search of summertime activities like pedal-boating ($5 per half-hour) the calm waters of the **Bassin Bonsecours**, a protected reservoir that cascades into the St Lawrence. The narrow **Parc des Écluses** that marks the start of the Lachine Canal and its **bike path** at the port's westernmost end is also popular for its funky floral sculptures. The activity all but dies out come winter, or at least moves indoors to the cavernous halls on the **Quai King-Edward**, where a portside hangar incorporates the interactive science exhibits of the **Centre iSci** and an **IMAX** theatre.

The staggered Cubist blocks across from the Vieux-Port comprise Habitat, a unique apartment complex built for Expo '67 by Moshe Safdie who later designed the new pavilion at the Musée des Beaux-Arts (see p.60).

Quai King-Edward

Map 4, E5–G7. Métro Place-d'Armes.

The lively **Quai King-Edward** at the southernmost end of boulevard Saint-Laurent is the hub of the Vieux-Port and a good place to start your waterfront explorations. The area immediately west of the quay is lined with a row of bright stalls whose stock of antique books and etchings occasionally yields a find. The real estate to the east of the quay is equally colourful, with caricaturists and musicians on hand to amuse passers-by. If you want to get away from the hubbub, walk to the southernmost end of the quay and take the stairs over the car park to reach a quiet **lookout** point. Here, you can get a rare panoramic view of the city stretching north to the mountain and south to the islands of the St Lawrence.

Centre iSci

Map 4, E5 & E6. 2 rue de la Commune, daily 10am–9pm; $9.95 adults, $7.95 under-12; Ⓦ*www.isci.ca*. Métro Place-d'Armes.

The port's only indoor attraction is the **Centre iSci**, located in two industrial hangars on Quai King-Edward. Divided into three exhibition halls, the interactive science museum focuses on the themes of life, information and matter, with displays heavy on multimedia technology – interactive touch screens, audio and video players are scattered throughout. Most of the exhibits are dull, and some are downright peculiar, like the enormous inflated barcoded tomato and hefty blow-up house that sway in the Life Lab. If you don't have kids, head instead for the seven-storey film screen of the neighbouring **IMAX Theatre** (☎496-4629; mid-April to early Sept daily 10.15am–10.15pm; early Sept to mid-April Tues–Sun 10.15am–10.15pm; $9.95 adults, $7.95 under-12; ⓦ*www.imaxoldport.com*).

Quai de l'Horloge

Map 4, I5. Métro Champ-de-Mars.

The only other pier worth visiting is the one located at the port's easternmost end, the **Quai de l'Horloge**. The Italian Renaissance building at the entrance to the pier was built to hold the offices of the Montréal Port Police, Canada's first police force. While the building is empty today, the L-shaped pier still does brisk business as the major departure point for several **boat cruises** (see pp.227–228) and is presided over by the simple **Tour de l'Horloge**, a sandstone clock tower that rises 65m above sea level. The views of Vieux-Montréal, the islands, and Mont Royal from its highest platform are superb, but it's a workout to get there – there are nearly 200 steps and the last 50 or so are quite narrow and steep. The lookout point on the grounds immediately east of the tower is an excellent spot to watch the annual fireworks competition (see Chapter 18, "Festivals").

QUAI DE L'HORLOGE

Downtown
Montréal

Downtown Montréal is the city's obvious commercial focus, thronged with businesspeople, shoppers and tourists throughout the day and well into the evening – at least during warmer months. And although it lacks the charm of Vieux-Montréal, the downtown area is dotted with enough old churches and museums to fill a few days' exploration. The other main draw is **nightlife**: this is where, around streets like rue Crescent and rue Bishop to the west and the Quartier Latin and the Village to the east, many of Montréal's best cinemas, music venues, bars and clubs are found.

In the winter, the crowds disappear from the streets, travelling below the surface to the temperate climate of the so-called **Underground City**, a vast labyrinthine network of shopping malls, Métro stations and other establishments that underlie much of downtown. The somewhat sterile corporate environment quickly loses its fascination, but if you're here during a January cold snap, you'll have no problem understanding its attraction.

Shaped like a long rectangle, the main thoroughfares

downtown run east–west, with **rue Ste-Catherine** offering the most in the way of shopping and entertainment. The boundaries of the region are somewhat amorphous, lying roughly between rue Sherbrooke and rue St-Antoine to the north and south, and extending to rue St-Denis to the east. The western border is harder to define, overlapping with the Golden Square Mile (see p.55), where downtown's commercial character gives way to more of the historic Anglophone enclave west of rue Peel.

A number of public spaces break up the long stretches of commercial establishments, helping keep the downtown core from feeling claustrophobic. Adjacent to rue Peel, **Square Dorchester** and **Place du Canada** are surrounded by old churches and modern skyscrapers, while nearby lies the area's distinctive focal point, **Place Ville Marie**. The cruciform skyscraper and its plaza mark the southern end of the city's truncated "Champs d'Elysées", **avenue McGill College**, which offers a vista of skyscrapers framing the view towards McGill University and Mont Royal to the north. Further east along rue Ste-Catherine, **Christ Church Cathedral** and **Square Phillips** lead to a broad plaza that encompasses the **Musée d'Art Contemporain de Montréal** and the performance halls of **Place des Arts**, and also serves as the site for some of Montréal's huge summer festivals. The pedestrianised rue de la Gauchetière, south of and parallel to rue Ste-Catherine, is lined with the restaurants and shops that comprise part of Montréal's small **Chinatown**. A half-dozen blocks to the east, the student bars and cafés of the **Quartier Latin** centred on **rue St-Denis** mark the eastern edge of downtown. Further along rue Ste-Catherine lies the **Village**, the hub of Montréal's vibrant gay community.

The area covered in this chapter is shown in detail on colour map 3.

DOWNTOWN MONTRÉAL

SQUARE DORCHESTER

Map 3, F6. Métro Peel.

Square Dorchester, on the east side of rue Peel between rue Ste-Catherine and boulevard René-Lévesque, is a good place to get your bearings as the Dominion Square Building on its north side is the site of Montréal's main **Infotouriste** office (see p.9). Originally a Catholic cemetery, the area was first laid out as Dominion Square in 1872 and subsequently partitioned by the widening of Dorchester Boulevard, which was controversially renamed boulevard René-Lévesque following the premier's death in 1987. The southern half of the square became Place du Canada (see overleaf), while the northern half was later renamed Square Dorchester to appease Anglophones upset that the street honouring Lord Dorchester, the British governor for much of the late 1700s, was so quickly renamed in honour of a separatist leader.

The grey-granite **Édifice Sun Life**, built in 1918 and for a quarter of a century the largest office building in the British Commonwealth, lords over the eastern side of the square. The principal tenant – the Sun Life Assurance Company – was among the many Canadian firms that moved their head offices out of Montréal around the time of the 1980 referendum on sovereignty. Behind the massive bronze doors, the cool marble and absence of trappings in the large lobby speak of old money.

BASILIQUE-CATHÉDRALE MARIE-REINE-DU-MONDE

Map 3, F7. Mon 7am–8pm, Tues–Fri 7am–7.15pm, Sat 8am–8pm, Sun 9.30am–7.15pm; free. Métro Bonaventure.

Facing the Édifice Sun Life and Square Dorchester, the **Basilique-Cathédrale Marie-Reine-du-Monde** (Cathedral-Basilica of Mary Queen of the World) is a scaled-down version of St Peter's in Rome, with faithful copies of the massive portico and copper dome. Although many think the statues crowning the facade are of the Apostles (as is the case with St Peter's), the thirteen figures actually represent the patron saints of the parishes that donated them. Bishop Ignace Bourget commissioned the building to replace the previous cathedral, St-Jacques, which was located in the present-day Quartier Latin and burned in 1852. He chose St Peter's as the inspiration to emphasize the dominant role of Catholicism in what was then the largest city in the new Dominion of Canada. Construction was delayed until 1870 due to a number of factors, including the uproar over his chosen site – a pre-dominantly Protestant Anglophone neighbourhood.

Inside it's not as opulent as you might expect from the grand exterior, though the high altar of marble, onyx and ivory is surmounted by a gilded copper reproduction of Bernini's baldachin over the altar in St Peter's. To your left on entering is the Chapelle des Souvenirs, which contains various relics collected by the enthusiastic Bourget, including the wax-encased remains of the immensely obscure St Zoticus, an early Christian martyr.

PLACE DU CANADA AND AROUND

Map 3, E8–F7. Métro Bonaventure or Peel.

Separated from Square Dorchester by boulevard René-Lévesque, the southern half of Dominion Square was renamed **Place du Canada** in 1967, Canada's centennial year. Its name made it an appropriate rallying point for national unity during the 1995 referendum on separation, when three days before the vote some 300,000 federalists gathered here – the largest political demonstration the country has ever seen. The (mostly) asphalt-covered square is dotted with various memorials and monuments, including an imposing bronze statue of **Sir John A. MacDonald**, Canada's first prime minister, plus a few bits of greenery, but most interest lies on the periphery. Head to the southwestern corner, where the Victorian **St George's Anglican Church**, at the intersection of rues Peel and de la Gauchetière (Tues–Sun 8.30am–5.30pm), is the only one of six Protestant churches constructed around the square between 1865 and 1875 that remains standing. Its solid neo-Gothic exterior gives way to a lofty interior with heavy wooden rafters supporting the gabled roof. A tapestry used at the Queen's coronation in Westminster Abbey in 1953 contrasts nicely with the darker wood fixtures, including the altar and choir hand-carved from English oak.

Gare Windsor, the large Romanesque structure facing the church's main entrance on rue de la Gauchetière, was Montréal's main rail terminus from 1887 until 1938, helping draw much business away from Vieux-Montréal to downtown. Just inside the doors on rue de la Gauchetière is a plaque bearing an eloquent tribute to the employees of the railway who perished in World War I (the eulogy is repeated at the base of the monument – a statue of an angel lifting a soldier to heaven – at the end of the otherwise bland concourse).

Although it continued to serve as a terminus for commuter trains until the mid-1990s (trains now stop a block to the west), the station's demise was finally sealed with the construction of the **Centre Molson** on the western side of the courtyard at 1200 rue de la Gauchetière O (Métro Lucien-L'Allier or Bonaventure). This 21,000-seat amphitheatre is home to ice hockey's **Montréal Canadiens**, the most successful team in the history of the National Hockey League. When there isn't a hockey game, it's the place for rock concerts, classical-music performances and family entertainment. Guided tours take place in English daily at 11am and 2pm ($7).

PLACE DU CANADA AND AROUND

RUE PEEL

Map 3, F5 & F6. Métro Peel.

Heading north on **rue Peel** from Square Dorchester quickly brings you to the corner of the city's main commercial thoroughfare since the early 1900s, **rue Ste-Catherine**. The intersection of the two is purportedly the busiest in the city and along the stretch east of here are the main shopping centres and department stores, interspersed with exclusive boutiques, souvenir shops and fast-food outlets. But for all its consumerist gloss, rue Ste-Catherine still has scattered seedy bits, with peepshows and strip clubs enlivening the streetscape.

Half a block further north along rue Peel stands the elegant **Cours Mont-Royal**, the largest hotel in the British Commonwealth when completed in 1922. Although no longer a hotel, it's worth taking a peek inside to gawk up at the fourteen-storey-high atria (surrounded by condos and offices), and to check out the lower four floors of shops, which include a number of expensive designers.

PLACE VILLE MARIE AND AVENUE McGILL COLLEGE

Map 3, G5 & G6. Métro McGill.

Heading back to rue Ste-Catherine and continuing east a block, you'll come across downtown's most visible landmark, the I.M. Pei-designed **Place Ville Marie**, Montréal's first true skyscraper and still one of the city's tallest at 46 floors. Sadly, there is no public viewing deck – in fact, none of Montréal's skyscrapers has one – but for the price of a drink you can check out the city from the top floor *Restaurant Club Lounge le 737* (see review on p.140); the entrance is from the rue University side of the tower.

THE UNDERGROUND CITY

Montréal's Underground City was planned as a refuge from weather that is outrageously cold in the winter and humid in the summer. It began with the mall beneath the Place Ville Marie in the 1960s. Montrealers flooded into the first climate-controlled shopping arcade, and, spurred by the opening of the Métro in 1966, the Underground City duly spread. With each newly constructed commercial development linking to the complex, it now has 31km of passages – the largest such pedestrian network in the world – providing access to the Métro, major hotels, shopping malls, transport termini, thousands of offices, apartments and restaurants, and a good smattering of cinemas and theatres to boot. Around half a million people pass through it each day, mostly on their way to and from work – the sixty building complexes linked to the system contain eighty percent of downtown's office space.

In the largest section of the system, you can walk all the way from the Centre Molson to La Baie, and from Cours Mont-Royal to as far as the Centre de Commerce Mondial on the edge of Vieux-Montréal. The other major components are the axis linking Place des Arts with the Palais des Congrès (the city's convention centre), and the area around Métro Berri-UQAM, which includes the bus station and the pavilions of the Université du Québec à Montréal (UQAM).

Although tourist-office hype makes the Underground City sound somewhat exotic, don't plan to make a day out of visiting: the reality is pretty banal and most Montrealers use it solely as a way to get from place to place. If you want cheap and quick food, though, check out the food courts on the lowest floor of any of the malls en route.

The base of the tower is integrated into the shopping mall that was the catalyst for the Underground City (see box, above). Set in the pavement in the centre of the mall's

THE UNDERGROUND CITY

landscaped roof is a granite compass indicating true north. It's not particularly exciting in itself, but because the city's street grid is tilted 45 degrees, most Montrealers would argue that north actually lies in the direction of avenue McGill College (which is geographically to the northwest). Now you can prove them wrong. Ignoring the compass and looking "north" beyond Gerald Gladstone's abstract copper sculpture, *Female Landscape*, you'll see one of downtown's best **views**. Framed by office towers are the gates leading to McGill University's main campus, with the cross atop the mountain visible in the distance beyond.

The *Queen Elizabeth Hotel*, directly south of PVM, is where John Lennon and Yoko Ono held their Bed-in For Peace (from room 1742) and recorded *Give Peace a Chance* on June 1, 1969.

Avenue McGill College and around

Map 3, G5 & G6. Métro McGill.

Redesigned in the early 1980s as a wide, tree-lined boulevard, **avenue McGill College** bustles with cafés overflowing onto the wide sidewalks. One block north of rue Ste-Catherine, on the eastern side of the street, stands one of the city's most notable sculptures – Raymond Mason's larger-than-life *The Illuminated Crowd*. The numerous white fibreglass figures, facing an illumination (both in the literal and metaphorical sense of "seeing the light"), are meant to represent the fragility of man – only a short distance separates the healthy folk in front from the particularly gruesome figures furthest from the light. It's somewhat ironic that the character at the front of the group is pointing across to the other side of the street, where Léa Vivot's charming bronze sculpture, *The Secret Bench*, depicts two youngsters cosying up to one another at the end of a park bench.

Continuing up avenue McGill College will bring you to the leafy campus of McGill University (see p.57).

Back on rue Ste-Catherine and just east of avenue McGill College, you'll be confronted with another juxtaposition. Across the road from the families streaming out of the Centre Eaton shopping mall is a two-storey-high neon sign fronting "Club Super-Sexe", featuring scantily clad "superwomen" (see p.175). Adjacent to the Centre Eaton, the Italianate building with shop windows set within ornamental columns and arches was where the venerable Eaton's department store stood for seven decades until the chain went into receivership in late 1999. The ninth-floor restaurant, *Le 9ᵉ*, is an Art Deco marvel, designed in 1931 by Jacques Carlu, and due to reopen once renovations have been completed.

CHRIST CHURCH CATHEDRAL

Map 3, G6. 635 rue Ste-Catherine O. Mon–Fri 8am–5.45pm, Sat 8am–4.30pm, Sun 8am–5pm; ⓦ*www.montreal.anglican.org/cathedral*; free. Métro McGill.

Although it's the seat of Montréal's Anglican diocese, **Christ Church Cathedral**, one block east of the Centre Eaton, is remembered by many Montrealers as the "floating church" – for two-and-a-half years, it was supported on concrete struts while developers tunnelled out the glitzy **Promenades de la Cathédrale**, a boutique-lined part of the Underground City. This curious development came about when the cathedral authorities, facing a shortage of funds, leased the land beneath the church, as well as that behind it, where the mirrored postmodern office tower, La

CHRIST CHURCH CATHEDRAL

Place de la Cathédrale, now reflects the symmetry of the 1859 church's tripartite neo-Gothic facade. Inside the cathedral, soaring Gothic arches are decorated with heads of saints, gargoyles and angels, but the most poignant feature is mounted to the left of the pulpit: the small Coventry Cross, made from nails salvaged from the bombed Coventry Cathedral in Britain.

One of the best features of the church is actually outside it – around back, you'll find benches set about a small and well-manicured public **garden**, centred around a trickling fountain that helps shut out the sounds of the city. The stone building separating the garden from rue University was the church's **rectory**, but has since been converted into *Le Parchemin* restaurant (see review on p.142).

SQUARE PHILLIPS AND AROUND

Map 3, H6. Métro McGill.

Spreading back from rue Ste-Catherine another block east, **Square Phillips** has little in the way of greenery, instead offering a line of market stalls towered over by a bronze statue at the square's centre of **Edward VII**. Thomas Phillips, a prominent merchant who bought the land in 1840, decreed that the buildings around the square should be the most beautiful in Montréal, and although they fall short of fulfilling his wish – the east side is a forgettable mishmash of cheap modern styles – a couple of the buildings fit the bill. The 1894 **Henry Birks and Sons building**, a jewellery store on the square's west side, has a lovely interior full of gilt columns and frothy blues and creams behind the smooth-cut sand-coloured stone of its facade. The dark red-sandstone building with the arched windows on the square's north side opened as Morgan's department store in 1890 and now houses **La Baie** (The Bay), a department store descended from the Hudson's Bay

Company, which operated the trading forts throughout the Canadian wilderness in the seventeenth to nineteenth centuries. To the south, the **Canada Cement Company Building**, defined by its classical columns and a scallop-effect parapet, was the first reinforced-concrete office building in Canada.

From the basement floor of La Baie, it's possible
to walk underground all the way back to the
Centre Molson, more than a kilometre away.

Immediately east of Square Phillips, **St James United Church** is tucked behind a row of shopfronts, leaving only a pair of large steeples and a neon sign advertising its presence at no. 463 on rue Ste-Catherine. The authorities of the city's largest Protestant church sold the land in front of the church in the 1920s to stave off bankruptcy, and its impressive sandstone bulk is still visible from the grotty churchyard around the west side of the block on rue City Councillors. The church's hours are sporadic, but it's worth ducking in, if possible, to see the bright and airy interior – even if paint is peeling off the ceiling in huge chunks.

ST PATRICK'S BASILICA

Map 3, H7. 460 boul René-Lévesque O. Daily 8.30am–6pm; free. Métro Square-Victoria or McGill.

Of Montréal's four basilicas, **St Patrick's**, a block south and east from Square Phillips, receives the least attention – although when the first Mass was celebrated on March 17, 1847, the church must have been an imposing sight on the hill overlooking Vieux-Montréal, where its Irish parishioners lived. Enter from the main south entrance, where the rather drab Gothic exterior gives way to a dramatic interior full of warm hues. Although at first glance the dozen pillars supporting the vault appear to be a red, veined marble, they are in fact each crafted from pine trees 30m tall. The combination of the pillars' polished glow, the oak pews, and the cream and peach colour of the ceiling and walls contrasts with the cool and distant tones of the **sanctuary**. It's hard to miss the elaborate sanctuary lamps over the main altar – the larger of the two weighs almost a tonne and is surrounded by two-metre-tall angels.

PLACE DES ARTS AND AROUND

Map 3, J5. Métro Place-des-Arts.

A couple of blocks east of Square Phillips, rue Ste-Catherine slopes down towards **Place des Arts**, Montréal's leading performing-arts centre, opened in 1963 and centre stage for events like the famous Festival International de Jazz de Montréal (see p.238). Place des Arts comprises five performance halls and the Musée d'Art Contemporain de Montréal in an ensemble of buildings set around a large plaza, with a series of gardens and fountains and a wide set of steps creating a seating area for tired tourists and for spectators during outdoor concerts. Note that the entrances to all the performance halls are via an underground concourse, best entered directly from the Métro or at 175 rue Ste-Catherine, where information on cultural events is available in the lobby.

For details of Place des Arts' resident symphony,
ballet, theatre and opera companies,
see Chapter 13, "Performing arts and film".

Place des Arts marks the northern point on one of the Underground City's main axes, with a tunnel connecting it to **Complexe Desjardins**, a collection of office towers and the *Hôtel Wyndham* (see p.115) surrounding the shopping mall on the opposite side of rue Ste-Catherine. An enormous central atrium hosts exhibitions on subjects of mainly local interest. Ahead, the next link in the chain is **Complexe Guy-Favreau**'s government office buildings. You can surface at the south side of the complex to explore Chinatown (see p.51) or continue to the hulking **Palais des Congrès**, the city's main conference centre on the edge of Vieux-Montréal.

Musée d'Art Contemporain de Montréal

Map 3, J6. 185 rue Ste-Catherine O. Tues–Sun 11am–6pm, Wed till 9pm; $6, free Wed evenings; ⓦ*www.macm.org*. Métro Place-des-Arts.

Occupying the west side of the Place des Arts plaza, the **Musée d'Art Contemporain de Montréal** was Canada's first museum devoted entirely to contemporary art. The city's foremost showcase for work by Québécois painters and sculptors, the museum also has a number of works by other Canadian and international artists. The building design is fairly low-key, although a photograph of a pair of lips smiling down from the rooftop adds a light-hearted touch. Inside, a two-storey rotunda links the main components including the *La Rotonde* restaurant (see review on p.142), whose terrace is often filled with diners enjoying live music.

The exhibit space is divided into two wings, one of which hosts temporary exhibitions of major artists and the other displaying recent acquisitions of works by current artists alongside highlights from the 6000-strong permanent collection (rotated two or three times a year). Among the most significant pieces are those of **Paul-Émile Borduas**, founder of *Les Automatistes*, a group that repudiated figurative art in favour of more imaginative and expressive representations, though his best-known paintings are his later abstracts, reduced to black blobs on a field of thick white paint. Fellow Automatistes represented here include **Jean-Paul Riopelle**, his paintings filled with vibrant energy and colour, laid on sharply with a palette knife to produce a mosaic-like effect.

The colourful stained-glass works of Marcelle Ferron, another Automatiste, adorn the Champ-de-Mars Métro station.

Their compatriot **Fernand Leduc** broke away to found the more abstract *Plasticiens* (Plasticists) in the 1950s, though you're more likely to see the rigorous abstraction typified by hard-edged bands of vertical colour produced in the 1960s by fellow member **Guido Molinari**. The museum's collection goes well beyond painting, however, with sculpture, photography, video and installation art as well as occasional multimedia performances. There is also a small, hard-to-find **sculpture garden**, entered through a partially hidden doorway in the last room of the temporary-works wing. It's worth the effort for the Henry Moore sculpture of an abstract human form, *Upright Motive no. 5*, standing amidst the greenery.

East of Place des Arts

As you follow rue Ste-Catherine east from Place des Arts, the blocks get increasingly seedy and there's not much of note along this stretch. The present-day Théâtre du Nouveau Monde, at the corner of rue St-Urbain, was once the notorious Gayety Burlesque Theatre, where Lili St-Cyr performed (see p.175). Further along, its intersection with **boulevard St-Laurent** has been a long-time hangout for prostitutes. Things don't get much more wholesome between here and the Quartier Latin, what with punkish youth hanging around places like the nightclub **Les Foufones Électroniques** (literally, The Electric Buttocks), and if you'd rather avoid the area, you can take the Métro two stops from Place-des-Arts station to Berri-UQAM in the Quartier Latin.

For reviews of *Foufones* and other clubs,
see Chapter 12, "Nightlife".

CHINATOWN

Map 3, J7 & K7. Métro Place-d'Armes.

Just south of rue Ste-Catherine, a large Chinese gate rises above boulevard St-Laurent, replete with lions' heads and Chinese characters, one of several gates that mark the entrances to Montréal's small **Chinatown**. Although the Chinese immigrants who constructed the nation's railway lines settled here in the mid- to late-nineteenth century, their descendants have dispersed throughout the city, leaving Chinatown to evolve into a primarily commercial and cultural centre. The traffic-choked blocks on boulevard St-Laurent contain a chaotic mix of produce shops and cheap restaurants, with crowds picking through the produce amid delivery vans double-parked along the sidewalks.

Although there is a token Chinese garden off of rue de la
Gauchetière, it's worth the trip to see the far more impressive
Chinese Garden at the Jardin Botanique – see p.83.

Extending westward as far as the plaza in front of the Palais des Congrès, the car-free portion of rue de la Gauchetière is quieter, though no less busy as crowds of pedestrians search out a place for dim sum or an evening meal (for reviews, see Chapter 10, "Eating"). Many of the city's Chinese residents

CHINATOWN

also venture here from the suburbs to stock up at grocery shops selling dry goods and herbal remedies.

QUARTIER LATIN

Map 3, M3–N6. Métro Berri-UQAM.

Like its Parisian counterpart, Montréal's bohemian **Quartier Latin**, on the eastern edge of downtown, derives its name from the fact that in the late-nineteenth century the area's large student population studied in Latin. Before it moved north of the mountain, the Université de Montréal was based here, and the scholastic tradition continued with the foundation of the **Université du Québec à Montréal** (UQAM) in 1969, now attended by 37,000 students. For most, though, the Quartier Latin's main appeal lies in just wandering through the boutiques or grabbing a drink at one of the many street-side terraces clustered on the stretch of **rue St-Denis** between rue Ste-Catherine and rue Sherbrooke to the north.

The university holds much of the sights, as such, including the **Centre de Design de l'UQAM** (Sept–May Wed–Sun noon–6pm; ⓦ*www.unites.uqam.ca/design/centre*) in the Dan Hanganu-designed concrete building broken by rectangular planes of glass at 1440 rue Sanguinet, where exhibitions on architectural, industrial, graphic and urban design are on display. Nearby, the modern brick **Pavilion Judith-Jasmin**, on the northeast corner of rue St-Denis and rue Ste-Catherine, incorporates the south transept and steeple of the former St-Jacques' church into its design. Inside, **La Galerie de l'UQAM**, 1400 rue Berri Tues–Sat noon–6pm; ⓦ*www.galerie.uqam.ca*; free), showcases artworks from its students as well as more established contemporary artists.

The cultural institutions continue along rue St-Denis north of boulevard de Maisonneuve, including the Beaux-

Arts **Bibliothèque Nationale** at 1700 rue St-Denis, which houses a satellite of Québec's national library, although planning for a larger edifice a block to the east (opposite the bus terminal on boul de Maisonneuve) is underway. The only bit of green space in the area lies immediately south of the bus terminal. Melvin Charney's whimsical steel sculptures of architectural elements mounted on stilts mark the northern edge of **Place Émilie-Gamelin**, a gently sloping park where summer concerts are often held, though drug dealers hang out here too.

The more upscale portion of rue St-Denis, north of rue Sherbrooke, is covered in Chapter 5, "Mont Royal and the Plateau".

THE VILLAGE

Map 2, I5. Métro Beaudry.

The **Village**, the heart of the city's gay and lesbian community, begins around rue Amherst, a few blocks east of the Quartier Latin, and extends along rue Ste-Catherine as far as rue Papineau. Montréal's gay district was once centred on rue Stanley downtown, but the city pressured bar owners out of the area in the run-up to the 1976 Olympics. The bars relocated to this run-down part of rue Ste-Catherine, and appearances have gradually improved, as has the city's attitude to the gay community – the local Métro stop, Beaudry, even incorporates the colours of the rainbow flag into its design.

The only real sights of particular interest are the **Écomusée du Fier Monde**, 2050 rue Amherst (Wed 11am–8pm, Thurs–Sun 10.30am–5pm; ☎528-8444; $5), an Art Deco former public bath with rotating art exhibitions, and the **Église St-Pierre-Apôtre**, 1201 rue de la

THE VILLAGE

53

Visitation, a delicate 1851 neo-Gothic church supported by flying buttresses. Within the latter's finely embellished interior lies the "Chapel of Hope", dedicated to those who have died of AIDS.

Listings of community resources, accommodation, bars and clubs can be found in Chapter 15, "Gay and lesbian Montréal".

Golden Square Mile

The **Golden Square Mile**, a dignified neighbourhood of limestone mansions that cascades down the slopes of Mont Royal and fuses with downtown's western core, was Montréal's epicentre of English privilege at the beginning of the twentieth century. Its name derives from the area it covers, roughly one square mile from rue University west to rue Guy, and avenue des Pins south to boulevard René-Lévesque, and the riches of its residents who, at the neighbourhood's zenith in 1900, possessed 75 percent of Canada's wealth.

Originally settled by fur merchants like James McGill – who maintained a summer home here and an "everyday house" in Vieux-Montréal – shipping, railroad and banking magnates began colonizing it for year-round living in the 1860s. Upon arrival, they built ostentatious mansions, embellishing them with an array of cornices, ornamental cherubs and bas-relief detailing that loudly announced their economic standing. But after the 1929 stock market crash, many of these residents were forced to flee west to smaller – but still relatively lavish – homes in nearby Westmount (see p.99). The neighbourhood's character changed drastically as the downtown core encroached, and skyscrapers sprouted up where mansions once had been. Thankfully, much of the area north of rue Sherbrooke has remained relatively untouched, and most of the mansions there maintain their sumptuous facades – even though they've nearly all been turned into university faculties, hospital wings and apartments.

To tour the neighbourhood in one continuous flow, which should take you no longer than an afternoon, head west on rue Sherbrooke from rue University; the streets branching off from here contain an assortment of heavyweight cultural institutions in just a few short blocks. The **Musée McCord d'Histoire Canadienne**'s glossy collection of Canadiana and the venerable **Musée des Beaux-Arts** are complemented by the leafy campus of **McGill University**, while the substantial **Centre Canadien d'Architecture** is the lone sentry marking the southwestern border.

The area covered by this chapter is
shown in detail on colour map 3.

MUSÉE McCORD D'HISTOIRE CANADIENNE

Map 3, G5. 690 rue Sherbrooke O. Tues–Fri 10am–6pm, Sat & Sun 10am–5pm; $8.50, free Sat before noon; ⓦ*www.mccord-museum.qc.ca*. Métro McGill.

On the corner of rues Sherbrooke and University sits the **Musée McCord d'Histoire Canadienne**, a handsome nineteenth-century limestone building that faces its one-time administrator, McGill University. Now private, the museum dedicated to Canadian history was opened in 1921 following the donation of wealthy magistrate David Ross McCord's collection of 15,000 artefacts. The current collection numbers nearly a million objects, photos and documents, although the majority of these only come out during high-calibre temporary exhibitions held on the ground floor.

MUSÉE McCORD D'HISTOIRE CANADIENNE

On the second floor, more than 800 pieces are permanently displayed in Simply Montreal, an exhibit addressing the city's social and commercial development. Though lacking cohesiveness – it seems as if nearly every aspect of Montréal life is touched on in only a few rooms – the exhibit does have its strong points. The real stunners are the gritty floor-to-ceiling black-and-white **photographs** of the city taken by Montréal photographer William Notman in the early 1900s. These anchor the displays in galleries three and four and provide the exhibit's most visceral contrasts: an image of rue St-Jacques bustling with streetcars and calèches is around the corner from a forlorn shot of workers' houses, with sagging wood frames and crooked stone chimneys. Equally sterling are the **aboriginal items**, such as a collection of wampum beads once used as trading currency and a delicately carved and painted Iroquois baby carrier. The array of memorabilia from elite Montréal families is also delightful, showing off things like an intricately detailed mourning necklace, with its onyx and pearl pendant worn to honour the dearly departed.

McGILL UNIVERSITY

Map 3, G4. 845 rue Sherbrooke O. ☏398-6555, ⓦ*www.mcgill.ca.* Métro McGill.

The greatest beneficiary of the Golden Square Mile's decline was Québec's first English-language university, **McGill University**, whose expansive campus inherited a number of mansions vacated by the neighbourhood's wealthy merchants. Their stone facades give the grounds a decadent air rare on most colleges, and its picturesque setting on the slopes and foreground of Mont Royal produce a quietude that's unexpected so close to the bustle of downtown.

While the campus spreads from rue Sherbrooke up to the mountain, and west from rue University to rue Peel, the main thrust of the university lies behind the semicircular **Roddick Gates** that enclose the top of avenue McGill College. The gates' colonnades open onto the campus's main road lined with grassy quads on either side, and on the right a **statue** of founder James McGill surveys the land. The main road leads directly to the Neoclassical **Arts Building**, the campus's first building, situated on a slight promontory at the northern end of the campus. It's distinguished from the rest by McGill's red-and-white flag atop its cupola – stand on the front steps for a fine view of downtown and the surrounding campus.

Musée Redpath

Map 3, F4. 859 rue Sherbrooke O. Mon–Fri 9am–5pm, Sun 1–5pm, closed Sat all year; June–Aug closed Fri also; free. Métro McGill.

Before reaching the Arts Building, the main road branches out, with the western fork cresting in front of the **Musée Redpath**, an unusual museum devoted to zoological and ethnological pursuits. The 1882 Greek Revival structure in which it is housed lays claim to being the province's first custom-built museum, and inside there's an impressive two-storey-high oval atrium with a wrapround mezzanine.

Architecture aside, though, it's an odd place with a hodgepodge collection of dusty fossils and ethnological tidbits covering two floors and lacking in context. Still, there are some interesting relics, like the 7m-long menacing Albertosaurus dinosaur skeleton known as "Zeller" that strides over the atrium's centre, and the 4m-long anaconda skeleton resting nearby. The top floor landing's shelves of cultural artefacts are poorly lit, but peer closely enough and you'll see some spooky Congo ritual masks and crusty Egyptian sarcophagi behind the glass. Extending out from the landing, the mezzanine's rounded walls are a taxidermist's dream with hundreds of stuffed birds, mammals and amphibians displayed. Among them is a soft and tawny-furred southern flying squirrel and a beautiful quetzel, a peacock-like bird whose long wispy tail glimmers with aqua-green and marine-blue tints.

ALONG RUE SHERBROOKE

Map 3, C4–G4. Métro McGill or Peel.

For decades, the stretch of **rue Sherbrooke** between rue Guy and rue University that forms the core of the Golden Square Mile was known as Canada's Fifth Avenue, as it was home to the country's chicest boutiques. Although the strip lost its five-star rating when much of the city's money shifted westward to Toronto years ago, it retains elements of its former shopping glory nonetheless, and Ralph Lauren hobnobs with Escada and Giorgio Armani, alongside Holt Renfrew, Canada's answer to Nieman Marcus. Those allergic to high-priced clothiers will still enjoy a stroll down this length of rue Sherbrooke, as impressive ornamental details like demonic gargoyles, wrought-iron entrance grilles, and detailed bas-relief carvings add to the street's architectural panache. One of the finest examples is the Beaux-Arts expanse of the **Ritz Carlton** hotel, built in 1911 and announcing its grandeur with a sinuous frieze of acanthus leaves and twinkling lights from the entranceway's chandeliers.

For more on rue Sherbrooke's shops,
see Chapter 14, "Shopping".

A HOUSE-HUNTING DETOUR

The Golden Square Mile's most noteworthy mansions are on the slopes of Mont Royal north of rue Sherbrooke, cradled by lush foliage and the mountain's rugged rock face. The roads around here are quite steep – although the superb views of downtown along the way offer plenty of excuses for a breather. Begin by heading to the north end of rue McTavish, McGill campus's western artery, to avenue des Pins ouest. On the north side of the street, at no. 1025, looms Ravenscrag, built for shipping magnate Sir Hugh Allan in 1864. The magnificent Tuscan-style villa, now home to a psychiatric institute, embodies the phrase "my home is my castle". Hemmed in by a weighty stone and wrought-iron gateway, the mansion's two sprawling wings connect to a central watchtower that rises high above the roofline. Allan himself often stood in the windowed tower to observe his ships docking at the port far below, and for decades its rough-cast stone facade welcomed Montréal's finest, along with royalty like Japan's Prince Fushimi, to waltzes in the grand Second Empire ballroom.

MUSÉE DES BEAUX-ARTS

Map 3, D4 & D5. 1379 and 1380 rue Sherbrooke O. Tues–Sun 11am–6pm, Wed til 9pm; special exhibits $10–15, free Wed after 6pm; permanent collection by donation; ⓦwww.mbam.qc.ca. Métro Guy-Concordia.

Canada's oldest art museum, the **Musée des Beaux-Arts** is renowned for the excellent quality of its visiting exhibits and the sheer size of its collection. Spanning two buildings and 65 rooms, seeing everything on display could easily take a full day, but doing so need not be a priority as the permanent collection is actually rather spotty. Certain aspects, like the post-1945 contemporary-art collection, are of high calibre, as are many of the pieces by renowned

Ten minutes west along avenue des Pins, at no. 1418, stands the Maison Cormier, its handsome Art Deco facade enhanced by a female statue above the door. The family of former Prime Minister Pierre Elliott Trudeau live there today and Trudeau died there in 2000. Across the street at no. 1415 is the Cuban Consulate's digs. The location hints at the longstanding friendship between Trudeau and Fidel Castro – a bond so strong that Castro was a pallbearer at Trudeau's funeral.

Four residences back east along avenue des Pins, a set of stairs on the south side of the street leads down to avenue du Musée. The three eclectic mansions closest to the base of the stairs on the left form the Russian Consulate, and it's thought the United States was closely monitored during the Cold War from here. Whatever the Russians were up to, they clearly didn't want anyone knowing about it: when fire broke out in 1987, they kept the firemen outside for fifteen minutes while they loaded document-filled boxes into waiting cars. From here, it's a five-minute walk to the bottom of avenue du Musée and the Musée des Beaux-Arts.

artists like Picasso, Rodin, El Greco and Dali. Unfortunately, these are surrounded by many lesser-known – and inferior quality – works. Note that the museum is planning to rearrange its permanent collection between 2001 and 2002, meaning the works mentioned below might be found elsewhere when you arrive. If you're looking for a particular piece, ask at the reception counters located on the buildings' main floors, where you can also pick up a museum map.

The Musée des Arts Décoratifs's collection of furnishings by Alessi, Philippe Starck, Charles and Ray Eames, and Arne Jacobson, formerly displayed in an annexe, is being moved into the Pavillon Hornstein.

MUSÉE DES BEAUX-ARTS

Pavillon Jean-Noël Desmarais

The best of the permanent collection and the temporary exhibits are housed in the modern **Pavillon Jean-Nöel Desmarais** on the south side of rue Sherbrooke ouest. Designed by Moshe Safdie, the pavilion merges the red-brick facade of a pre-existing apartment building into a new wing built of Vermont marble. Begin on the fourth floor, where pieces from the museum's **European decorative arts** and **Old Masters** from the twelfth-to nineteenth-century collections are on display. Stand-outs in the first few rooms include Salvador Dali's amusing silver *Chess Set*, with thumbs for pawns and various fingers as the remaining pieces, and James Tissot's splendid oil painting *October*, featuring an elegant young lady tucked amongst golden autumn foliage. Later rooms showcase English painter Thomas Gainsborough's immense *Portrait of Mrs George Drummond* looking demure at her country estate, and Rembrandt's *Portrait of a Young Woman*, her face brilliantly illuminated against an almost black background. The collection of late-sixteenth-century works matches El Greco's ethereal *Ecstasy of St Francis* with Hendrick de Clerk's orgiastic aftermath of *Moses Striking the Rock*, while the gallery showcasing the museum's religious altarpieces has a Jan de Beer triptych with pastoral overtones as the centrepiece.

The temporary exhibition halls that mount the museum's high-calibre shows are down a floor. To the left of these are two small galleries, the first of which displays a fine collection of **Impressionist** pieces by Monet, Cézanne, Sisley, and a gloomy Degas alongside three Renoirs, whose *Vase of Flowers* overflows with vibrant colours. The second gallery here hosts **twentieth-century European Art**, with stand-outs by Giacometti, Matisse, Modigliani and Dali, whose pre-Surrealist *Portrait of Maria Carbona* faces Picasso's sexually charged *Embrace*, a Cubist take on entwined lovers.

In the basement, the superb **contemporary art post-1945** collection has a strong accent on works by Canadian artists. Jack Bush, Alex Colville, Christopher Pratt and Michael Snow are all represented, but the best of the pieces belong to Québécois artists. Look for Claude Toussaint's acrylic *Gong 96*, depicting a pastel-hued bulls-eye – stare at it too long and you may go cross-eyed. Nearby hangs Jean-Paul Riopelle's magnificent oil painting *Austria*, its hundreds of geometric daubs of colour surrounding a starkly white centre. But pride of place goes to **Automatiste** Paul-Émile Borduas, who gets an entire gallery in the back. Examine his pieces counterclockwise to follow his artistic progression – early works are much more fluid and bright than later pieces, which are sparsely coloured but highly textured. These culminate with *Black Star*, its putty-coloured background heavily sculpted and layered with his painting knife.

An underground passageway connects the two pavilions
from the post-1945 contemporary art galleries.

Pavillon Michal et Renata Hornstein

The older of the two buildings, the elegant Beaux-Arts **Pavillon Michal et Renata Hornstein** on the north side of rue Sherbrooke ouest, houses the thrust of the museum's **Canadian collection** in its second-floor galleries, which are reached by ascending the main hall's majestic grand staircase. The furthest gallery to the left is crammed with decorative arts, the showstopper being an outrageously extravagant white-oak Renaissance revival sidebar; dog's heads protrude on both sides of a central mirror while their catch – fish and fowl – hang by their feet and tails on the lower side panels. The middle gallery is busy with Inuit

MUSÉE DES BEAUX-ARTS

soapstone carvings; *Finger Pulling Game*, a palm-sized Iqaliut soapstone showing two hunched men with bony forefingers cocked for action, is particularly delightful.

The main gallery's collection of Canadian paintings pre-1945 is less than spectacular and confusing to boot, as numerous dividing walls break up the flow. There are some noteworthy mentions, starting with Cornelius Krieghoff's two warmly rendered scenes of domestic aboriginal life, *Indian Hunter and the Family* and *Indian Family in the Forest*. Paul Kane's *Mah-Min*, a menacing-looking Indian chief in full regalia, is also worth a nod, as are the series of landscapes by the **Group of Seven**, a group of Canadian artists that set the standard for landscape paintings throughout much of the twentieth century. Tom Thompson, the inspiration behind the group's creation, has several works here, including his magnificent *In the Northland*, which resonates with the orange hues typical of northern Canadian autumns. Emily Carr's *Indian War Canoe*, inset with a frog-like mascot on the bow, is symbolically hung just outside the area devoted to the Group – while they admired her work tremendously, she met them near the end of their heyday and never became an official member. Heading towards the back of the gallery, you'll find Adrian Hébert's *Montreal Harbour*, a good portrayal of Vieux-Port activity in the 1920s, before reaching three bizarre pieces by Alfred Pellan on the back wall, including his disturbing *Mad Love* awash in bloody red.

South on rue Crescent from the museum, nineteenth-century town houses host some of the city's most upscale boutiques; closer to rue Ste-Catherine, bars and dance clubs take over (see Chapter 11, "Drinking", and 12, "Nightlife").

MUSÉE DES BEAUX-ARTS

CENTRE CANADIEN D'ARCHITECTURE

Map 3, A6. 1920 rue Baile. June–Sept Tues–Sun 11am–6pm,
Thurs til 9pm, closed Mon; Oct–May Wed & Fri 11am–6pm,
Thurs 11am–8pm, Sat & Sun 11am–5pm, closed Mon & Tues; $6,
free Thurs after 5.30pm. Ⓦ*www.cca.qc.ca*.
Métro Guy-Concordia or Atwater.

Situated on the southwestern outskirts of the Golden
Square Mile, the significant collection of architectural
prints, drawings and scale models belonging to the **Centre
Canadien d'Architecture** (CCA) is housed in an
immensely formal building set back from landscaped
grounds. The cold, grey-limestone facade, designed by
Peter Rose, is broken up by few windows, a minimalist
approach echoed in the angular metal-and-glass portico
over the entrance to the grounds themselves. But what the
CCA lacks in detail on its side facing rue Baile it more than
makes up for on the side that fronts boulevard René-
Lévesque. Here, two Golden Square Mile-era houses col-
lectively known as the **Shaughnessy House** have been
ingeniously incorporated into the building, and their refurbished interior chambers offer the most luxurious sitting
areas in the city. Outfitted with marble fireplace mantles
and archways supported by grooved columns, the setting
may make you linger long enough to forget about seeing
the exhibits.

**One-hour guided tours of the building and the
Shaughnessy House are offered on weekends with
the price of admission; call Ⓣ939-7026 for times.**

The CCA mounts anywhere from three to eight exhibitions a year using pieces from its archives – past shows have
focused on the works of Frank Lloyd Wright, Frederick
Law Olmsted and Carlos Scarpa, with whimsical displays on

Disney theme parks and garden implements also receiving critical acclaim. If you're in town between exhibits, there is no permanent collection to tour as such, though museum staff insist the architecture of the Shaughnessy House fills that function. The CCA's **gardens**, on the south side of boulevard René-Lévesque, are also open to the public (daily 6am–midnight; free), and are scattered about with an incongruous collection of architectural chunks and columns.

Mont Royal
and the Plateau

No neighbourhood is as emblematic of Montréal as **Plateau Mont-Royal**, a dense urban area that manages to capture the city's duelling Anglophone and Francophone traditions, as well as its immigrant legacy. The Plateau Mont-Royal, called just the Plateau by most, occupies the east flank of **Mont Royal**, and the edge of the plateau where the land drops down towards the St Lawrence is clearly visible along the district's southern border, rue Sherbrooke. It extends in the east and north as far as rue d'Iberville and the Canadian Pacific Railway tracks respectively. The northwest corner of this area, though, is taken up by a different neighbourhood, **Mile End**, adjacent to the town of **Outremont**.

Most of the area covered by this chapter is shown in detail on colour map 5.

The Plateau's tight grid of streets was laid out shortly after the first horse-drawn trams began trundling through what had been a mostly rural landscape in 1860. The district's main arteries developed along the tram routes, prompting the building boom of the Plateau's characteristic town houses. While the eastern half of the Plateau has remained steadfastly Francophone, the western part has been home to a rotating cast of immigrants since the late 1800s, although, as of late, yuppies have been the largest group of arrivals.

While pretty much devoid of standard tourist attractions, the neighbourhood is nonetheless a fabulous place to wander about. The main drags – **avenue du Mont-Royal**, **rue St-Denis** and especially **boulevard St-Laurent** – hum with a constant energy, and the area is home to many of the city's finest restaurants, bars and clubs. Add to that a wide-selection of trendy boutiques and charming green spaces, **Square St-Louis** and larger **Parc Lafontaine** in particular, and you've got yourself a great day out.

Contrasting with this very urban landscape is the neighbourhood's chief attraction: its proximity to the **Parc du Mont-Royal**, which covers the summit of Mont Royal and its southern and eastern slopes. Wound about with heavily used trails, the park draws active Montréalers from all over the city, many of whom stop to ogle the spectacular views of downtown from the various lookout points. The large, rounded hill dominates the city's skyline and Montréalers' perceptions to the extent that, although it rises to a height of only 233m and actually comprises three separate summits – Mont Royal, Westmount and Outremont – everyone simply calls it **the mountain**.

Confusingly, Montréalers refer to "the mountain" or "Mont Royal" when talking about the whole mass, just the summit of Mont Royal or even the Parc du Mont-Royal itself.

The largest green space on the mountain, though, is not the park, but the two huge **cemeteries** on the northern slopes, while beyond these are the Université de Montréal and the enormous dome of the **Oratoire St-Joseph**.

AVENUE DU MONT-ROYAL, RUE ST-DENIS AND AROUND

Map 5, G3–I6. Métro Mont-Royal.

The Mont-Royal Métro station exits directly onto Place Gérald-Godin, a paved plaza named after a Québécois poet whose "Tango de Montréal" is excerpted on the wall of a nearby building. **Avenue du Mont-Royal**, running along the front of Place Gérald-Godin, has become increasingly gentrified of late, with a collection of boutiques, cafés and restaurants catering to a diverse population. But as you head further east, the district's make-up becomes increasingly Francophone and more down-market, reflecting the traditionally working-class population.

The yellow Tourisme Plateau Mont-Royal **information kiosk** across from Métro Mont-Royal station dishes out brochures and maps throughout the summer (June to early Sept daily 10am–7pm; early Sept to Oct Sat & Sun only; ⓣ840-0926 ext 34, ⓦ*www.tpmr.qc.ca*).

To get a flavour of the distinct, early-twentieth-century residential architecture typical of the Plateau, take a stroll down some of the side streets that branch off of avenue du Mont-Royal, notably avenue de Christophe-Colomb and rue Fabre. Wrought-iron balconies, ornate parapets and *tourelles* (turret-like dormers) adorn the brick and greystone town houses, but the most notable features are the rows of exterior staircases – built outside despite the snow to save interior space.

Many of the same architectural details appear on the more bourgeois greystone town houses lining north–south running **rue St-Denis**, two blocks west of the Mont-Royal Métro station. Long *the* shopping street for the city's Francophones, rue St-Denis continues to draw well-heeled shoppers with its array of fashion boutiques, French bookstores, interior-design shops and a multitude of cafés, bars and bistros. Three blocks south of avenue du Mont-Royal, rue St-Denis crosses red-brick-paved **avenue Duluth**. Lined with *apportez votre vin* (bring your own wine) restaurants, this street makes for the most pleasant route for the ten-minute walk to Parc Lafontaine to the east.

Reviews of Plateau-area restaurants begin on p.146.

Parc Lafontaine

Map 5, H4–I6. Daily 6am–midnight. Métro Mont-Royal or Sherbrooke.

The Plateau's most central park, **Parc Lafontaine**, offers a green respite from the crowded streets nearby. In its western half, a promenade makes for a lovely stroll around two large man-made ponds, while to the east a network of lamp-lit pathways are shaded by tall trees. Locals swarm to the place in warmer times to bask in the sun, take a lazy turn on a pedal-boat or cruise around on rollerblades. The outdoor **Théâtre de Verdure**, on the western side of the ponds, regularly stages free summertime performances that range from classical concerts to Shakespeare (see p.182). In winter the frozen-over ponds create a perfectly romantic scene for **ice skating** (see Chapter 16, "Sports and outdoor activities").

SQUARE ST-LOUIS AND RUE PRINCE-ARTHUR

Map 5, F6. Métro Sherbrooke.

Back on rue St-Denis, and just before it runs into rue Sherbrooke, is **Square St-Louis**, Montréal's most attractive square. The elegant ensemble of grey-stone Victorian residences with fanciful *tourelles* – some painted in vivid red or purple – that border it were originally occupied by the city's Francophone elite. Accordingly, the square itself has a formal layout, centred around a large fountain with pathways radiating outward beneath the overarching trees.

On the opposite side of avenue Laval from the square begin the five pedestrianized brick-paved blocks of **rue Prince-Arthur**, lined with restaurants and bars with plenty of outdoor seating. Tourists crowding around the street performers and artists' stalls set up here can make it a bit difficult to navigate, but even Montrealers occasionally get caught up in the hubbub and settle back with a pitcher of sangria to watch the busy parade.

THE MAIN

Map 5, E3–E7. Métro Sherbrooke or Saint-Laurent; bus #55.

The pedestrianized part of rue Prince-Arthur ends at the no-less-crowded **boulevard St-Laurent**, jammed with revellers passing to and from the many bars and restaurants on the city's most famous strip. Appropriately known as "**The Main**", boulevard St-Laurent, the traditional divide between the Catholic, French-speaking east of the city and the Protestant, English-speaking west, captures much of the city in microcosm, reflecting its ethnic diversity and attracting citizens of all stripes with its pulsing vibe. The nonstop stream of automobile traffic moving northward echoes the movement of the immigrants who walked up the Main from the port, stopping, as legend has it, when they heard their own language being spoken. Eastern Europeans, Jews, Greeks, Hungarians, Portuguese and Latin Americans have all passed through, leaving behind a trail of wonderful ethnic shops and restaurants. The "discovery" of the area's cheap rents and ethnic flavour by artists and students in the 1970s and 80s gave it a hip reputation that has led to rapid gentrification.

In 1792, boulevard St-Laurent was chosen as the official divide between east and west, with east–west street numbers subsequently designated so that they increase from zero the further away you travel.

There's not really anything specific to see here – the street's charm is appreciated by just wandering along – though you might want to check out trendy **ex-Centris**, the multimedia cinema at no. 3536 on the Main's flashiest block, south of rue Prince-Arthur. Behind the cinema's colonnaded facade are bizarre ticket booths where you're face-to-face with a video image of the ticket-seller (eerily, real human hands pass you your ticket).

Northwards from rue Prince-Arthur, you'll find more of the Main's former life – bakeries, butchers, kitchenware and fabric shops – struggling against the tide of new bars and cafés. One classic storefront that won't be going anywhere soon though is **Schwartz's**, a tiny deli further up the Main at no. 3895. No visit to the city would be complete without a classic Montréal smoked-meat sandwich, and this unassuming spot, open since 1930, is the best place to tuck into one (see pp.133–134 for a review).

MILE END AND OUTREMONT

Map 5, B1–E2; map 2, F2–H3. Bus #51, #80 or #535.
Further along The Main, north of avenue du Mont-Royal,

the Plateau blends into **Mile End**. Extending from rue Hutchison in the west towards rue St-Denis, the neighbourhood's more pronounced ethnic character and cheaper rents are drawing businesses that were once lower down on the Main, earning it the "new Plateau" label. The district's commercial flavour is concentrated along **avenue du Parc**, a bustling street with excellent Greek restaurants, while Jewish bagel bakeries are the main draw on **avenue Fairmount** and **rue St-Viateur**, not far from the city's largest community of Hassidic Jews.

The black-clad men with curls peeking out of their hats provide a striking contrast to the fashionably attired bourgeois Francophones who have colonized the slopes of **Outremont** just to the west. The main shopping and promenading street for Outremont's stylish set is lively **avenue Laurier**, full of chic cafés, restaurants and upscale boutiques.

For a different ethnic flavour, catch bus #55 to Little Italy, half-a-dozen long blocks north of avenue Laurier on the Main – see p.154.

PARC DU MONT-ROYAL

Map 5, A6–D3. Daily 6am–midnight. Ⓦ*www.lemontroyal.com*. Bus #11, #80, #129 or #535.

Rising up north of downtown and visible from much of the city, the mountain is crowned by **Parc du Mont-Royal**. Opened in 1876, the park's creation was the result of demands for the mountain's preservation after a number of its trees were cut for firewood after a particularly harsh winter. Occupying some 544 acres – a fifth of the mountain's total area – it was designed by the American landscape architect Frederick Law Olmsted, whose works include

New York City's Central Park and Golden Gate Park in San Francisco.

Ascending the mountain

From the intersection of boulevard St-Laurent and rue Rachel, head west to **Parc Jeanne-Mance**, where a path continues on past soccer fields to Parc du Mont-Royal's main access point – easy to spot by the **Sir George-Étienne Cartier monument**, topped by a winged angel and guarded by four reclining lions. The surrounding plaza draws hundreds on summer Sundays from noon until dusk for the **Tam Tams**, a large drumming jam session and improvised market with hippyish overtones.

North of the monument, **chemin Olmsted**, the gravel path designed by Olmsted for horse-drawn carriages, ascends the 4.5km up to the Chalet and cross in a series of gentle looping slopes. The lazy hour-long stroll up the main path offers several memorable vistas of the city below, but there's a shortcut halfway along if time is limited. Just after the two-kilometre mark, look for the 200-odd steps that lead up to the Chalet – a treacherous climb when covered in snow and ice, and exhausting at any time.

Atop the mountain

If you stick to chemin Olmsted, the trees open out into a large grassy expanse surrounding the man-made **Lac aux Castors** (Beaver Lake) twenty minutes further along. Pedal-boats ($6 per half-hour) rather than beavers glide across the surface of the former swamp, and the immediate area is popular for winter activities like sledding (Wed–Fri 10am–5pm, Sat 10am–8pm, Sun 10am–6pm; $7, $3.50 for children under 13), and skating on the lit trails running amongst the nearby trees. On the slope above the lake to the east is the **Maison Smith**, a squat stone structure housing an information centre and exhibition on Mont Royal (daily 9am–5pm; ☏843-8240, ⓦ*www.lemontroyal.com*).

You can rent snowshoes, cross-country skis, ice skates and bicycles in season from the pavilion next to Lac aux Castors (☏843-8240).

Five to ten more minutes of walking up chemin Olmsted brings you to the rustic mountaintop **Chalet** (daily 10am–8pm) and the nearby 30m-high **cross**, one of the city's most recognizable landmarks and visible from miles around. The Chalet's long, low, stone building is a good spot to warm up on colder days, with a passable canteen, toilets and a gift shop. The chief attraction, though, is the large semicircular plaza in front of the Chalet that offers outstanding **views** of downtown's skyscrapers and beyond. It's possible to walk east along chemin Olmsted to the base of the cross, although it's not nearly as impressive up close. The illuminated metallic structure, erected in 1924 by the St-Jean-Baptiste Society, recalls the wooden one that Paul de Chomedey, the founder of Montréal, planted on the mountaintop in 1643 in honour of the fledgling colony being spared from a flood.

THE CEMETERIES

Map 5, A1–B4; Map 2, D3–F4. Métro Côte-des-Neiges or bus #11. The winding paths amidst large pockets of trees and shrubs make the 165-acre Protestant **Cimetière Mont-Royal**, founded in 1847, another wonderful place to wander around. Easily accessed from the car park behind the Maison Smith in Parc du Mont-Royal, the cemetery draws relatively few people, and the surrounding ridges help cut out most of the city's noise. The **reception centre**, located at the bottom of the slope next to the north entrance off boulevard Mont-Royal, has a guide for bird-watchers (145 species of birds have been spotted here) in addition to a map listing the burial sites of prominent citizens – the Molson brewing family's mausoleum is particularly impressive.

The adjacent (but not directly connected) **Cimetière Notre-Dame-des-Neiges** has been the resting place for the city's Catholics since 1855. The most impressive aspect is simply its vast scale – with nearly a million resting souls, it is one of the largest cemeteries in North America. There's a gate on chemin Remembrance opposite Lac aux Castors, but for information about the gravesites you'll need to visit the main reception, a fifteen-minute walk away. To get there, head west along chemin Remembrance and turn right on chemin de la Côte-des-Neiges; you can also take bus #165, #166 or #535 directly to the cemetery from Métro Guy downtown.

- -

It's a five-minute walk to the Oratoire St-Joseph from the Cimetière Notre-Dame-des-Neiges' northwest corner, where a gate opens onto avenue Decelles. Turn right as you exit and then immediately left on chemin Queen-Mary.

- -

ORATOIRE ST-JOSEPH

Map 2, C3. 3800 chemin Queen-Mary. Daily 7am–9pm; free; Ⓦ*www.saint-joseph.org*. Métro Côte-des-Neiges or bus #165, #166 or #535.

Towering over the northwestern slopes of Mont Royal is the immense granite **Oratoire St-Joseph**, a monumental domed shrine set on a promontory far back from the street. Upon approaching, you may well find yourself passing pilgrims in search of physical cures heading up the structure's hundred-odd steps on their knees. Such displays of devotion are the norm from visitors who often feel divinely inspired by the life of its late founder, Frère André Bessette (see box, p.79).

The sheer size of the structure almost matches its mythical aura. Topped by a remarkable 45m-high copper dome second only to that of St Peters basilica in Rome, the interior chambers are so dispersed that escalators link the complex's main sights, including the hypnotic **Votive Chapel**, majestic **basilica** and an **exhibition** on Frère André that features one of Montréal's most bizarre spectacles.

Enter through the doors to the left of the main portico, where detailed guidebooks are available free of charge.

Inside the Oratory

The ground-floor **Votive Chapel** is the oratory's eeriest room – the flames of 10,000 votive candles illuminate a colossal collection of wooden canes, crutches and braces. Left behind by healed pilgrims, their numbers make a statement even hard-line skeptics would have difficulty explaining. A central statue of St Joseph with his arms outstretched stands between two doorways leading to a simple room containing Frère André's **tomb**, where parishioners can often be found touching the black-marble slab in an attempt to establish a connection with the man.

The landing at the top of the first set of escalators leads to an outdoor terrace with terrific views, and the oratory's gardens, landscaped by Frederick G. Todd, the man behind Île Ste-Hélène (see p.92) and Québec City's Plains of Abraham (see p.269).

Tucked away on a mezzanine two floors up from the chapel is the Frère André **exhibition**. Here, three rooms central to his life have been re-created with their original furnishings. His bedroom, with its tiny bench-like bed and small roll-top desk, illustrates his ascetic ways. The main draw on this floor is on the other side of the exhibition where, amazingly, a gold box atop a marble column holds Frère André's **heart**. It has been preserved as a sign of admiration, and some pilgrims have claimed it has twitched in their presence.

Further up is the **basilica**, an enormous space with a soaring domed ceiling that reaches 60m high. After the heavy iconography found in the lower levels, the basilica's lack of frills is quite refreshing. Its cruciform layout is simply ornamented by six wooden carvings of the apostles mounted at the end of each transept and a few stone carvings, depicting Christ's procession with the cross, inset in the connecting corridors. A corridor behind the altar accesses the most richly decorated part of the basilica, the **Chapel of the Blessed Sacrament**, painted from floor to ceiling in gold leaf and anchored by chunky green-marble columns. The doors to the right lead outside to Frère André's rustic **chapel**, with decor common to Québec's hinterlands, particularly the cross over the small altar – it's festooned with vanity-mirror lightbulbs.

As you leave the chapel, the driveway exits onto Summit Crescent, leading to Summit Circle and the Westmount lookout (see p.100).

INSIDE THE ORATORY

MONTRÉAL'S MIRACLE MAN

The founder of the Oratoire St-Joseph, the Blessed Brother André, is one miracle away from sainthood. Pope John Paul II recognized the first of his necessary two posthumous miracles in 1982, after a cancer-stricken New Yorker returned home from the Oratory disease-free. Still, André's early years didn't portend such greatness. In 1870, at the age of 25, he was asked to leave the religious order of the Holy Cross because he was too sickly to perform the manual labour asked of him. After the bishop of Montréal intervened, he was allowed to stay as a lay brother and was given the lowest job on the order's totem pole: porter of Collège Notre-Dame, a boys' school facing where the Oratory stands today.

It was here that André's extraordinary curative powers began to show, as after tending to ailing parishioners many would soon heal completely. He attributed his abilities to the oil he applied to their afflictions – an unguent that came from a lamp below a small statue of St Joseph in the college chapel. As knowledge of André's abilities spread, thousands of sick pilgrims began visiting the school. To make room, he built a primitive chapel in St Joseph's name at the top of the oratory's grounds in 1904, using $200 saved, in part, from tips received for cutting the boys' hair. More than four hundred cures were recorded here in 1916 alone.

Brother André never took credit for the cures pilgrims received, but always deferred to St Joseph's divine generosity. Indeed, André's devotion to St Joseph was so intense that he deemed the chapel an insufficient monument to his patron saint, and began canvassing for donations to build the massive shrine that stands today. André never saw it finished – he died in 1937, 18 years before the basilica was inaugurated. Impressively, one million mourners came to see his body laid out in the Votive Chapel.

Parc Olympique and Jardin Botanique

O n a clear day, the **Parc Olympique**'s striking architectural forms act like a magnet, enticing visitors from Montréal's downtown core to the Hochelaga-Maisonneuve neighbourhood, six kilometres to the east. Rising on the slope above the district's residential and industrial tracts, the flying-saucer-shaped **Stade Olympique** anchors the site of the 1976 Olympic Games. Climbing up the stadium's eastern side is the **Tour de Montréal**, an inclined tower with terrific views from its observation deck. Another relic of the Games, the nearby Vélodrome was transformed in 1992 into the **Biodôme**, an indoor zoo of sorts that re-creates four distinct ecosystems.

While the sheer scale of the stadium may first draw your attention, the real reward for venturing this far is the colourful **Jardin Botanique**, one of the largest botanical gardens in the world. Among its gardens and greenhouses are a Ming Dynasty replica **Chinese Garden**, a traditional **Japanese Garden** and the unique **Insectarium**, crawling with all manner of six and eight-legged creatures. Leave time as well for a tour of the elegant **Château Dufresne**, a restored Beaux Arts residence built in the early twentieth century.

The "Nature Package" lets you visit the Biodôme, Jardin Botanique and Insectarium for $15.75, while the "Get an Eyeful" pass also includes the Tour de Montréal for $23.50. These are available only at the attractions themselves.

The easiest way to reach this area from downtown is the fifteen-minute Métro ride on the green line to the Viau or Pie-IX (pronounced "pee neuf") stations, though you can also cycle along the rue Rachel bike path – it's about twenty minutes from rue St-Denis. The gardens and the park cover a huge area but fortunately a shuttle bus (free; 2–3 per hour) links each attraction with the Métro stop. Places to **eat** are a bit thin on the ground, and your best bet is to pack a lunch beforehand for a picnic in the gardens.

THE PARC OLYMPIQUE

The 1976 Olympics resulted in one of the city's most recognizable landmarks – and also one of its biggest follies. French architect Roger Taillibert was enlisted to create the **Parc Olympique**, the Games' massive arena and housing complex, and was told money was no object. Indeed, then-mayor Jean Drapeau even declared: "It is as unlikely that Montréal will incur a debt as for a man to bear a child." Biology has yet to catch up, but the complex ended up costing $1.4 billion – $300 million of which is still outstanding.

The Stade Olympique

Map 2, M3. Daily: mid-Feb to mid-June & mid-Sept to mid-Jan 10am–5pm; mid-June to early Sept 10am–9pm; closed mid-Jan to

mid-Feb; tower: $10, tour: $5.50, both: $12.50;
Ⓦ*www.rio.gouv.qc.ca*. Métro Viau or Pie-IX.

At the centre of the Parc Olympique looms the **Stade Olympique**, home to a varied line-up of rock concerts, monster truck races, trade shows and baseball games. It's an impressive sight, with huge concrete ribs rising out of an asphalt expanse to enclose the stadium's shell. Locals refer to the stadium as the "Big O" – ostensibly because of its shape or for the "O" in Olympic, but more usually for the fact that the city still owes so much money for its construction. And things look to be getting worse as the **Expos**, the Major League Baseball team who play here, are looking to move. There are half-hour **guided tours** (12.40pm & 3.40pm; ☏252-4737 or 1-877/997-0919), but for the time being at least, the best way to see the stadium is in the cheap seats during an Expos game (see pp.222–223 for details).

Tickets for tours and the funicular are sold in the Tourist Hall in the base of the tower.

Adjoining the stadium and rising above it in a graceful arc is the 175m-high **Tour de Montréal**, the world's tallest inclined tower. Although it was designed to hold the steel cables that raise the stadium's 65-tonne roof, at the time of the Games it was still just a concrete stump – the upper section was completed in 1987, and the movable roof was installed soon after (it never really worked properly, though, and was replaced by a fixed roof in 1998). A funicular rumbles along the tower's spine, rewarding riders with a panoramic view across the city from the top – on a clear day you can see as far as the Laurentians to the west. The tower's lower floor houses an interesting **exhibition** of photographs on Montréal's development throughout the twentieth century that makes the tower's ticket price some-

THE STADE OLYMPIQUE

what more worthwhile – though you can get an equally striking view from atop Mont Royal for free.

Biodôme de Montréal

Map 2, M3. Daily 9am–5pm, summers until 7pm; $10; Ⓦ*www.ville.montreal.qc.ca/biodome*. Métro Viau.

The Olympic Park's Vélodrome, the scalloped-roof structure south of the tower, is now the **Biodôme**, an environmental museum comprising four distinct ecosystems. Tallibert's design has proven as well suited for its current role as it was for cycling, as the large, column-free roof span allows visitors to wander freely through the flora- and fauna-filled zones.

While touring the hot and humid **tropical rainforest** section keep an eye out for the sloths; they move so slowly that their fur grows mould, quite unlike the lively marmosets and tamarins that swing through the trees above. It's noticeably cooler in the **Laurentian forest** portion, where you can look at a beaver dam and take a televised peek inside its lodge. Beyond that, in the **St Lawrence marine ecosystem** gulls fly overhead, touching down on an impressive tidal rock pool complete with foaming waves and a multicoloured population of anemones, crabs, lobsters and starfish. In the final **Polar zone** there are both Arctic and Antarctic ecosystems – puffins bob and dive along a replica Labrador coast while close by four species of penguins waddle amusingly on snow-covered slopes.

JARDIN BOTANIQUE DE MONTRÉAL

Map 2, L2–M3. Daily: 9am–5pm, mid-June to early Sept until 7pm; $10 (May–Oct), $7.25 (Nov–Apr); Ⓦ*www.ville.montreal.qc.ca/jardin*. Métro Pie-IX.

With its harsh winters, Montréal seems an unlikely locale

for one of the world's largest botanical gardens, but the **Jardin Botanique de Montréal** is just that, second in size only to London's Kew Gardens. Begun in 1931, the 75 hectare site comprises some thirty thematic gardens and ten greenhouses that can easily take a full day to explore. The **main gate** at the corner of boulevard Pie-IX and rue Sherbrooke provides the most dramatic approach, passing by a procession of colourful flowerbeds and a statue of founder Brother Marie-Victorin on the way to the Art Deco administration building. Behind the latter is the **reception centre**, where you can find out where and what's in bloom.

Between May and October, a free mini-train travels from the reception centre to the Insectarium and Tree House every fifteen minutes from 9.30am to 5pm.

The exhibition greenhouses

The reception centre leads to the **Molson Hospitality Greenhouse**, where fan palms, bamboo and other sub-tropical plants provide a backdrop to introductory displays on plant biology. From here, the rest of the greenhouses branch off in two narrow rows. The hot and humid east wing begins with a simulated **tropical rainforest** canopy, the fake tree limbs hosting several types of bromeliads, rootless plants which collect water in their funnel of leaves to survive. The next conservatory may look similar, but the **tropical economic plants** flourishing here – which provide everything from coffee to medicines – help illustrate our dependency on the rapidly disappearing rainforests. Next door in the most striking greenhouse, scores of multi-coloured **orchids** and **aroids**, such as the elegant calla lily, appear to have colonized an ancient ruin, the walls of which were actually built from salvaged Vieux-Montréal cobblestones.

The pathways in the east wing are narrow, and, when crowded, you may find yourself rushing over to the more varied, and less busy, west wing. First up is the **begonias and gesneriads** conservatory, whose bright flowers contrast greatly with the **arid regions** room next door, where a desert landscape supports spiky aloe, prickly pears and giant cacti straight out of a Road Runner cartoon. Further on, the footbridge and ponds of the aptly named **Garden of Weedlessness** create a memorable stage for the impressive Chinese *penjings* (dwarfed trees), tended and pruned with exacting care, while the two-tiered **Main Exhibition Greenhouse**, at the end of the row, showcases everything from springtime perennials to a carved pumpkin competition.

The outdoor gardens and arboretum

The first part of the Jardin Botanique to be developed, the **Exhibition Gardens**, bordering boulevard Pie-IX, are laid out in a formal French manner with a central axis interrupted by vine-covered pergolas and decorative fountains. Nearest to the reception centre are the perennial garden and the economic plant garden, installed to educate visitors on the uses of plants such as indigo and camomile. The axis terminates with a cluster of smaller gardens, including a collection of **poisonous plants** – fortunately fenced off.

The path opposite the Garden of Innovations leads to the **alpine garden**, where hardy dwarf conifers poke out of the scree and delicate alpine poppies cling to a pseudomountainous landscape. A small waterfall flows into a brook, along whose banks lies the English-style **Flowery Brook** garden of lilies, irises and peonies. The brook itself feeds the ponds at the centre of the Jardin Botanique, one of which borders on the new **First Nations Garden**, celebrating native-peoples' relationship with the land.

Beyond the ponds and covering more than half of the botanical garden's area is the **arboretum**, a popular spot for local birdwatchers and, in winter, cross-country skiers. It's at its loveliest in autumn when many of the 200-odd species of trees and shrubs turn fiery shades of yellow and orange. In the far northeast corner here, the **Tree House** interpretation centre holds a unique collection of dwarf North American trees, cultivated in the same manner as Japanese bonsai.

The Chinese and Japanese gardens

The true highlights of the Jardin Botanique are the two gardens based on the traditional landscaping principles of China and Japan. To get to them, head east from the reception centre, where you'll first come across the **rose garden** and then the **marsh and bog garden**, whose lotuses and water lilies are laid out in a grid of ponds with sunken pathways so you can see the plants up close.

From here, a pathway to the left leads through a grand pagoda-like arch guarded by stone lions to the **Chinese Garden**'s entrance courtyard, where a full-moon gate provides a perfect frame for the ensemble of seven pavilions interconnected by pathways and bridges – all often filled with human traffic. The design is a replica of a Ming Dynasty garden, and the most arresting feature is the Tower of the Condensing Clouds, a delicate 14m-high pagoda perched on the rock face above a small lake. The tree peony blooms – described by Marco Polo as "roses the size of cabbages" – are another startling sight, though you'll only see these bursts of soft pink if you visit in June. Throughout the year, Scotch pine and some twenty species of bamboo provide a green backdrop to numerous *penjings* (dwarfed trees), magnolias, azaleas and artfully placed stones, many of which were imported from China.

Far more serene, the **Japanese Garden** is a short walk to the northeast. The simple compositional elements of water, rock, plants, bridges and lanterns reward you with carefully planned views along the perimeter of its pond – save perhaps from the north side, with the Olympic Stadium in the distance. The garden might be best appreciated from the **Japanese Garden Pavilion**, especially during the occasional tea ceremonies (☎872-1400 for schedule). Designed in the style of a traditional family home, the pavilion has within its precincts a Zen garden and a collection of bonsai, the oldest of which are around 350 years old – almost the age of Montréal itself.

Insectarium

Much shorter-lived than the ancient bonsai are the inhabitants of the nearby **Insectarium**, a building shaped like a stylized housefly and devoted solely to insects and arthropods. The upper level is the more educationally oriented, with interactive displays on insect physiognomy standing alongside a collection of mounted butterflies – though in summer, it's more fun to see them in action in the adjacent **butterfly house** where local species flit about. There's also a transparent beehive that lets you see the busy inhabitants go about their work.

In November, the adventurous might come for the **insect-tasting** sessions when local chefs sauté scorpions and wrap other critters in pastry or chocolate (☎872-1400).

The bulk of the collection is downstairs, where some of the mounted beetles look like beautifully wrought jewellery, though the horned rhinoceros beetles might put you

THE CITY OF MAISONNEUVE (1883–1918)

The neighbourhood directly south of the Parc Olympique was, for 35 years, the independent city of Maisonneuve. Influenced by the City Beautiful reform movement, prominent citizens such as the Dufresne brothers hoped the city, created by wealthy Francophones who decided they would be better off on their own rather than being amalgamated by Montréal, would be a model industrial city. Buoyed by its proximity to both the St Lawrence River and railways, Maisonneuve did indeed become a major independent manufacturing centre, albeit short lived.

The City Beautiful reform movement believed in part that a beautiful city would encourage moral and civic virtue in its citizens. Maisonneuve's elite thus began construction on wide boulevards and elegant Beaux Arts public buildings. Architect Marius Dufresne was instrumental in designing many of these, including the Bain Morgan, an ornate public bath fronted by classical Ionic columns, and Marché Maisonneuve, a large public market topped by a copper-covered cupola and chateau-style corner towers. Both remain standing today and face onto the plaza at the intersection of rue Ontario est and avenue Morgan, a kilometre south of the Stade Olympique.

Despite the wealth generated by local industry, such grand projects ultimately led to the municipality's bankruptcy in 1918, and the city of Maisonneuve was soon annexed by Montréal. It's still a working-class district today, and if you'd like to visit, a free guidebook with suggested walking tours is available from the Hochelaga-Maisonneuve tourist office (Tues–Fri 9.30am–noon & 1.30–4.30pm, ☎256-4636, ⓦ*www.tourismemaisonneuve.qc.ca*), located in the Marché Maisonneuve at 4375 rue Ontario E.

off ever wanting to visit the tropics. The live scorpions, tarantulas and giant centipedes are hardly more comforting, even behind glass.

LE CHÂTEAU DUFRESNE

Map 2, L3. 2929 av Jeanne-d'Arc. Thurs–Sun 10am–5pm; $6.
Métro Pie-IX.

In contrast to the fluid forms of the Stade Olympique across boulevard Pie-IX, the Beaux Arts **Château Dufresne** presents a mannered and dignified sight. Inspired by the Petit Trianon palace at Versailles, the symmetrical facade gives no indication that there are actually two separate residences within, built between 1915 and 1918 for two brothers influential in the development of Maisonneuve (see box, opposite). The west wing housed the mansion's architect Marius Dufresne, while the east was home to his elder brother Oscar, an industrialist who headed the family's shoe-manufacturing company.

The entrance is in back, where a small exhibit on the history of the building and the Dufresnes gives a bit of context, although the free guided tours in the afternoon (Thurs & Fri 3pm; Sat & Sun 1.30pm & 3.30pm) best bring the period to life. The tour begins by ascending a staircase to the main foyer of **Oscar Dufresne's residence**, where his visitors must have been impressed by the gold-damask walls and opulent marble staircase. A hallway leads past Oscar's study to a large drawing room designed with business rather than socializing in mind, its decorative restraint limited to a few features like the elaborate candelabra set against the mahogany-panelled walls. Before heading down the hall, check out the small salon to your left – the decidedly secular decoration is the work of Guido Nincheri, the Italian artist whose works feature in more than a dozen Montréal churches. Keep an eye out for the "modern" touches in what initially appear to be classical scenes on the pastel-shaded walls – the nude in one is framed by electricity poles, still a novelty back in the early 1900s.

A winter garden occupies the rear of the apartment, and

through the breach made in the partition wall you can see its mirror image in **Marius Dufresne's residence**. Once inside the second brother's home, you'll notice almost immediately that it's less austere, and the eclectic mix of styles and comfortable design indicate a more intimate and domestic lifestyle. There's also more scope for whimsy, as the "Turkish lounge" with its bacchanalian frieze, plush cushions and houka attests.

Parc Jean-Drapeau

The roars and rumbles that spill out from the city's amusement park and annual Grand Prix do much to obscure the more simple outdoor pleasures found on **Parc Jean–Drapeau**, the collective name of the two islands across from Vieux-Montréal. With a combined 268 hectares of greenspace – dotted with canals, parks and public art – the park is a popular urban escape, especially during the summer months as the breeze from the St Lawrence provides a welcome respite from the heat. Breaking up all the greenery are various buildings left over from the 1967 World Fair that drew some 50 million visitors to Île Ste-Hélène and Île Notre-Dame.

Note that you're unlikely to hear Montrealers refer to the islands as Parc Jean-Drapeau, a name recently given to commemorate former Mayor Jean Drapeau, the man responsible for Expo '67, who died in 1999. Instead, you're more likely to hear them referred to by their individual names.

The area covered in this chapter is shown on colour map 2.

ISLAND PRACTICALITIES

Parc Jean-Drapeau is easily reached from downtown. The most efficient way is on the Métro's yellow line to the Jean-Drapeau station on Île Ste-Hélène. Île Notre-Dame is accessible from here by walking over one of the two bridges that connect the islands, or by taking bus #167 that stops due east of the Métro station and makes a tour of both islands. From mid-May to early October, a ten-minute ferry ride connects Île Ste-Hélène with the Quai Jacques-Cartier in the Vieux-Port (call ☎281-8000 for schedules; $3.50). The bike path from the Vieux-Port will get you there in about thirty minutes; head west and take the turn-off to Cité du Havre that passes under Hwy 10 and over the Pont de la Concorde. You can also drive over either of the two bridges though on-island parking is scarce and costs $10. A seasonal information booth near the Métro gives out maps of the islands (May to early Sept daily 9am–6pm; ⓦwww.parcjeandrapeau.com). While it's possible to walk around the islands, riding a bike or rollerblading are the best ways of getting around; a kiosk near the Métro station rents either for $7.50/hour.

ÎLE STE-HÉLÈNE

Map 2, I7–K6. Métro Jean-Drapeau.

Île Ste-Hélène, named after the wife of explorer Samuel de Champlain, who stumbled onto its shores in 1611, is the larger and more historic of the park's two islands. Most notably, the island was the last French possession in North America surrendered to the British in 1760; soon after, the British built a military garrison along its shores, but eventually ceded the island to Canada. Montréal purchased it in 1908, promising to turn the land around the military camp into a public park.

The city made good on its vow, and the island now provides visitors with ample spots to lounge about and picnic. Designed by Frederick G. Todd, who also landscaped the gardens at the Oratoire St-Joseph (p.76) and Québec City's Plains of Abraham (p.269), the park spreads out around a 45m-high grassy hillock, and is circled by one main road, the chemin du Tour de l'Île. The biggest draw, the city's **amusement park**, lords over its easternmost point while the remains of the **military fort** are nearby along the northern shore. On the southern side looms the aluminium sphere that encloses the **Biosphère**, an engaging ecological museum.

La Biosphère

Map 2, J7. 160 chemin du Tour de l'Île. June–Sept daily 10am–6pm; Oct–May Tues–Sat 10am–4pm; $8.50; Ⓦ*www.biosphere.ec.gc.ca/cea/*. Métro Jean-Drapeau.

A few metres east of the Métro exit along the chemin du Tour de l'Île, architect Buckminister Fuller's geodesic dome, built to house the United States pavilion during Expo '67, rises out of the greenery, its hulking orb evoking the ghostly remains of a futuristic planet. Composed of thousands of interlocking aluminium triangles, the sphere was left to decay following the World Fair, and lost its protective acrylic cover to fire in 1976. It was spruced up in 1992, and the **Biosphère**, an interactive centre with a focus on water ecosystems, and the St Lawrence and Great Lakes in particular, moved in.

Using the raised platforms that remained inside the dome, the Biosphère created a structure resembling an oil rig with four large interior halls dedicated to watery pursuits. Several of the permanent installations employ a playful tone that aims to amuse as much as educate: there's a squirtgun firing range, a scale that measures your weight in water, and a soothing Water Delights hall where you can bang on

LA BIOSPHÈRE

tonal water drums or soak your feet in a tiled Roman bath – towels are nearby. Still, the best reason to visit may just be the **view** of the city and islands through the dome's metallic trusses from the fourth-floor observation deck.

Fort de l'Île Ste-Hélène and Musée Stewart

Map 2, J6. 20 chemin du Tour de l'Île ☎861-6701. Mid-May to mid-Sept daily 10am–6pm; mid-Sept to mid-May Wed–Mon 10am–5pm; $6; ⓦwww.stewart-museum.org. Métro Jean-Drapeau.

A twenty-minute walk around the winding chemin du Tour de l'Île from the Biosphère will get you to the grounds of Montréal's only **fort**, its U-shaped layout situated close to the river's edge. Built by the British between 1820 and 1824 as a defence against the threat of American invasion, its four low-lying buildings are made of stone culled from the island's core and surrounded by fortifications indented with loopholes and parapets. On the parade grounds between the walls is a heavy bronze **cannon** bearing George II's royal coat of arms; lost during a storm in 1760, it was recovered in 1957, during the creation of the St Lawrence Seaway.

The complex never saw battle and got heavy use as an ammunitions storehouse instead. The British withdrew in 1870, and Canadian soldiers patrolled the fort until the end of World War II, when the barracks served as a prison camp for some 250 Nazis and deserters. Opened as a museum in 1955, the fort is staffed in the summer by costumed guides that lead informative, thirty-minute tours. To get the most out of a summer visit, arrive in the early afternoon, when ceremonial military corps perform drills on the parade grounds.

The only building open to the public is the ammunitions storehouse, now known as the **Musée Stewart**. Inside, there's an extensive collection of military memorabilia, full

PUBLIC ART ON THE ISLANDS

Among the more unique attractions in Parc Jean-Drapeau are several mammoth pieces of public art, their soaring steel and stone frames providing a striking contrast to the green, natural landscape. While dotted about both islands, the most exceptional examples are clustered on the western tip of Île Ste-Hélène, including Mexican sculptor Sebastián's fiery-red *Puerta de la Amistad*, on the chemin du Tour de l'Île west of the Métro. The openings between its three columns play tricks on the eyes – depending on where you stand, one shrinks and the other expands. Around 100m northwest stands Alex Calder's grey-steel stabile *Man*. At 20m high and 29m wide, it's the largest work ever produced by the American sculptor, and its lumbering mass of sweeping wings and curved angles is poised over a belvedere with terrific views across to the city. Over by the ferry wharf, five white-granite pillars rising high up from the ground comprise *Imaginary Village* by Portuguese sculptor João Charters de Almeida, looking strangely like a modern version of Roman ruins. Back from Calder's piece, a path leads to the island's southwestern side to *Phare du Cosmos* by Yves Trudeau, a 9.5m-high sculpted robot whose chunky torso sits atop a tripod base. His head and body used to move; nowadays his mini-telescopic eyes are permanently transfixed on the Pont de la Concorde.

of uniforms and their accoutrements – French *justeaucorps* and pointy tricorn hats included – and all manner of threatening pistols, revolvers, rapiers and bayonets, some of which are etched with their owner's insignias.

La Ronde

Map 2, J6 & K6. Mid- to late May Sat & Sun 10am–9pm; early to mid-June daily 10am–9pm; mid-June to early Sept daily

10.30am–11pm; $29.50 full-access, $15.25 grounds only. Métro Jean-Drapeau and bus #167.

The shrieking sounds that can be heard all over the island's eastern points emanate from **La Ronde**, the city's amusement park, whose best thrill-ride is *Le Monstre*, the world's highest wooden double-track roller coaster. Close behind in thrills is *Orbite*, a rocket-launch simulator that shoots passengers 45m in the air before dropping them with a stomach-lurching plummet. While the line-ups for rides are usually short, and the diversions good fun, the 35 rides and the land they're situated on have, unfortunately, become quite dingy over the years due to financial neglect – though plans are afoot to spruce the place up.

La Ronde hosts a spectacular fireworks competition every June through July (see Chapter 18, "Festivals").

ÎLE NOTRE-DAME

Map 2, H8–J7. Métro Jean-Drapeau.

Man-made **Île Notre-Dame** rose from the St Lawrence in the span of ten months, its elongated teardrop shape consisting of silt and rock dredged from the construction of Île Ste-Hélène's Métro line. Today, its major draws are the massive **casino** along its shores and, for three days every June, the **Grand Prix**, which turns the island into a giant pit stop of fumes, screeching tires, and concession stands. The entire island is in fact circled by the 4.42km **Circuit Gilles-Villeneuve** racetrack, which when not in use by F1 drivers is open to the public for rollerblading, cycling and cross-country skiing. More worthwhile, though, are Île Notre Dame's **parklands** – its 122 hectares are ideal for strolling as they're delightfully laced with canals overarched with wooden footbridges.

Casino de Montréal and around

Map 2, I8. 1 av du Casino. Daily 24hr; ⓣ392-2746,
ⓦ*www.casinos-quebec.com*. Métro Jean-Drapeau and bus #167.

The diamond-shaped building that held Expo '67's French pavilion presides over Île Notre-Dame like the centrepiece of a giant engagement ring. Shielded from the sun by aluminium shards, the five-storey building is a marvel of concrete, steel and glass, and served a stint as the Palais de Civilisations, a museum showcasing treasures from ancient cultures, before being repurposed as a **casino** in 1993. It quickly proved too small to serve its growing clientele, and was expanded in 1996 to include the sawed-off pyramid formerly home to the World Fair's Québec pavilion to the east. The casino is now home to a whopping 3000 slot machines and 120 gaming tables and the place teems with players day and night.

Most of Île Notre-Dame's outdoor activities are clustered around the casino, and clearly signposted along the island's footpaths. The chunk of land immediately north envelops the perennially blooming Jardins des Floralies, a **garden** whose park benches and calming fountain invite lingering stays (May–Oct 6am–midnight). Due east, you'll find the city's only **beach**, the Plage des Îles (late June to late Aug 10am–7pm; $7.50; ⓣ872-6222), forming a sandy crescent moon along the eastern edge of the man-made lake in the island's centre.

You can rent peddleboats to cruise the canals at the Pavillon des activités nautiques on the beach and at the snack bar situated in the Jardins des Floralies for $9/hour.

CASINO DE MONTRÉAL AND AROUND

Westmount and the Lachine Canal

To encounter a small-town atmosphere not easily found in central Montréal, it's necessary to venture to some of the city's western neighbourhoods. **Westmount**, which borders the Golden Square Mile, has a picturesque, English vibe complete with Victorian houses and tree-lined streets, while to the south, **Pointe St-Charles** and **St-Henri** are throwbacks to the industrial era, their landscapes crossed by railroad tracks and dominated by tenement housing.

The contrast between Westmount and its southern neighbours is most keenly felt while travelling along the **Lachine Canal bike path** that starts from the Parc des Écluses in Vieux-Montréal (see p.34). The mansions belonging to the city's Anglo-Saxon elite look down – literally – over the city's poorer neighbourhoods flanking the canal's shores. At the end of the 11km bike path lies the town of **Lachine**, offering yet another eye-catching contrast as the skyline of this once booming fur-trade town is a miniature version of Vieux-Montréal's, silver dome and church spires included.

**The areas covered in this chapter are
shown on colour maps 1 and 2.**

WESTMOUNT

Map 2, C4–D5. Métro Atwater.

The wealthy residential neighbourhood of **Westmount**, tumbling down from the slopes of the mountain's western peak, became the new epicentre of Anglo-Saxon wealth after the stock market crash of 1929 forced Golden Square Milers to settle permanently into their one-time summer cottages. The choicest of these grand "cottages" remain perched high up on the mountain slopes, and while it's a hike to see them, the views from up top make the effort well worth it.

Westmount's few sights are clustered within a seven-block radius of avenue Greene, itself lined with upscale boutiques and presided over by a triad of impersonal black-and-glass towers known as **Westmount Square**. The Atwater Métro station's underground passageway connects to the Square's shopping concourse, from where you can exit onto avenue Greene. Once outside, turn right and then left onto boulevard de Maisonneuve to reach Westmount's architectural standout, the chunky Romanesque **Église St-Léon** at the corner of rue Clarke anchored by a gabled bell tower. The interior is a visual feast of Italian marble floors, columns embellished with Florentine mosaics, and superbly coloured frescoes on every inch of the domed ceiling painted by Guido Nincheri. His altar painting is the most intriguing work, as the church's namesake is shown standing with Attila the Hun; he's hardly the personage you'd expect in a religious portrait, but Pope St-Léon was instrumental in convincing Attila to leave Italy.

Guido Nincheri's decorative flair also
adorns the Château Dufresne; see p.89.

One block north of the church, and another one west on rue Sherbrooke ouest, is the neo-Tudor **Hôtel de Ville** (City Hall), at no. 4333. There's not much to see inside; more action is found at the rear, where the locals doffed in sporty whites frequently play croquet or lawn bowls on the village green. West of here is the oldest public library in the province, the **Westmount Library**, 4574 rue Sherbrooke O (Mon–Fri 10am–9pm; Sat & Sun 10am–5pm), its leaded windows engraved with the names of influential writers and philosophers. There's a cheerful domed **greenhouse** inside with goldfish-filled pools and park benches; the door at its western end leads to the ground-floor atrium of **Victoria Hall**, where local artists' works are showcased.

More upscale boutiques are found west of the
library on rue Sherbrooke ouest. For a list of
Westmount's best shops, see Chapter 14, "Shopping".

The lookout and around

Map 2, D4.

No one road leads directly up to Westmount's **lookout**. From the library, head northward through Parc King-George to avenue Westmount, and take it eastward until you reach avenue Aberdeen. From here, strike north to the curvy **avenue Bellevue**, Westmount's most enchanting street. Its heady hairpin turns wind past gingerbread houses, ivy-covered brownstones, and stone cottages before reaching **avenue Sunnyside**, home to the neighbourhood's ritziest private residences. The rambling medieval-looking mansion at no. 12-14 is perhaps the grandest of all – its gabled peaks poke through the trees behind a finely crafted gridiron gate etched with blooming lilies. Across the street, the first of two sets of steep stairs leads to the lookout on rue Summit Circle where an impressive panorama takes in the tony neighbourhood. The twelve-hectare **Summit Park** behind the lookout is a popular bird sanctuary, particularly in the month of May when high concentrations of passerines stop here during migration.

Follow Summit Circle westward and you'll arrive at Summit Crescent, which accesses the rear of the Oratoire St-Joseph (see p.76).

POINTE ST-CHARLES

Map 2, E7 & F8. Métro Charlevoix.

Slightly more than a kilometre west of the Vieux-Port lies gritty **Pointe St-Charles**, a community severed from downtown by the Lachine Canal and a string of major highways. The Pointe, as it's affectionately called, developed a rough reputation thanks to a working-class, largely Irish population that settled here in the early part of the 1800s to help build the canal and later worked in the now-defunct factories along its shores. Though pretty run-down nowadays, the Irish legacy is ever present in the shamrocks that emblazon the neighbourhood's bar and corner-store signs; the wrought-iron Celtic crosses gracing the gables of **Grace Church** at 2083 rue Wellington are particularly pleasing.

The rue Charlevoix turn-off breaches the canal and puts you right on the Pointe's main north–south artery.

POINTE ST-CHARLES

Maison St-Gabriel

Map 2, E8. 2146 Place Dublin. Late June to early Sept Tues–Sun
10am–5pm; Mid-April to late June & early Sept to mid-Dec
Tues–Sun 1.30–4.30pm; $5; ☎935-8136. Métro Charlevoix.

In the Pointe's south end stands its main attraction, the
Maison St-Gabriel, a picturesque duo of seventeenth-
century fieldstone buildings tucked behind a monstrous
1960s apartment complex. The lovely manor house,
trimmed by two stone chimneys and capped by a petite bell
tower, once served as the school and residence of the King's
Wards (see box, opposite); livestock was sheltered in the
rustic barn nearby. The estate's location here seems unexpected given the Pointe's industrial tenor, but there was little else around when Sœur Marguerite Bourgeoys purchased the land in 1668, and founded the school. Besides
housing her order of nuns, the house also served as a neighbourhood school and farm.

Sœur Marguerite Bourgeoys also established the
Chapelle Notre-Dame-de-Bon-Secours on the eastern
edge of Vieux-Montréal see p.30.

Th current house dates from 1698 – the original burned
five years earlier – and opened as a **museum** in 1966.
Members of the congregation founded by Bourgeoys give
informative, thirty-minute guided tours of the rooms, each
boasting unique pieces dating from the early eighteenth
century. Most unusual are the two large shelf-like sinks
made of black stone; the one in the kitchen is 1.5m-wide
and drains outside the house. The girls' dormitory is also of
interest as its tiny canopy beds are stacked high with pillows
so the girls would sleep virtually upright lest death come
and take them while lying down – a common superstition
at the time. During summer Sundays, the grounds are given

MAISON ST-GABRIEL

THE KING'S WARDS

When France settled Québec in the mid-1600s, the majority of residents were male bachelors recruited to defend against Iroquois attack; the few women on hand were either married or in the service of the church. The lack of eligible women vexed the men, who responded by carousing with native women. This behaviour was quickly deemed unsuitable, and a scheme was soon hatched to provide the colony with "honest" wives. King Louis XIV sent almost 800 women, to become known as the King's Wards (*filles du roi*), to New France between 1663 and 1673. Most were orphans who, in return for their services, had their passage paid for and received a royal dowry of useful household items that enhanced their marriage value.

The first contingents were dispersed between Montréal, Québec City and Trois Rivières, but many of the post-1668 arrivals resided at the Maison St-Gabriel. There, under the guidance of Sœur Marguerite Bourgeoys and members of her congregation, the girls learned domestic skills – latter-day home economics – while awaiting betrothal.

The plan was a success: the colony's population doubled between 1666 and 1672, and the king was able to phase out the programme which, in any case, had proved a drain on the royal treasury.

over to costumed performances and weaving and lace making demonstrations (call for information).

ST-HENRI

Map 2, C6 & D6. Métro Lionel-Groulx.

The neighbourhood of **St-Henri**, 800m west of the Pointe, is the perfect spot for a pit stop if travelling along the canal's bike path. Not far off the trail – there are signs pointing the way – is the Art Deco **Marché**

Atwater (138 ave Atwater; Mon–Wed & Sat 8am–6pm; Thurs–Fri 8am–9pm; Sun 9am–5pm), highlighted by a large clock tower and holding a public market brimming with stalls selling mouthwatering foodstuffs. One of the finest is the Première Moisson, a delectable gourmet shop at the market's southern end selling heavenly patés – among other sundry treats like dainty pastries and prepared salads – that are perfect for lunching along the canal. Also worth a peek is the section of rue Notre-Dame ouest north of the market, between rue Atwater and rue Guy, known as "rue des antiquaires" due to the numerous **antique shops** that line the street; see pp.195–196 for more details.

While browsing is the main trade in St-Henri nowadays, the neighbourhood's blue-collar history has its roots in leather tanneries. Though there's little left of the bygone era, its working-class roots are still evident a few blocks west of the market, on **rue St-Augustin**, a narrow residential street lined with quaint clapboard houses dating from the 1870s. Some have recently been covered with unattractive aluminium siding, but the restored private residences at nos. 110 and 118 recall a rustic charm with their small front porches, tiny dormer windows and brightly painted exteriors.

LACHINE

Map 1, D5. Métro Angrignon and bus #195.

The canal's bike path ends in the scenic town of **Lachine**, which sits on land granted to Robert Cavelier de La Salle in 1667 by the Messieurs de St-Sulpice, the priests that governed Montréal for over a century. La Salle was so obsessed with finding a passage to China that Montrealers mockingly referred to his territory as "La Chine" (China) – the name stuck even though he never

LACHINE

found the route, although he somehow managed to chart Louisiana instead.

Lachine grew up to be an important fur-trading post due to its location near the **Lachine Rapids**, which hindered ships from travelling to Montréal prior to the canal days, thus shipments were unloaded here for transportation to Montréal by land. Those days are remembered in Lachine's major attraction, the **Commerce-de-la-Fourrure-à-Lachine**, an interactive historical museum lodged in a former fur storehouse, while the once unnavigable rapids are now plied by rafts and jet boats (see Chapter 16, "Sports and outdoor activities").

The grassy 3km peninsula Parc René-Lévesque that juts out from the end of the bike path has a fantastical collection of contemporary sculptures and offers prime views onto Lachine's attractive skyline.

Lieu historique national du Commerce-de-la-Fourrure-à-Lachine

Map 1, D5. 1255 boul St-Joseph. April to mid-Oct, Mon 1–6pm, Tues–Sun 10am–12.30pm & 1–6pm; mid-Oct to Dec Wed–Sun 9.30am–12.30pm & 1–5pm; $2.50. ⓣ637-7433, ⓦ*www.parkscanada.gc.ca/fourrure*. Métro Angrignon and bus #195.

The **Commerce-de-la-Fourrure-à-Lachine** historical museum occupies an attractive low-lying fieldstone building built in 1803 as a storehouse for the country's leading fur company, the North West Company. Inside, the museum is jam-packed with hands-on exhibits dealing with the fur trade. The costumed mannequins guarding some of the displays are pretty cheesy, but you do get to handle some exquisite furs, the softest of which are beaver – a nearby price list notes a keg of rum bought three. There's also a weigh-station that determines your qualifications as a *voyageur*; their measurements were capped at 178cm and 63kg (5'7"/139lbs) so as not to upset the canoe in which they spent up to 18 hours a day. A fine example of their water transport, a 12-metre-long birchbark canoe, is also on display.

LISTINGS

9 Accommodation   109

10 Eating   125

11 Drinking   156

12 Nightlife   169

13 Performing Arts and Film   181

14 Shopping   194

15 Gay and lesbian   214

16 Sports and outdoor activities   221

17 Kids' Montréal   229

18 Festivals   235

19 City Directory   242

Accommodation

Montréal does not want for **accommodation**. Across the city, thousands of rooms are available, and each year more options surface. Still, the days of being able to score cheap rooms in upmarket **hotels** year-round are no longer, as the increasing number of visitors to the city have been matched by higher prices. During the high season, which runs from mid-May to early-September and again around Christmas, you should reserve well in advance – especially if you're coming on Grand Prix weekend or during the Jazz Fest (see Chapter 18, "Festivals"). Throughout the rest of the year, though, when vacancies are higher, good weekend specials can sometimes be found.

Due in large part to increasing hotel rates, **bed and breakfasts** are becoming increasingly popular and many of them are tucked into handsome greystones in ideal Plateau and Quartier Latin locations. Budget-conscious travellers also have a good selection of options, as Montréal's universities open their residence doors in summer, and several decent **hostels** are open year-round.

HOTELS

The major problem of Montréal's **hotel** scene is a shortage of quality mid-range accommodations – we've listed the

ACCOMMODATION PRICE CODES

Accommodation prices vary throughout the year, with the highest rates from mid-May to early-September, and again around Christmas. Our listings for hotels and B&Bs feature a code (eg ❸) for the least expensive double room in high season, excluding special offers.

❶ up to $50 ❷ $50–75 ❸ $75–100 ❹ $100–150
❺ $150–200 ❻ $200–250 ❼ $250–300 ❽ $300+

The prices do not include tax, which totals about 15 percent (some of which may be refundable – see p.245), plus there's an additional $2 per night occupancy tax.

best of a small supply below. If you're willing to spend a minimum of $150 a night, there are plenty of quality upmarket hotels to choose from. And if you're on a tight budget, somewhat shabby bargain hotels abound, many fortunately concentrated in energetic neighbourhoods like the Plateau and Quartier Latin. Hotels around the bus station in the Quartier Latin are especially cheap, but the immediate area is a popular drug-dealing spot that attracts unsavoury types day and night. Downtown finds an assortment of **chains** geared towards corporate travellers with a few winning independent hotels thrown into the mix. In contrast, Vieux-Montréal's **inns** are intimate and wonderfully atmospheric, but at a price – you're paying for the history of your surroundings as well as exclusive amenities.

VIEUX-MONTRÉAL

Auberge Bonaparte
Map 4, C4. 447 rue St-

François-Xavier ☎ 844-1448, ⓦ www.bonaparte.com.
Métro Place-d'Armes.
A handsome upscale inn,

steps from the Basilique Notre-Dame, built in 1886 and shaded by smart burgundy awnings. Inside, the quarters are decked out with wrought-iron headboards, hardwood floors, high ceilings and French dormer windows; the more expensive overlook the private gardens of the Séminaire de Saint-Sulpice and have a jacuzzi. The ground-floor restaurant serves up rich French fare (see p.138). Breakfast included. ❹

Auberge les Passants du Sans Soucy

Map 4, C5. 171 rue St-Paul O ⓣ842-2634.

Métro Place-d'Armes.

Vieux-Montréal's longest-running inn, housed in a greystone building built in 1723, is full of personal touches like flowerpots on the windowsills and lace curtains throughout. Brass beds and hardwood floors contribute to the romantic atmosphere, and some rooms have wooden beams and stone walls. Breakfast, served in a skylit nook, is included. ❹

Auberge de la Place Royale

Map 4, D5. 115 rue de la Commune O ⓣ287-0522, ⓦ*www.aubergeplaceroyale .com*. Métro Square-Victoria or Place-d'Armes.

The standard rooms have exposed stone and queen beds, but look onto a back lane. Pay a bit more and you can get a view of the Vieux-Port, along with four-poster bed and whirlpool tub. All the rooms, though, are a bit dowdy. Breakfast, served on a sidewalk terrace in summer, is included. ❺

Auberge du Vieux-Port

Map 4, F4. 97 rue de la Commune E ⓣ876-0081 or 1-888/660-7678, ⓦ*www.aubergeduvieuxport .com*. Métro Place-d'Armes.

An 1882 waterfront warehouse dotted with 27 loft-style rooms offering spectacular views onto the Vieux-Port or rue St-Paul from large casement windows. Original stone walls, hardwood floors and brass headboards add to the rooms' overall appeal. Three

HOTELS: VIEUX-MONTRÉAL

large lofts are also available, with full kitchen and washer/dryer, that can sleep up to four. Breakfast included. ⑤–⑦.

Inter-Continental

Map 4, B2. 360 rue St-Antoine O ⑨987-9900 or 1-800/361-3600, ⑩*www.interconti.com*. Métro Square-Victoria.

It's plush and expensive, but well worth the price. The rooms have huge floor-to-ceiling windows overlooking either Vieux-Montréal or downtown, and each comes equipped with marble bathrooms, modem hook-ups, and in-room movies and video games. Impeccable service is a guarantee, and you have a choice of either free breakfast or parking. ⑥

Pierre du Calvet

Map 4, H3. 405 rue Bonsecours ⑨282-1725 or 1-866/544-1725, ⑩*www.pierreducalvet.ca*. Métro Champ-de-Mars.

The *Pierre du Calvet* is housed in one of Vieux-Montréal's finest buildings (see pp.29–30 for more details), and the accommodation is as fine as the exterior – guestrooms include oriental rugs, gas fireplaces and original masonry walls. The ground floor has a superb wood-panelled library and sunken dining room – trio of mounted deer heads included – and breakfast is served in a plant-filled greenhouse that's home to several squawking parrots. ⑥

Place d'Armes

Map 4, D3. 701 Place d'Armes ⑨842-1887 or 1-888/450-1887, ⑩*www.hotelplacedarmes.com*. Métro Place-d'Armes.

The location of this eight-storey boutique hotel can't be beat – it's right on Place d'Armes, kitty-corner to the Basilique Notre-Dame. The spacious rooms are sleekly tailored in neutral tones, and extras like in-room CD player, high-speed Internet access and cocktail hour by the lobby fireplace complete the package. ⑤

DOWNTOWN AND THE GOLDEN SQUARE MILE

- - - - - - - - - - - - - - - - - - - -

Château Versailles

Map 3, B4. 1659 rue Sherbrooke O ⓣ933-3611 or 1-800-361-3664, ⓦwww.versailleshotels.com. Métro Guy-Concordia.

Spacious, individually decorated rooms in four greystones built in the 1800s. The deluxe suites have classy touches like chandeliers and gas fireplaces, while the sleek, standard rooms have perks that include CD players, modem hook-up and fancy toiletries. Book early, as it's extremely popular, and ask about weekend specials when doing so. Breakfast included. ❻

Comfort Suites

Map 3, D6. 1214 rue Crescent ⓣ878-2711 or 1-800/221-2222, ⓦwww.choicehotel.ca. Métro Guy-Concordia.

This place gets packed during the June Grand-Prix weekend as its rue Crescent location puts guests right in the thick of the three-day F1 street party. All the rooms are junior suites with pull-out sofa, and can sleep four. Street-facing rooms have private balconies with a bird's-eye view of the festivities. ❺

Le Germain

Map 3, F5. 2050 rue Mansfield ⓣ849-2050 or 1-877/333-2050, ⓦwww.hotelgermain.com. Métro Peel.

Every last detail in this boutique hotel has a designer touch to it, even the smart staff uniforms, which are the output of Québec fashion designer Philippe Dubuc (see p.199). The airy rooms feature dark woods, down duvets and a sheer glass wall that divides the bed from the shower (there is a wrap round shower curtain for privacy-seekers). In-room extras like CD player and VCR add to the package. Breakfast included. ❻/❼.

Manoir Ambrose

Map 3, E4. 3422 rue Stanley ⓣ288-6922 or 1-800/565-5455, ⓦwww.manoirambrose.com. Métro Peel.

Two adjoining nineteenth-century Victorian houses on a quiet street offering budget accommodation with character, albeit in slightly tatty condition. Some of the high-ceilinged rooms have air conditioning and private bathroom, for a bit extra. Breakfast included. ❷/❸

Marriott Château Champlain

Map 3, E7. 1 Place du Canada ⓣ878-9000 or 1-800/200-5909, ⓦ*www.marriotthotels.com/ YULCC/*. Métro Bonaventure. Popular with executive travellers as it's huge, well-appointed and connected to the Underground City (see p.43), this Marriott's most distinctive features are the rooms' unusual half-moon windows. Ask for quarters facing Place du Canada – the views are excellent. ❻

Hôtel de la Montagne

Map 3, D5. 1430 rue de la Montagne ⓣ288-5656 or 1-800/361-6262, ⓦ*www.hoteldelamontagne.com*. Métro Peel.
The lobby is something out of an *Arabian Nights* fantasy: two large sculpted elephants guard the front desk while a nearby flowing fountain, complete with golden water nymph, shines under a massive crystal chandelier. After this spectacle, though, the guestrooms are disappointingly standard. The lively singles' bar *Thursdays* is on the main floor. Breakfast included on weekends. ❺

Queen Elizabeth

Map 3, E8. 900 boul René-Lévesque O ⓣ861-3511 or 1-800/441-1414, ⓦ*www.cphotels.ca*.
Métro Bonaventure.
The grande dame of Montréal's big hotels, the *Queen Elizabeth* doesn't quite command the same kind of clientele as it did in the days when John Lennon and Yoko Ono staged their "Give peace a chance" bed-in here. Nowadays, its thousand-plus rooms play host to convention-goers, and the place can seem quite desolate when nothing corporate is going on. ❻

Ritz-Carlton

Map 3, E4. 1228 rue Sherbrooke O Ⓣ 842-4212 or 1-800-363-0366, Ⓦ*www.ritzcarlton.com*. Métro Peel.

Staying here has nothing to do with the room quality, which is perfectly standard, and everything to do with the brand name. Still, the lobby is spectacular, the charming garden-side restaurant is a lovely oasis in summer, and the hotel is located near the city's finest shopping. ❽

Le St-Malo

Map 3, A6. 1455 rue du Fort Ⓣ 931-7366, Ⓦ*www.colba.net/~stmalo*. Métro Guy-Concordia or Atwater.

A reasonably priced option on the western edge of downtown. The building lacks charm, but the fourteen rooms are well lit and come with cable television; the cheapest are on the small side. ❷

Travelodge Montréal-Centre

Map 3, K6. 50 boul René-Lévesque O Ⓣ 874-9090 or 1-888/515-6375, Ⓦ*www.travelodge.com*. Métro Place-d'Armes or St-Laurent.

There's not a lot of character here, but it's modern, clean and well located on the outskirts of Chinatown, close to Vieux-Montréal. Cable television and in-room coffee maker included. ❹

Wyndham

Map 3, J6. 1255 rue Jeanne-Mance Ⓣ 285-1450 or 1-800/361-8234, Ⓦ*www.wyndham.com*. Métro Place-des-Arts

A glass elevator silently whisks you up the outside of the building to the elegant third-floor lobby with marble floors so polished they squeak. The 600 expansive rooms lack personality but come with modem hook-ups and free newspapers. When the Jazz Festival is on (see p.238), you won't find a better location – the third-floor terrace overlooks the main stage. ❼

QUARTIER LATIN

Le Breton
Map 3, N4. 1609 rue St-Hubert ☏524-7273 or 1-888/336-3613, ⓦ*www.contact.net/publix/breton*. Métro Berri-UQAM.
A clean and friendly European-style hotel with well-priced though smallish rooms near the bus station and gay Village. Most rooms have a private bathroom, and all have cable television and free continental breakfast. Good family rates are available. ❷

Castel St-Denis
Map 3, M4. 2099 rue St-Denis ☏842-9719, ⓦ*www.castelsaintdenis.qc.ca*. Métro Berri-UQAM or Sherbrooke.
A good budget hotel right on trendy rue St-Denis in the heart of the Quartier Latin. Though the rooms lack flair, they're clean and include private baths, air conditioning and cable television. ❷

Manoir des Alpes
Map 3, N6. 1245 rue St-André ☏845-9803 or 1-800/465-2929, ⓦ*www.hotelmanoirdesalpes.qc.ca*. Métro Berri-UQAM.
A friendly, good-value hotel in a Victorian-era building that's seen better days. The adequate rooms include cable television, parking and breakfast; a couple of them have exposed brick and whirlpool tubs as well. ❸

Manoir St-Denis
Map 3, M4. 2006 rue St-Denis ☏843-3670 or 1-888/567-7654, ⓦ*www.hotel-manoir-stdenis.com*. Métro Berri-UQAM.
Bargain-basement lodging at the Quartier Latin's busiest intersection. Many of the rooms are dark, but they're reasonably clean and include private bathroom, cable television and mini fridge; the sagging front terrace overlooks the action. Breakfast included. ❷

Le St-Denis
Map 3, M6. 1254 rue St-Denis ☏849-4526 or 1-800/363-3364, ⓦ*www.hotel-st-denis.com*. Métro Berri-UQAM.

One of the city's finest mid-range hotels has an excellent location on busy rue St-Denis, immaculate rooms, friendly service and a funky downstairs café. Cable television and in-room coffee maker are part of the price; full bath or whirlpool tub are extra. ❸

PLATEAU MONT-ROYAL

Auberge de la Fontaine

Map 5, H4. 1301 rue Rachel E ⊤597-0166 or 1-800/597-0597, ⓦ*www.aubergedelafontaine .com.* Métro Mont-Royal.

This hotel scores high on charm and location, right across from Parc Lafontaine and close to the restaurants and shops of av du Mont-Royal. Its modern rooms are brightly painted, have queen or twin beds, and private bathrooms. Extras like private balcony and jacuzzi are also available. Breakfast and parking included. ❺

Casa Bella

Map 3, I4. 264 rue Sherbrooke O ⊤849-2777

or 1-888/453-2777, ⓦ*www.hotelcasabella.com.* Métro Place-des-Arts.

A surprisingly good and affordable option in a three-storey limestone town house a few short blocks west of boul St-Laurent. The rooms are basic but include continental breakfast, parking and most have private bathrooms. Ask for rooms at the back as they're quieter. ❷/❸

Château de l'Argoat

Map 5, G7. 524 rue Sherbrooke E ⊤842-2046, ⓦ*www.hotel-chateau-argoat.qc.ca.* Métro Sherbrooke.

A fanciful cream-coloured fortress offering 26 spacious and attractive rooms with eye-catching details like decorative mouldings, quaint chandeliers and large windows. All have private bath, but in the cheaper rooms they're quite cramped. Breakfast and parking included. ❷

HOTELS: PLATEAU MONT-ROYAL

Hôtel de L'Institut
Map 5, G6. 3535 rue St-Denis
ⓣ282-5120 or 1-800/361-5111,
ⓦwww.*hotel.ithq.qc.ca*.
Métro Sherbrooke.
Though the exterior is a
modernistic eyesore, *L'Institut*
is nonetheless an interesting
choice since it's the training
ground for students attending
Québec's Institute of Hotel
and Tourism Management.
Accordingly the quality is high
and the standards are strict.
The suites have delightful
views onto Square St-Louis.
Breakfast included. ❺

Hôtel de Paris
Map 5, G7. 901 Sherbrooke E
ⓣ522-6861 or 1-800/567-7217,
ⓦwww.*hotel-montreal.com*.
Métro Sherbrooke.
A mansion near rue St-Denis
with a lively ambience to go
along with the great-value
accommodation. There's a
balcony café to hang out in,
and the rooms have cable
television, telephone and
private bathroom; some have
air conditioning. Several
apartments (❹) with
kitchenettes are available for
longer stays. ❷

Pierre
Map 5, G7. 169 rue
Sherbrooke E ⓣ288-8519
or 1-877/288-8577,
ⓦwww.*pjca.com/hotelpierre*.
Métro Sherbrooke.
A darkly lit bargain hotel
with few amenities near rue
St-Denis. Its eleven rooms are
individually decorated in
styles ranging from rustic
weekend cabin to Seventies
disco fever, so ask to see them
first if you're picky about
decor. Laundry room and
kitchenette are on the
premises. ❸

Renaissance Hôtel du Parc
Map 5, D6. 3625 av du Parc
ⓣ288-6666 or 1-800/363-0735,
ⓦwww.*duparc.com*. Métro
Place-des-Arts and bus #80.
Upmarket accommodation at
the foot of Mont Royal with
added premiums like a sauna
and steam room. The
quarters are spacious and
well-appointed, many with
mountain views, and popular
with tour groups. The wood-
panelled lobby with fireplace
is especially warm and
inviting come winter. ❺

Résidence du Voyageur

Map 5, G7. 847 rue Sherbrooke E ⓣ527-9515; Ⓦ*www.wworks.com/~ resvoyager.* Métro Sherbrooke. A good-value hotel just east of rue St-Denis on busy rue Sherbrooke. The air-conditioned rooms have private bathrooms, telephones and cable TV, and the rock garden out front adds a whimsical touch. Rates include parking and breakfast. ❸

BED-AND-BREAKFASTS

Quebecers, who have a peculiar penchant for motels, have been slow to take to **bed & breakfast** accommodation. In recent years, however, that trend has started to wane as B&Bs have proven they can provide superior accommoda-tion for less – many of them charge under $100 a night. In addition to highly personalized service, B&Bs are also most often found on quiet, leafy side streets rather than the main drags. You can make reservations directly with the ones listed here, or use an agency to make the booking for you (see box, overleaf).

Angelica Blue

Map 3, L6. 1213 rue Ste-Elisabeth ⓣ844-5048 or 1-800/878-5048, Ⓦ*www.angelicablue.com.* Métro Berri-UQAM. An attractive B&B on a pretty side street near the Quartier Latin. The five rooms have lots of character – exposed brick walls, high ceilings and original antiques – and all the rooms are en suite. An additional two-bedroom apartment (❻) with full kitchen and private entrance can sleep a family of five. ❸

Bienvenue Bed & Breakfast

Map 5, F5. 3950 av Laval ⓣ844-5897 or 1-800/227-5897, Ⓦ*www.bienvenuebb.com.* Métro Sherbrooke.

B&B AND SHORT-TERM RENTAL AGENCIES

L'Appartement-In Montréal ☎284-3634 or 1-800/363-3010. Studios, 1-bedroom and 2-bedroom apartments with kitchenettes, air conditioning, phones and TVs, on the edge of the Plateau. Daily, weekly and monthly rates include access to outdoor pool and sauna, though parking is extra. $114 studio/$154 2-bedroom per night for seven-week stay.

Bed & Breakfast à Montréal ☎738-9410 or 1-800/738-4338, ⓦwww.bbmontreal.com. Montréal's original B&B agency lists good-quality houses downtown, in the Quartier Latin, and Québec City, starting at $60.

Downtown B&B Network in Montréal ☎289-9749 or 1-800/267-5180, ⓦwww.bbmontreal.qc.ca. Dependable agency that nearly always has a vacancy either downtown or in the Quartier Latin, starting at $85.

Fédération des Agricotours ☎252-3138, ⓦwww.agricotours.qc.ca. An excellent service listing quality-inspected B&Bs throughout Montréal and province-wide should you be moving on afterwards. Rates start at $65.

Vacances Canada ☎270-4459. Lists basic studio apartments in the Plateau area for $325/month.

Montréal's original B&B is in a handsome Victorian house on a picturesque street. The twelve rooms don't live up to the exterior though, as they're quite plain with industrial carpeting on the floors. Several have private bathrooms; those that don't do have in-room sinks. ❸

À la Maison de Pierre et Dominique
Map 5, F6. 271 Square St-Louis ☎286-0307, ⓦwww.pierdom.qc.ca. Métro Sherbrooke.
A charming navy-blue-trimmed house facing Square St-Louis with three tastefully decorated rooms and a

cheerful breakfast area. None of the rooms have private bathrooms, and there's a small sitting area. **❸**

Marmelade

Map 3, K7. 1074 rue St-Dominique ⊤876-3960, ⓦ*www.total.net/~marmelad*. Métro Place-d'Armes or St-Laurent.

An inviting five-room B&B on the outskirts of Chinatown with bonuses like sloped ceilings, a flower-filled terrace come summer, and two indoor lounges for the rest of the year – one with a cosy fireplace. Shared bathrooms. $100 deposit required. **❸**

Petite Auberge les Bons Matins

Map 3, D7. 1393 av Argyle ⊤931-9167 or 1-800/588-5280, ⓦ*www.bonsmatins.com*. Métro Lucien-l'Allier.

Located on a tree-lined street near the Centre Molson, this well-appointed B&B has a dozen large, en-suite rooms, each with picture windows, and additional details like arched ceilings and polished hardwood floors. Several have a fireplace. **❸**

Au Portes de la Nuit

Map 5, F7. 3496 av Laval ⊤848-0833, ⓦ*www.bbcanada.com/767.html*. Métro Sherbrooke.

Well-situated on one of the Plateau's most attractive streets, this Victorian house has five comfortable rooms; three with private bath. The least expensive share facilities; the priciest has wood-beamed ceilings and exposed brick walls. **❷**

Le Zèbre

Map 5, F6. 3767 av Laval ⊤844-9868, ⓦ*www.bbcanada.com/2728.html*. Métro Sherbrooke.

Located in the heart of the Plateau with three large and attractive rooms, *Le Zèbre*'s sitting room is elegantly furnished with a marble fireplace and bright bay window. Shared bathroom. Open mid-March to mid-Oct only. **❸**

BED-AND-BREAKFASTS

UNIVERSITY RESIDENCES AND HOSTELS

Montréal has several large **universities** scattered about the city and from about mid-May to mid-August they open their residences to visitors. These provide excellent value if you're not picky about frills, though you will get a linen service, access to a kitchenette, and a common room with cable television. The city also has a number of youth **hostels** and "Y's" offering primarily dormitory style accommodation, most of which should be booked far in advance come summer.

Auberge Alternative du Vieux-Montréal

Map 4, B5. 358 rue St-Pierre
☎282-8069, Ⓦ www.auberge-alternative.qc.ca.
Métro Square-Victoria.
Montréal's finest hostel is located in a refurbished 1875 Vieux-Montréal warehouse. The common room, with its exposed masonry wall and modern cooking facilities, is a great place to lounge, and the dormitories sleep from six to twenty on bunk beds. The top floor is women-only; the mixed floor below has arched windows and wood floors. Singles and doubles also available. Rates include Internet access and laundry facilities. $18/dorm, $45/single.

Auberge de Jeunesse Internationale de Montréal

Map 3, C7. 1030 rue Mackay
☎843-3317 or 1-800/663-3317,
Ⓦ www.ajmontreal.qc.ca.
Métro Lucien-l'Allier.
A well-equipped downtown hostel with over 200 beds. Dorms sleep a maximum of ten, and single, double and family quarters are also available. The lounge has a pool table and cable television, and reservations are advised between June and September. Member of Hostelling International. $19/dorm, $52/single (with membership card).

Auberge de Paris
Map 5, G7. 874 rue Sherbrooke E ☎522-6861 or 1-800/567-7217.
Métro Sherbrooke.

A new youth hostel with tiny bunk rooms in the Plateau district. Guests have access to cooking facilities, laundry room, café, garden and TV room. The second floor has a few single and double rooms. Check-in after 10pm is at the *Hôtel de Paris* across the street (see p.118). $19/dorm, $55/single.

Concordia University
7141 rue Sherbrooke O ☎848-4757, Ⓦ*www.concordia.ca*.
Métro Vendome and bus #105.

Sparse and clean single and double rooms seven kilometres west of downtown with shared kitchenettes, free local calls and linen service provided. Mid-May to mid-Aug; $20/single, $40/double.

Le Y des Femmes (YWCA)
Map 3, D7. 1355 boul René-Lévesque O ☎866-9941 ext 505, Ⓦ*www.ywca-mtl.qc.ca*.
Métro Lucien-l'Allier.

Women-only accommodation is available in this downtown YWCA in single, double, triple or six-bed dormitories. There are lots of extras here (laundry facilities, indoor swimming pool, and computer-equipped lounges), but coming home in twos at night is advised, as women have been assaulted in the vicinity. $22/dorm, $46/single.

McGill University
Map 3, G2. 3935 rue University ☎398-6367, Ⓦ*www.residences.mcgill.ca/summer.html*. Métro McGill.

Up to 900 single rooms in four residence buildings near downtown with shared kitchenettes and lounge areas. Sheets and towels are provided, as is free Internet access. Very popular among visiting Anglophones and, consequently, often full. Mid-may to mid-Aug only; $37.50.

Vacances Canada
Map 2, H3. 5155 av de Gaspé ☎270-4459. Métro Laurier.

UNIVERSITY RESIDENCES AND HOSTELS

Up to 200 beds are available all year, double that in July and August at the Collège Français, a college residence with two to six beds per room. The northern Plateau location makes it very popular, and it's frequently booked-up by Francophone school groups. $11.50/dorm, $18.50/double.

YMCA Centre-Ville

Map 3, E5. 1450 rue Stanley
ⓣ849-8394 ext 0,
ⓦ*www.ymcamontreal.qc.ca*.
Métro Peel.

Expensive, mixed YMCA – with single and double rooms and shared bathrooms – located downtown. Rates include health centre and swimming-pool access, and there's a ground-floor cafeteria serving three meals daily. $46/single, $56/double.

UNIVERSITY RESIDENCES AND HOSTELS

Eating

One of Montréal's greatest pleasures is **eating** out. On top of the expected array of authentic French cuisine, there's a huge selection of international foods in which to indulge. To house this wide range, the city has thousands of restaurants in a variety of guises, from cosy breakfast spots and speedy lunch-time diners to upscale and formal dining extravaganzas. Where the city truly excels is between these extremes – a bewildering array of moderately priced restaurants, often clustered close together, make it easy to just walk along and see what takes your fancy.

If you've come looking for local Québécois cuisine, you may have to look long and hard – apart from a few traditional standbys such as *tourtière* (meat pie), *fèves au lard* (baked beans with fatty bacon) and the fast-food *poutine* (fries smothered in gravy and topped with cheese curd) such cuisine is nearly nonexistent. What you will find though are what locals consider quintessentially Montréal delicacies, adopted from the European Jews who settled here in the early twentieth century. Top of the list is **smoked meat**, beef brisket cured in brine and then smoked (similar to pastrami or corned beef), which is sliced thick and piled high on rye bread. Another Montréal great is the rather prosaic **bagel** – denser and chewier than those found elsewhere – boiled first in honey water before being baked in a traditional wood-burning oven and sprinkled with sesame seeds; see p.207 for a review of the city's finest.

Montrealers tend to grab a quick fry-up **breakfast** or a croissant or muffin with their coffee on weekday mornings, but weekend **brunch** is an altogether different affair. Long and drawn out, the meal is an antidote to the previous night's partying and most places serve until mid-afternoon. **Lunches** offer the chance to try cheaper two or three-course *spécial de midi* (lunch special) menus at the city's pricier restaurants, but lighter and healthier options like soups, salads and sandwiches at a café or snack bar are more typical.

A complete index of restaurants by cuisine begins on p.136.

Dinner tends to be later in Montréal than many North American towns, with restaurants filling up between 7 and 8pm and serving until around 10 or 11pm. Most offer a three-course *table d'hôte*, which works out cheaper than ordering an individual starter, entrée and dessert à la carte. Many of the city's priciest dining places are **downtown**, where gastronomic French restaurants and higher-end ethnic eateries are tucked away on the side streets around rue Ste-Catherine. Over in **Chinatown**, rue de la Gauchetière is thronged with people seeking out not only Cantonese and Szechuan dishes, but also cheap and filling Vietnamese food. There are a few good options in **Vieux-Montréal**, as well, but many of the establishments here are overpriced tourist joints that don't offer much in the way of imaginative cuisine. The best place to eat out is on the **Plateau**, where stylish restaurants serve up innovative cuisine on rue St-Denis and boulevard St-Laurent just above Sherbrooke. Greek-style tavernas serving *brochettes* (shish kebabs) and a mix of other ethnic spots vie for the tourist trade on **rue Prince-Arthur** but you should head north a few blocks to

avenue Duluth, where more authentic cuisine from Portugal, Italy, Afghanistan and even the tiny Indian Ocean island of Réunion can be found. The majority of restaurants on both these streets invite you to *apportez votre vin* (bring your own wine), a practice quite common in Montréal; see p.206 for recommendations on where to pick up a bottle. For authentic Greek food, head up to **Mile-End**, where you'll also find the best bagel bakeries. Adjacent **Outremont** is full of cafés, bistros and slightly pricier but good-value ethnic eateries on and around avenue Laurier.

If you want to grab a **late-night** bite, there are numerous places scattered along rue Ste-Catherine and in the Plateau. Less conveniently, many smaller restaurants close Sunday and/or Monday, and places that cater to the business lunch crowd may not be open for lunch on the weekend; call ahead to avoid disappointment.

CAFÉS, BRUNCHES AND LIGHT MEALS

Nowhere is Montréal's European flavour more evident than in its small **cafés**, where you can usually sit and read or talk undisturbed for hours while sipping on a drink. The majority of the cafés listed below also dish out delicious **snacks** such as *croque monsieur* and *panini*, and some go as far as serving light bistro fare. These latter cafés typically serve up excellent weekend brunches as well, and the Plateau and avenue Laurier in particular have great spots to linger lazily over crepes, *pain doré* (French toast) or more lunch-like dishes.

For a completely different brunch experience,
head to Chinatown and get stuffed on dim sum –
see pp.143–144 for the top choices.

In addition to cafés and coffeehouses, you can seek out one of the city's many **diners** for deli-style meals, or try healthier food like soups, salads and sandwiches in smaller spots spread around the city. A number of bars also serve up grub at lunch or in the early evening (see Chapter 11, "Drinking").

VIEUX-MONTRÉAL

Bio Train
Map 4, A3. 410 rue St-Jacques ⓣ842-9184.
Métro Square-Victoria.
Self-serve health-food restaurant with tasty soups and hearty sandwiches. The muffins here – especially the tangy cranberry variety – make great snacks.

Le Cartet
Map 4, A6. 106 rue McGill ⓣ871-8887.
Métro Square-Victoria.
If the weather's decent, head here for healthy sandwiches and complete boxed lunches to go – it's not far from the Vieux-Port's many green spaces. Otherwise you'll have to fight for one of the two tables.

Eggspectation
Map 4, C3. 201 rue St-Jacques O ⓣ282-0119.
Métro Place-d'Armes.
Map 5, D1. 198 av Laurier O ⓣ278-6411.
Métro Laurier or bus #80.
Map 3, D6. 1313 boul de Maisonneuve O ⓣ842-3477.
Métro Peel or Guy-Concordia.
A variety of antique objects are scattered about the brick walls in the Vieux-Montréal, downtown and Mile End branches of this great local chain that's packed at weekends. Look for the cheaper "Classics" buried in the menu between the scrumptious crepes, French toast, eggs Florentine and the like. Open 6am to 3pm.

Titanic
Map 4, B4. 445 rue St-Pierre ⓣ849-0894.
Métro Square-Victoria.
Businesspeople and tourists

alike fill the large communal tables crammed into this small Italian-style deli serving pizza, sandwiches and healthy-sized salads from 8am to 3pm.

DOWNTOWN AND GOLDEN SQUARE MILE

Ben's Delicatessen
Map 3, F5. 990 boul de Maisonneuve O
Ⓣ844-1000. Métro Peel.
Lithuanian Ben Kravitz opened his deli in 1908 and his sons and grandsons still run this Montréal institution. Its gaudy 1930s interior continues to draw people into the wee hours for tasty smoked-meat sandwiches, but the yellowing celebrity photos on the wall attest to an earlier, more prosperous time. Open Mon–Thurs & Sun 7am–4am, Fri & Sat 7am–5am.

Marché Mövenpick
Map 3, G6. 1 Place Ville Marie
Ⓣ861-8181.
Métro Bonaventure or McGill.

Labyrinthine "marketplace" that combines some of the tackiest motifs of the countries whose cuisine is on offer here, including Italian pastas, Japanese sushi and Swiss *rösti* potatoes. Take a ticket (and map), pick and choose from the different food stands, then pay as you leave. Open until 2am.

Montréal Pool Room
Map 3, K6. 1200 boul St-Laurent Ⓣ875-0819.
Métro St-Laurent.
A Montréal institution: nothing much but a steel counter facing the grill where steamies (hot dogs) have been the order of the day since 1912.

Café République
Map 3, J6. 93 rue Ste-Catherine O Ⓣ840-0000.
Métro St-Laurent.
Popular with media types, this relaxed café is close to Place des Arts and does a fine cup of coffee. Good for light lunches – burgers, pizzas and salads – at decent prices.

CAFÉS, BRUNCHES AND LIGHT MEALS

Reuben's Deli

Map 3, F6 & E6. 892 and 1116 rue Ste-Catherine O ⓣ844-1605.

Métro McGill or Peel.

One of the best downtown delis, with great big jars of pimentos in the window and a wealth of smoked meats served up in a frantic atmosphere with friendly service. A favourite with local business types, and thus packed at lunch time. Open from 7am.

Café Toman

Map 3, C5. 1421 rue Mackay ⓣ844-1605.

Métro Guy-Concordia.

The irrepressible Czech owner will insist you try the desserts here, and with reason – the strudel is terrific. A mostly student crowd comes for simple sandwiches and tasty soups in what feels, with its dove-grey walls and white-plaster mouldings, like an East European parlour.

QUARTIER LATIN AND THE VILLAGE

La Brioche Lyonnaise

Map 3, M5. 1593 rue St-Denis ⓣ842-7017.

Métro Berri-UQAM.

The smell of freshly baked French pastries like flaky *mille-feuille* and chocolate eclairs from morning to midnight should lure you in to this café-patisserie. Try, too, the savoury crepes filled with egg, ham and cheese.

Kilo

Map 2, I5. 1495 rue Ste-Catherine E ⓣ596-3933.

Métro Beaudry.

The healthy salads and sandwiches served here are merely teasers for the wild array of killer desserts on offer – the cheesecake is particularly deadly.

La Paryse

Map 3, M4. 302 rue Ontario E ⓣ842-2040.

Métro Berri-UQAM.

Delicious hamburgers – try Le Spécial, which is topped with cream cheese and bacon

– served up in a friendly, 1950s-style diner.

Café Le Pélerin

Map 3, M4. 330 rue Ontario E ⊤845-0909.

Métro Berri-UQAM.

Some of the best coffee in the city, but if that's all you're after drop by in the late afternoon as it's packed at lunch for the sandwiches, *croques* and other light bistro dishes. Brunch served until 2pm on the weekend.

Presse Café Village

Map 2, I5. 1263 rue Ste-Catherine E ⊤528-9530.

Métro Beaudry.

One of the best spots in the Village for people-watching, especially with its front window rolled up, this busy 24hr café serves up fine basic salads and sandwiches along with Internet access for $5 per hour.

Le Resto du Village

Map 2, I5. 1310 rue Wolfe ⊤524-5404. Métro Beaudry.

Down a side street from rue Ste-Catherine, this small *apportez votre vin* diner serves

filling comfort food such as *pâté chinois* (shepherd's pie) and *poutine* to a largely gay crowd. It's open 24 hours and packs up quickly once the nearby clubs close.

Zyng

Map 3, M4. 1748 rue St-Denis ⊤284-2016.

Métro Berri-UQAM.

Create your own meal by choosing a meat, shrimp or tofu base and one of eight seasonings, then fill your bowl from an assortment of veggies and hand it to a nearby chef who whips it all up. It's not haute cuisine, but it's cheap and the tight-packed tables ensure a good conversational buzz.

PLATEAU MONT-ROYAL

- - - - - - - - - - - - - - - - - - -

Aux Deux Marie

Map 5, G4. 4329 rue St-Denis ⊤844-7246. Métro

One of the better of the many rue St-Denis cafés, *Aux Deux Marie* roast their own coffee beans and serve cheap cakes and snacks to go with

CAFÉS, BRUNCHES AND LIGHT MEALS

the finished brew. An expanded menu, including sandwiches, burgers and pasta, is served in the cosier, exposed-brick upper level.

Beauty's

Map 5, E3. 93 av du Mont-Royal O ⓣ849-8883. Métro Mont-Royal or bus #55.
A brunch institution that's been serving meals to customers snuggled up in cosy booths for nearly sixty years. The "Beauty's Special" – bagel, lox, tomato, red onion and cream cheese – is the best such combo in the city. Be prepared to get up extra early on the weekend to avoid the line-up.

La Binerie Mont-Royal

Map 5, F3. 367 av du Mont-Royal E ⓣ285-9078. Métro Mont-Royal.
Just four tables in this hole-in-the-wall diner, which prides itself on traditional Québécois cuisine. The house specialty is *fèves au lard* (baked beans), doused with ketchup, vinegar or maple syrup, and other worthwhile dishes include a mean *tourtière*

and the *pouding au chômeur* ("unemployed pudding") – a variation on bread pudding. Cheap breakfasts served from 6am. Closed Sun.

Le Café Cherrier

Map 5, G6. 3635 rue St-Denis ⓣ843-4308. Métro Sherbrooke.
An older Francophone crowd congregates here for guilt-free weekend brunches – the buttery eggs Benedict oozes calories – so you'll be hard-pressed to find a table on the terrace. *Croques* and quiches fill the afternoon gap before the fuller bistro menu is available in the evening.

Les Gâteries

Map 5, G7. 3443 rue St-Denis ⓣ843-6235. Métro Sherbrooke.
Opposite Square St-Louis, the warm ochre-and-yellow interior of this café makes for a great spot to indulge in one of the excellent cakes on offer – a big slice of dark chocolate *mousse royale* goes for $4. If you want something less sweet, the typical standbys – sandwiches, *croques* and quiches – are also available.

Café Laïka

Map 5, E4. 4040 boul St-Laurent. ☎842-8088.
Bus #55 or Métro Sherbrooke or Mont-Royal.

The sleek interior draws urbane hipsters from the Plateau for daily specials and *cafés au lait*. Floor-to-ceiling windows open onto the street in summer, and a small brunch selection, including eggs Florentine and crepes, is available on the weekends.

Mondo Fritz

Map 5, E5. 3899 boul St-Laurent ☎281-6521.
Bus #55 or Métro Sherbrooke.

Great little place for fries and a beer, as there's a wide array of dips for the former and a large, international selection of the latter. Good spot for vegetarians: both the *poutine*, served with a meat-free gravy, and the garden burgers are worth a try.

Porté Disparu

Map 5, H3. 957 av du Mont-Royal E ☎524-0271.
Métro Mont-Royal.

Folksy café with dark wood furnishings and exposed brick walls that's a good place to read or hang out. Cheap and generous three-course lunch specials for around $7, occasionally accompanied by impromptu piano playing. Schedule of evening gigs is posted at the door.

Café Santropol

Map 5, E5. 3990 rue St-Urbain ☎842-3110. Bus #55 or Métro Sherbrooke or Mont-Royal.

This outstanding and mostly vegetarian café on the corner of av Duluth has a lovely "secret garden" back terrace, and retains its charm in winter thanks to a cosy atrium. Massive inventive sandwiches (the "Midnight Spread" contains honey, peanut butter, cream and cottage cheeses, nuts, raisins and bananas) on chewy dark bread are accompanied by loads of fresh fruit. Vegetarian pies, salads and soups also available.

Schwartz's

Map 5, E5. 3895 boul St-Laurent ☎842-4813. Bus #55 or Métro Sherbrooke.

A small, narrow deli with

CAFÉS, BRUNCHES AND LIGHT MEALS

only ten tables that's been serving colossal sandwiches since 1930, *Schwartz's* consistently (and deservedly) tops the "best smoked meat" list – choose the *gras* style for the full-fat experience. There's usually a line-up out the door and surly service, but it's well worthwhile.

Le Toasteur
Map 5, H6. 950 rue Roy E ⓣ527-8500. Métro Sherbrooke.
Cute little brunch place with a retro Fifties feel and tables jammed in close together. It's packed at weekends when locals down rich eggs Benedict or simpler fry-ups. Superb, but expect a queue.

OUTREMONT AND MILE END

Café Ciné-Lumière
Map 5, E1. 5163 boul St-Laurent ⓣ495-1796. Métro Laurier or bus #55.
Antique Parisian decor sets the stage for cheap French food, along with a wide selection of mussels and movies shown on a large

screen – which are listened to through headsets – at 7pm.

La Croissanterie Figaro
Map 2, G3. 5200 rue Hutchison ⓣ278-6567.
Bus #80.
Delightful café with marble-topped tables and dark wood fixtures that added the *Figaro* to the name, though everyone still just calls it *La Croissanterie*. The wrap round terrace is the perfect place for pastries and coffee.

La Petite Ardoise
Map 5, D1. 222 av Laurier O ⓣ495-4961.
Métro Laurier or bus #80.
The *ardoise* (blackboard) in question is reflected in the blackboard-green walls (surrounded by honey-coloured wooden mouldings) and in the intellectual make-up of the Francophone Outremont regulars. The secluded garden terrace is an idyllic spot to sip your *café au lait*.

Wilensky's Light Lunch
Map 2, G3. 34 av Fairmount O ⓣ271-0247.

Métro Laurier or bus #55.
A lunch counter whose decor hasn't changed since 1932, and that includes the till, the grill and the drinks machine – you can still get an old-fashioned cherry or lemon coke. The $4 Wilensky Special includes bologna and three types of salami on a kaiser roll. Open Mon–Fri 9am–4pm.

RESTAURANTS

While it's easy to splurge on an expensive French **restaurant** in Montréal, the multitude of less formal ethnic spots can be just as satisfying and far more memorable, not to mention a good deal cheaper. The listings are divided by neighbourhood, but you'll also find a list cross-referenced by cuisine beginning overleaf. It's a good idea to reserve in advance, but there are enough choices on rue St-Denis, rue Prince-Arthur, avenue Duluth, boulevard St-Laurent and avenue Laurier to stroll around and see what grabs you.

In French, an appetizer is called an *entrée*,
while the main course is a *plat principal*. See the glossary
beginning on p.313 for more words likely to be on the menu.

RESTAURANT PRICES

The restaurant listings are price-coded into four categories: inexpensive (under $15), moderate ($15–25), expensive ($25–40) and very expensive (over $40). This assumes a three-course *table d'hôte* for one person, not including drinks, tax or tip. Taxes total just over 15 percent, and a 15 percent tip is standard and may occasionally be included on the bill as a service charge.

RESTAURANTS BY CUISINE

Afghan
Khyber Pass   p.149

African
Le Nil Bleu   p.151
La Piton de la Fournaise p.151
Souvenirs d'Afrique   p.152

Belgian
Witloof   p.153

Chinese
Hong Kong   p.143
Jardin de Jade   p.143
La Maison Kam Fung   p.144
Lotté   p.143
Zen   p.143

International/Eclectic
Area   p.144
L'Avenue   p.147
Club Lounge 737   p.140
Côté Soleil   p.148
Saloon   p.146
Toqué!   p.152
Union   p.139

Fondue
Fonduementale   p.149

French
Au 917   p.146
Le Café des
  Beaux-Arts   p.139
Bonaparte   p.138
Les Chenêts   p.140
La Colombe   p.147
Le Continental   p.148
Crêperie Bretonne
  Ty-Breiz   p.148
L'Express   p.149
Fouquet's   p.141
Le Grand Café   p.141
Laloux   p.150
Le Café du
  Nouveau-Monde   p.142
Le Parchemin   p.142
Au Petit Extra   p.145
La Rotonde   p.142

German
Checkpoint Charlie   p.147

Greek
Arahova Souvlaki   p.153
La Cabane Grecque   p.147
Milos   p.155
Terrasse Lafayette   p.155

Indian

| Masala | p.138 |

Italian

Amelio's	p.146
Boccacinos	p.140
Da Emma	p.138
Eduardo	p.148
Il Piatto Della Nonna	p.149
Lucca	p.154
Lugrano	p.150
Pizzeria Napoletana	p.154
Quelli Della Notte	p.154

Japanese

Katsura	p.141
Mikado	p.155
Yakata	p.155

Malaysian

| Nantha's Cuisine | p.151 |

Mexican

| Mañana | p.150 |

North American

Bar-B-Barn	p.139
Bâton Rouge	p.139
Laurier BBQ	p.153
Mike Bossy Restaurant	p.141

Portuguese

Ferreira Café Trattoria	p.140
Tasca	p.152
Le Vintage	p.153

Seafood

| Chez Delmo | p.138 |
| Maestro SVP | p.150 |

Steakhouses

| Moishe's | p.151 |
| Queue de Cheval | p.142 |

Thai

Bato Thai	p.145
ChuChai	p.147
Fou d'Asie	p.145
Red Thai	p.152

Tibetan

| Chez Gatsé | p.145 |

Vegetarian

| ChuChai | p.147 |
| Le Commensal | p.145 |

Vietnamese

Fou d'Asie	p.145
Pho Bac 97	p.144
Pho Viet	p.146

RESTAURANTS BY CUISINE

CHAPTER TEN

VIEUX-MONTRÉAL

Bonaparte

Map 4, C4. 443 rue St-François-Xavier ⓣ844-4368.
Métro Place d'Armes.
Moderate.
Located on a picturesque cobblestone street, the rich-red carpeting and dark-panelled wainscotting of this French restaurant provides a perfect backdrop to dishes like rack of lamb in port wine or lobster stew with a vanilla sauce; if you're feeling indulgent try the seven-course tasting menu ($52.50). No lunch on weekends.

Chez Delmo

Map 4, C3. 211 rue Notre-Dame O ⓣ849-4061.
Métro Place d'Armes.
Expensive–very expensive.
Seafood is the forte here, as evidenced by two long oyster bars up in front. In the back dining room, typically brimming with local stock-exchange workers, the fish and seafood dishes don't come cheap, but they do come perfectly cooked – the

chowder is also a treat. Closed Sun.

Da Emma

Map 2, G7. 777 rue de la Commune ⓣ392-1568.
Métro Square-Victoria.
Expensive–very expensive.
Fantastic Roman cooking served up in a stylishly renovated basement in one of Montréal's oldest buildings. Standout mains include fettucine *al funghi porcini* and succulent *abbachio* or *maialino al forno* (huge chunks of lamb or suckling pig). Save room, if you can, for the home-made sorbets and addictive tiramisu.

Masala

Map 4, B5. 373 Place d'Youville ⓣ287-7455.
Métro Square-Victoria or Place-d'Armes.
Moderate.
Punjabi and Kashmiri dishes are prepared with style and skill in this loft space. It's actually a cooking school – a group of at least four or more can book a two-hour class for $35 a head – but you can sample the food (and home-made mango ice cream) by

calling ahead for the $10 lunch. Groups of six or more are required for a dinner reservation, but if you're just a few, call to see if there's a group you can join. *Apportez votre vin.*

Union

Map 4, A7. 600 rue d'Youville ⊤286-9851. Métro Square-Victoria. **Moderate.**
A hopeless place to eat at in the evening (see "Drinking", p.159 for the reason why), *Union* draws loads of workers from nearby multimedia companies for its fusion/bistro lunch especially when it's nice enough to sit on the terrace. Try the *moules frites* or cappelini with sun-dried tomatoes and goat's cheese. Weekend brunch. Closed in the winter.

DOWNTOWN AND THE GOLDEN SQUARE MILE

- -

Bar-B-Barn

Map 3, C6. 1201 rue Guy ⊤931-3811. Métro Guy-Concordia. **Moderate.**

A fun, lively and loud restaurant serving tasty ribs in a faux Western setting. The hundreds of business cards stuck in the log rafters attest to its popularity with the local business world, and it's always packed to the hilt.

Bâton Rouge

Map 3, J6. 160 rue Ste-Catherine O ⊤282-7444. Métro Place-des-Arts. Inexpensive–moderate.
Huge portions of ribs, fries and other American standards with a slight Cajun touch. Good value considering the central location.

Le Café des Beaux-Arts

Map 3, D5. 1384 rue Sherbrooke O ⊤843-3233. Métro Peel or Guy-Concordia. **Moderate.**
Second-floor lunch spot in the Musée des Beaux-Arts where the food – French bistro with a Québécois touch – and table service are equally good. There's a wide range of wines by the glass and stand-out meals include the lamb shank and the portobello mushroom risotto.

Dinner is only available Wednesday evenings.

Boccacinos

Map 3, G6. 1251 av McGill College ☎861-5742.
Métro McGill. **Moderate.**

A great spot for a bite downtown, with loads of tables on two floors and a good, crowded buzz – the place is heaving at lunchtime. There's a range of breakfasts starting at $4 served until 3pm, or choose from pizza, pasta, salads and light meals like grilled swordfish.

Les Chenêts

Map 3, D5. 2075 rue Bishop ☎844-1842.
Métro Peel or Guy-Concordia.
Expensive–very expensive.
Superior French cuisine served up in a warm candle-filled room adorned with copper cookware. Highlights include wine-soaked escargots and good game dishes, such as pheasant breast smothered in wild mushrooms. With an extensive wine list, referred to by staff as "the bible", selecting a vintage to

accompany your meal won't be easy; there are also some 360 varieties of cognac.

Club Lounge 737

Map 3, G6. 1 Place Ville Marie ☎397-0737.
Métro McGill or Bonaventure.
Expensive.
The prices may be sky-high, but so is the 360° view, perched 737 feet above sea level with the city spread out below. There are exotic touches like Thai and Indian on the menu, but French predominates – try the pan-fried fillet of beef or the lovely poached salmon. There's also a club and lounge with an outdoor terrace downstairs.

Ferreira Café Trattoria

Map 3, E5. 1446 rue Peel ☎848-0988.
Métro Peel. **Very expensive.**
Portuguese *azulejos* (glazed tiles) hint at the authenticity of the delicious cooking here, notably fish dishes like the grilled sardines coated in sea salt. If you're on a budget, drop by for the two-course weekday lunchtime special

($22–25) served up in a lively atmosphere. Comprehensive port and wine selection. Closed Sun; no lunch Sat.

Fouquet's

Map 3, D5. 2180 rue de la Montagne ☎284-2132. Métro Peel. Expensive.
Trading on its century-old Parisian namesake's fame – illustrated by photos of celebrities who ate there – prices are a bit higher than they should be, though lunch is an OK deal ($16–24). That said, the classic French menu (try the veal medallions with truffles) is tempered with a Mediterranean influence – the risottos and pastas actually giving vegetarians some choice here. You can buy and smoke Cuban cigars in the red-carpeted piano lounge upstairs. Closed Sun.

Le Grand Café

Map 3, H6. 1181 Union ☎866-1303. Métro McGill. Moderate–expensive.
The rattan chairs yell bistro, and the lunch menu delivers here, though with a few Asian-fusion twists like dumplings and sashimi thrown in. The evening is more classic French – think duck *confit* and rack of lamb – and the prices jump accordingly, though the wine list is reasonable. Closed Sun.

Katsura

Map 3, D5. 2170 rue de la Montagne ☎849-1172. Métro Peel. Expensive.
Large and popular downtown Japanese restaurant where kimono-clad waitresses bring sushi, sashimi and chicken or steak teriyaki to your table. Traditional Japanese paintings add a subtle touch to the understated decor. No lunch on the weekend.

Mike Bossy Restaurant

Map 3, H6. 1175 Place du Frère-André ☎866-5525. Métro McGill or Square-Victoria. Moderate–very expensive.
The oak-panelled dining hall in this mansion offers the appropriate surroundings for a rich, meaty dinner; go for the generous portions of juicy prime rib of roast beef carved at your table. The

downstairs bistro is cheaper, if less grand.

Le Café du Nouveau-Monde

Map 3, J6. 84 rue Ste-Catherine O ⓣ 866-8669. Métro Place-des-Arts. Moderate.

A place to see and be seen, as much to sample the high-quality bistro fare like a simple *bavette* with salad, though food is a bit richer upstairs, where you can dine on the likes of duck *confit*. There's always a good buzz before show-time in the adjacent theatre, and if it's sunny out the terrace is always packed. Closed Sun; open until midnight other nights.

Le Parchemin

Map 3, G5. 1333 rue University ⓣ 844-1619. Métro McGill.

Inexpensive–expensive. Classic French dishes with *nouvelle* touches like seared tuna or tender chicken in a honey-almond sauce are served in this light-filled former presbytery built in 1876. It's the same menu and price for the *table d'hôte* at lunch but those on a budget can pick a dish from the bistro menu and a glass of wine for $10–13.

Queue de Cheval

Map 3, E7. 1221 boul René-Lévesque ⓣ 390-0090. Métro Lucien-l'Allier or Peel. Very expensive.

Just north of the Centre Molson, this high-end steakhouse is one of the best in the city. Specials such as the arctic char – flown in fresh – cost a small fortune, but the main draw is the beef, like the juicy porterhouse steak, which they dry-age in house. With two waiters to a table, service is attentive to say the least.

La Rotonde

Map 3, J6. 185 rue Ste-Catherine O ⓣ 847-6900. Métro Place-des-Arts. Moderate–expensive.

Wrapped around the atrium of the Musée d'Art Contemporain, it can be a bit noisy here – but the food is worth it. Provençal and southern French dishes like the roasted duck breast in a pear and honey sauce draw a busy evening crowd. Cheaper at lunch – the $10 Salade Fidji, topped with ham, chicken and tropical fruit, is a meal in itself. Closed Mon in the winter.

Zen

Map 3, F5. *Hôtel Omni*, 1050 rue Sherbrooke O ℡ 499-0801. Métro Peel. **Expensive.**
Spicy Szechuan dishes are the order of the day in this elegantly minimal restaurant, with specialties like crispy duck, beef with ginger and green onion and a particularly good General Tao chicken. Your best bet, though, is the "Zen experience" – for $27 you choose as many dishes as you want but the more you order, the smaller each portion served. There's a $15 lunch special, as well.

CHINATOWN

- - - - - - - - - - - - - - - - - -

Hong Kong

Map 3, K7. 1023 boul St-Laurent ℡ 861-0251.

Métro Place d'Armes. **Moderate.**
The vast menu at this Chinese restaurant is one reason it's packed with Chinese-Canadians. Despite the army of roasting ducks in the window, it's seafood this place is best known for – try the Cantonese-style lobster, flavoured with ginger, garlic and soy sauce.

Jardin de Jade

Map 3, K7. 67 rue de la Gauchetière ℡ 866-3127. Métro Place d'Armes. **Inexpensive.**
It's a bit of a factory, but the all-you-can-eat buffet is a bargain at $6.95 for lunch, $11.25 for dinner. The wide selection gives you a chance to try a variety of Cantonese and Szechuan dishes, from dumplings to spicy stir-fried beef.

Lotté

Map 3, L6. 215 boul René-Lévesque E ℡ 393-3838. Métro Champ-de-Mars. **Inexpensive–moderate.**
On the eastern edge of Chinatown, the large banquet

hall on the second floor of the *Days Inn* hotel is crowded with Chinese-Canadian families choosing dim sum dishes from the passing trolleys. The dumplings, like shrimp and coriander in a translucent rice wrapper, are wonderful.

La Maison Kam Fung
Map 3, K7. 1008 rue Clark. Métro Place d'Armes. Moderate.
Montréal's vast temple to dim sum, right in the heart of Chinatown. Well-priced menu but not dirt-cheap, and you'll have to fight back the urge to grab spring rolls and fried seafood dumplings every time they wheel the trolley by. There are often long queues for dim sum (served 7am–3pm) so get there early. If you go in the evening, opt for the Peking duck or fresh seafood.

Pho Bac 97
Map 3, K7. 1016 boul St-Laurent ⊤393-8116. Métro Place d'Armes. Inexpensive.
This small canteen-style Vietamese restaurant is typically crowded as they don't cheat on the Tonkinoise fixings, so expect plenty of coriander, basil and mint with your noodles and beef, chicken or veg. The iced coffee, laced with condensed milk, is serious rocket fuel.

QUARTIER LATIN AND THE VILLAGE

Area
Map 2, I5. 1429 rue Amherst ⊤890-6691. Métro Beaudry. Expensive.
Well-designed restaurant with a stylish and airy atmosphere – ornamented by creamy-grey banquettes and chairs and minimalist floral arrangements against the white and exposed-brick walls – reflected in the presentation of the shredded duck *confit* with mushrooms and asparagus and other French and Asian fusion dishes. Closed Monday and open for dinner only at the weekend.

Bato Thai

Map 2, I5. 1310 rue Ste-Catherine E ⓣ524-6705. Métro Beaudry.

Inexpensive–moderate.

Thai restaurant in the Village with horrendously slow service, but the food's worth the wait – especially the satay chicken served with deep-fried spinach. Lunchtime specials start at $6, but it's closed for lunch on the weekend.

Chez Gatsé

Map 3, M4. 317 rue Ontario E ⓣ985-2494.

Métro Berri-UQAM.

Inexpensive.

Tibetan restaurant serving *mômos* (Tibetan ravioli stuffed with cheese, beef or veg), egg-noodle *thukpas* with beef and veg, and curry-spiced beef and chicken *shaptas*. If you like the decor, you can buy your own handicrafts in the store upstairs.

Le Commensal

Map 3, M4. 1720 rue St-Denis ⓣ845-2627.

Métro Berri-UQAM.

Inexpensive.

Choose from dozens of vegetarian dishes, including salads, couscous, stir-fried tofu and lasagne from the buffet, then pay by weight ($1.59 per 100g) and enjoy your meal in the large, glazed front room looking onto the street. Open daily until 11pm. There's a downtown branch at 1204 av McGill College (ⓣ871-1480; Map 3, G6).

Fou d'Asie

Map 3, M4. 1732 rue St-Denis ⓣ281-0077.

Métro Berri-UQAM. Moderate.

More stylish than many of its Quartier Latin neighbours, this Asian fusion restaurant applies Thai and Vietnamese flavours to beef, chicken and seafood, served up with noodles. The sushi bar is also a popular draw.

Au Petit Extra

Map 2, I5. 1690 rue Ontario E ⓣ527-5552. Métro Papineau. Moderate.

Large, lively and affordable bistro with amazing food and an authentic French feel, reflected in the selection of sweetbreads and kidneys, in

RESTAURANTS: QUARTIER LATIN AND THE VILLAGE

addition to the tasty duck breast and fish dishes. There's also a good range of wines at affordable prices. Closed for lunch on the weekend.

Pho Viet

Map 2, I5. 1663 rue Amherst ⓣ522-4116. Métro Beaudry. Inexpensive.

Literally a hole-in-the-wall, this barely furnished Vietnamese restaurant is nonetheless popular with those in the know, especially for its beef or chicken Tonkinoise soup. Lunch during the week only and closed Sunday. Reservations recommended for dinner. *Apportez votre vin.*

Saloon

Map 2, I5. 1333 rue Ste-Catherine E ⓣ522-1333. Métro Beaudry. Inexpensive–moderate.

A reliable menu of pizzas, burgers, salads and brunch draws a mixed crowd of young and old, gay and straight to this two-level Village hangout, but it's the grilled chicken served Thai-style that stands out.

PLATEAU MONT-ROYAL

- - - - - - - - - - - - - - - - - -

Amelio's

Map 5, D7. 201 rue Milton ⓣ845-8396. Métro Place-des-Arts or bus #24. Inexpensive.

Hearty pastas and pizzas – including their unusual five-cheese "white pizza" – are served in this tiny restaurant tucked away in the heart of the McGill University student ghetto. The service is friendly and the raspberry cheesecake heavenly. *Apportez votre vin.*

Au 917

Map 5, H4. 917 rue Rachel E ⓣ524-0094.

Métro Mont-Royal.

Inexpensive–moderate.

French bistro whose reliable menu and comfortable atmosphere make it one of the better bring-your-own-wine restaurants on the Plateau. Standards like well-prepared filet mignon and *boeuf bourguignon* should satisfy the meat-eater in you. Evenings only.

L'Avenue

Map 5, G3. 922 av du Mont-Royal E ⊤523-8780.
Métro Mont-Royal. **Moderate.**
Extremely popular restaurant among the hip Plateau set, full of stylish decor from the giant silver starfish scaling the facade to a wall of water in the bathroom. Huge portions of thoughtfully prepared updates on diner food – like goat's cheese and wild-mushroom topped hamburgers – share the menu with salads and pastas. Long queues for weekend brunch.

La Cabane Grecque

Map 5, F6. 102 rue Prince-Arthur E ⊤849-0122.
Métro Sherbrooke.
Inexpensive–moderate.
Bring-your-own-wine *brochetterie* serving heavy meals – the standard is chicken or beef shish kebabs on a bed of rice accompanied by Greek salad. If it's full, try *La Caverne Grecque* directly opposite – they're virtually indistinguishable.

Checkpoint Charlie

Map 5, E4. 50 rue Rachel E ⊤842-0191.
Bus #55 or Métro Mont-Royal. **Moderate.**
Third location of this long-time favourite, where the beer steins hanging over the open kitchen hint at the menu of German sausages and Wiener schnitzel, though there are a few surprises such as Peking duck and rabbit prepared *à la française*. The apple schnapps makes for a great finish. Closed Sun & Mon; no lunch Sat.

ChuChai

Map 5, F4. 4088 rue St-Denis ⊤843-4194. Métro Mont-Royal or Sherbrooke. **Moderate.**
Terrific and fresh vegetarian Thai food featuring a wide-array of tasty mock meats, including a delicious crispy "duck". Get the divine deep-fried seaweed as an accompaniment.

La Colombe

Map 5, G5. 554 av Duluth E ⊤849-8844. Métro Sherbrooke or Mont-Royal. **Expensive.**
Open for dinner only, this

RESTAURANTS: PLATEAU MONT-ROYAL

small, stylish bistro attracts a well-heeled Francophone crowd and serves a higher level of cuisine than the average *apportez votre vin* restaurant. Fresh seasonal ingredients accompany mains like venison or *jarret d'agneau* (lamb shank) served *au jus*. No smoking. Closed Mon.

Le Continental

Map 5, G4. 4169 rue St-Denis ☎845-6842.
Métro Mont-Royal. **Expensive.**
An always packed French bistro that has a few Italian dishes thrown into the à-la-carte-only menu – fish bisque, lamb medallions and steak frites are tops. The retro decor attracts an artsy crowd, and those eating at the bar add to the talkative buzz. Finish off with the decadent chocolate-mousse cake. Open for dinner only until midnight Sun & Mon, until 1am other nights.

Côté Soleil

Map 5, G5. 3979 rue St-Denis ☎282-8037. Métro Sherbrooke or Mont-Royal.
Inexpensive–moderate.

Light, Mediterranean-influenced bistro fare, including a delicious roasted goat's-cheese salad, served in a welcoming space with exposed-brick walls. Great terrace for surveying the St-Denis scene.

Crêperie Bretonne Ty-Breiz

Map 5, H4. 933 Rachel E ☎521-1444. Métro Mont-Royal. **Moderate.**
Despite the incredibly tacky decor with pictures of Bretagne and traditional costumes, this family-style creperie has drawn a local following for over four decades. The large crepes are the real thing, filled with ingredients like sausage, apples or asparagus in Bechamel sauce. Open from 11am.

Eduardo

Map 5, G5. 404 av Duluth E ☎843-3330. Métro Sherbrooke or Mont-Royal.
Inexpensive–moderate.
Cheap Italian restaurant featuring huge portions of veal, trout in lemon sauce

and spaghetti with shrimps, clams and scallops in a rosé sauce served in a dark and cosy space with back-lit stained-glass windows. Even though the tables are packed close together you can still expect a queue. No lunch on the weekend. *Apportez votre vin.*

L'Express

Map 5, G5. 3927 rue St-Denis Ⓣ845-5333.

Métro Sherbrooke.

Moderate–expensive. Fashionable Parisian-style bistro whose hectic but attentive service adds to the atmosphere. Try the steak tartare if you're feeling adventurous; otherwise opt for the safer steak frites or *confit canard* (slow-roasted duck). Table reservations are essential – though you might be able to squeeze in at the bar unannounced. Open til 1am, 2am on weekends.

Fonduementale

Map 5, G4. 4325 rue St-Denis Ⓣ499-1446.

Métro Mont-Royal. Expensive. Set in a red-brick Victorian

two-storey house, the main dining room is fitted with late nineteenth-century lights and mouldings and warmed by a fireplace in winter, and there's a blooming outdoor terrace in summer. The fondue here is exquisite – especially *Le Mental*, featuring chunks of venison and caribou, and chocolate fondues for dessert.

Il Piatto Della Nonna

Map 5, F4. 4268 rue St-Denis Ⓣ843-6069.

Métro Mont-Royal. Inexpensive. Tiny family-run restaurant serving well-prepared Italian specialities from Calabria like charcoal-grilled veal sausage and roast rabbit and lamb. The small terrace out front in summer is a great spot to knock back a pasta fagiola for lunch.

Khyber Pass

Map 5, G5. 506 av Duluth E Ⓣ844-7131. Métro Sherbrooke or Mont-Royal. Moderate. The cosy furnishings and music here feel as authentic as the menu of Afghan specialties, including kebabs, koftas and kormas, though

RESTAURANTS: PLATEAU MONT-ROYAL

the *sabzi khalaw* – lamb shank with spinach and three kinds of basmati rice – stands out. Dinner only. *Apportez votre vin.*

Laloux

Map 5, F6. 250 av des Pins E ⓣ287-9127. Métro Sherbrooke. Moderate-expensive.

Creamy buttercup-yellow walls lined with gilt mirrors add an elegant touch to this Parisian-style bistro serving pricey – and exquisite – *nouvelle cuisine.* The chef likes to contrast flavours, serving foie gras with grapes for instance. Follow it up with the marvellous sweetbreads, but leave room for the chocolate cake with tarragon ice cream, a memorable sweet/zesty/bitter medley.

Lugrano

Map 5, G3. 775 av du Mont-Royal E ⓣ524-5470. Métro Mont-Royal. Moderate-expensive.

Stylish Italian eatery whose contemporary seating plays off against the porcelain and glassware displayed in antique cabinets against the exposed-brick and cream-coloured walls. The veal is superb and the imaginative pastas – such as linguine *nero pescatore* (seafood piled on black linguine) – are worth a try as well. No lunch on the weekend; closed Mon.

Maestro SVP

Map 5, E6. 3615 boul St-Laurent ⓣ842-6447. Métro Sherbrooke or bus #55. Expensive.

If you're in the mood for oysters, this is the place – some fifteen species are served up in a myriad of ways. Try them Rockefeller (pesto, cheese and white sauce) or raw with lemon one-by-one ($1.50–8). If you're a couple, the $62 "Maestro Platter" is another sure bet, loaded with clams, mussels, calamari, shrimp, king crab and lobster.

Mañana

Map 5, G7. 3605 rue St-Denis ⓣ847-1050. Métro Sherbrooke. Moderate.

Tuck into tasty beef fajitas and vegetarian quesadillas in this cosy spot opposite Square

St-Louis, surrounded by Mexican masks, sombreros and colourful woven tablecloths.

Moishe's

Map 5, E5. 3961 boul St-Laurent ℗ 845-3509. Bus #55 or Métro Sherbrooke. Very expensive.

This steakhouse with dark, panelled walls has been a favourite haunt of Montréal's business community since 1938. Excellent (and huge) charcoal-broiled steaks, but very expensive (the filet mignon is $40, rib steak a more affordable $31.50), with notoriously bad-tempered service. Open for dinner only; reservations recommended.

Nantha's Cuisine

Map 5, E5. 9 av Duluth E ℗ 845-4717. Métro Sherbrooke or Mont-Royal. Moderate.

Man-about-the-Plateau Nantha opened his Malaysian restaurant after running a small kitchen out of *Copacabana* (see "Drinking", p.165), bringing with him the recipe for tasty samosas

and noodle dishes (in both meat and veggie). Don't worry if it looks empty – everyone heads upstairs first, where a DJ spins on some nights.

Le Nil Bleu

Map 5, F6. 3706 rue St-Denis ℗ 285-4628. Métro Sherbrooke. Moderate.

You get to eat your plate at this Ethiopian restaurant: spicy doro wat stew with beef, chicken, lamb or just vegetables is served on top of *injera*, a fermented flat bread that's like a cross between a sponge and a pancake. Open for dinner only.

La Piton de la Fournaise

Map 5, G5. 835 av Duluth E ℗ 526-3936. Métro Mont-Royal or Sherbrooke. Moderate.

This cute little restaurant features the cuisine of Réunion – the French island colony between Africa and India – and the mix of the three cuisines is flavoured with turmeric, ginger, garlic and Thai pepper, applied to dishes like the shark or octopus stew. Evenings only;

RESTAURANTS: PLATEAU MONT-ROYAL ●

closed Sunday and Monday.
Apportez votre vin.

Red Thai

Map 5, E7. 3550 boul St-Laurent ⊤289-0998. Métro Sherbrooke or Saint-Laurent. **Expensive.**

This restaurant serves up delightful Thai in a decor straight out of *Anna and the King*. They've got a sizzling seafood plate, Mekong scampi and chicken satay, and you can sample cheaper "Bangkok lunch" specials until 3pm.

Souvenirs d'Afrique

Map 5, G3. 844 av du Mont-Royal E ⊤598-8181. Métro Mont-Royal. **Moderate.** The specialities here span the continent from Angola to Zanzibar, with the decor to match: African textiles and carved wooden masks create a wonderful accompanying atmosphere to dishes like *mafe* (beef in peanut sauce with rice and yam chips) and *tieboun bien* (salmon with rice). Closed for lunch weekdays.

Tasca

Map 5, F5. 172 av Duluth E ⊤987-1530. Métro Sherbrooke or Mont-Royal. **Moderate.** Authentic tapas restaurant filled with Portuguese families, especially at weekends when an accordionist plays. Pick a few dishes from the wide range of charcoal-grilled fish and seafood to share – try the octopus, either grilled or marinated in a herb and onion sauce.

Toqué!

Map 5, F5. 3842 rue St-Denis ⊤499-2084. Métro Sherbrooke. **Very expensive.** World-renowned Chef Normand Laprise holds court and the results are a mouth-watering fusion of styles prepared with market fresh ingredients. Try the seared foie gras and perhaps the local venison with sautéed craterelle mushrooms, wilted spinach and crushed Roseval potatoes. Ultrachic, high-end, and unforgettable – if you can get a seat. Dinner only; reservations are essential.

Le Vintage

Map 5, G3. 4475 rue St-Denis
ⓣ849-4264. Métro Mont-
Royal. Moderate–expensive.
Set in a cosy, stone-walled
half-basement, this
Portuguese restaurant serves
up tapas in addition to a long
list of fish and seafood dishes,
notably the cod grilled with
fried onions and olive oil, and
succulent calamari, grilled or
stuffed with chorizo sausage.
Closed for lunch on the
weekend.

Witloof

Map 5, G6. 3619 rue St-Denis
ⓣ281-0100. Métro Sherbrooke.
Moderate.
Belgian bistro tailor-made for
carnivores – the menu
features many forms of game,
steak tartare, mussels, horse
flank and blood pudding *à la
Bruxelloises*. Wash it all down
with a Belgian beer on a
terrace facing Square St-
Louis. No lunch on
weekends; closed Sun in
winter.

MILE END AND
OUTREMONT

Arahova Souvlaki

Map 2, G3. 256 rue St-Viateur
O ⓣ274-7828. Bus #80.
Inexpensive.
Superb, inexpensive choice
for authentic Greek cuisine.
The basic dishes are the best,
such as the souvlaki, chicken
shish kebabs and fried
calamari, all of which are
served up in a taverna-style
restaurant with pictures of the
old country hung about.
Open until 5am Fri & Sat,
2am other nights.

Laurier BBQ

Map 5, D1. 381 av Laurier O
ⓣ273-3671. Bus #80.
Inexpensive.
Great hunks of rotisserie
chicken, served drizzled with
the delicious house barbecue
sauce, have made this cosy
family-run restaurant a
favourite for over half a
century. If you're after
comfort food, the home-
made macaroni and cheese
with meat sauce is hard to
beat.

LITTLE ITALY: A CULINARY TOUR

The vibrant neighbourhood of Little Italy is a marvellous place to poke about, especially if you've got food on the brain. The city's largest outdoor market, the Marché Jean-Talon (see p.208), is here and the whole area is dotted with cafés and restaurants dishing out authentic Italian cuisine and some of the city's strongest coffee. While it's a short ride away from the downtown core to Métro Jean-Talon, and a half-hour walk from the Plateau, most people bus it on the #55 that runs up boulevard St-Laurent. You'll know you've arrived when you see Italian flags waving everywhere.

Café Italia, 6840 boul St-Laurent ⓣ495-0059 (Map 2, G1). Inexpensive. Boisterous Italian debates and mismatched tables await at this atmospheric café that froths up cappuccino with a potency nearing jet-fuel.

Lucca, 12 rue Dante ⓣ278-6502 (Map 2, G1). Moderate. A rustic trattoria where the constantly changing daily menu emphasizes refreshing antipasto combinations, delicious grilled meats and light seafood. Reservations recommended.

Pizzeria Napoletana, 189 rue Dante ⓣ276-8226 (Map 2, H1). Moderate. A casual restaurant with a lively outdoor terrace in the summer and hearty pizzas – try the sausage and mushrooms *tutta bella* – and pastas on the menu for $9–14.50. *Apportez votre vin*.

Quelli Della Notte, 6834 boul St-Laurent ⓣ271-3929 (Map 2, G1). Expensive. Stylish restaurant complete with grand staircase spiralling down to a cigar lounge. Standouts on the dinner menu include grilled striped bass and home-made ravioli stuffed with veal and porcini mushrooms. No lunch Sat; closed Sun.

Mikado

Map 5, D1. 368 av Laurier O
ⓣ279-4809. Bus #80.
Moderate–expensive.
Excellent sushi in a smashing
modern Japanese decor that
draws a fun but well-dressed
crowd. The grilled salmon
and chicken teriyaki are tasty
alternatives if you prefer your
food cooked. They have a
second restaurant at 1731 rue
St-Denis (ⓣ844–5705; Map
3, M4) in the Quartier Latin.

Milos

Map 2, G3. 5357 av du Parc
ⓣ272-3522. Bus #80.
Very expensive.
Milos may be expensive, but
it's the finest Greek restaurant
in the city. The seafood is
exceptionally fresh and dishes
are prepared simply and
skilfully - try the grilled
Mediterranean sea bass or
delicately seasoned grilled
lobster. Reservations are
essential.

Terrasse Lafayette

Map 5, D2. 250 rue Villeneuve
O ⓣ288-3915. Bus #80.

Inexpensive–moderate.
A great little neighbourhood
restaurant, popular for its
wraparound terrace, where
you can tuck into *pikilia*
(Greek hors d'oeuvre platter),
fried calamari and tender
pitta bread stuffed with
chicken or souvlaki. The
Greek specialities are best,
though the spinach, shallot
and feta pizza is really good as
well. *Apportez votre vin.*

Yakata

Map 5, E1. 5115 boul St-
Laurent ⓣ272-8667.
Métro Laurier or bus #55.
Expensive.
The fish swimming in the
aquarium here aren't the ones
that the chefs roll up at the
bar, but you might wonder
given how fresh the sushi is.
The tempura prawns and
scallops are other tasty
choices, while for a satisfying
finish try the green-tea ice
cream. No lunch at
weekends; reservations
recommended for dinner.

RESTAURANTS: MILE END AND OUTREMONT

Drinking

With its 3am closing time and minimum (suggested) drinking age of 18, Montréal's vibrant **bar scene** has earned it a reputation as the party capital of Canada. Starting with a bustling *5 à 7* happy-hour, many bars remain packed well into the early hours, especially on the weekend – which for many here begins on Thursdays.

Not all the best bars are long-countertop-with-stools-type joints – several of the places listed below are part café or restaurant (but best for drinking), and may have a small dance floor or host bands on some nights. Likewise, many clubs and live-music venues keep things lubricated with cocktails and pitchers of beer.

Without a doubt, the best spot to bar hop is the Plateau, where on weekends it feels like the whole city has come to party. There's a great mixing of Francophones and Anglophones, although the smaller bars on and around **rue St-Denis** tend to have a more Gallic flair, while **boulevard St-Laurent** has everything from flashy resto-bars to grungy student watering holes, with some fabulously hip lounges sprinkled in between. The downtown scene is also reliable, if less exciting, with bars catering to businesspeople and McGill and Concordia students dotted about. The action here centres on **rue Crescent**, where the block north of rue Ste-Catherine is choked with bars and pick-up joints, but there's less testosterone and a more neighbourly feel in parallel **rue Bishop**'s watering holes. The Quartier Latin's terrace-fronted bars on rue **St-Denis** draw a rollicking crowd, while nearby Vieux-Montréal is low on the drinking radar – except for the terraces lining **Place Jacques-Cartier**, which often have a festive vibe. In **Mile End** and **Outremont** you're better off with a glass of wine in a café or restaurant on avenue Laurier, though there are a few bars dotted about, notably on avenue Bernard.

For café and restaurant reviews, see Chapter 10, "Eating"; live-music venues and dance clubs are covered in Chapter 12, "Nightlife". Bars in the Village are covered in Chapter 15, "Gay and lesbian Montréal".

Note that you should tip the bar staff 15 percent – the perks constitute the main whack of their wages. And, if you're planning on a long night, leave the car behind; **drinking and driving** penalties are harsh and taxis are cheap and plentiful.

5 à 7

Thanks in part to Montréal's economic upswing, there's been a resurgence of bars throughout the city offering happy-hour specials, like two-for-one beers, once the work day is done. Rather than referring to "happy hour", you're more likely to hear Montrealers say such-and-such bar has a great *5 à 7* (*cinq à sept*) – literally 5pm to 7pm, the standard time for cheap booze – though many bars are stretching things to *4 à 8*. Unlike many other North American cities, the deal rarely extends to food, though a few places may offer cheap nibbles. Instead, the best spots are simply packed full of people in a boisterous mood.

VIEUX-MONTRÉAL

La Cage aux Sports
Map 4, A4. 395 rue Le Moyne
ⓣ288-1115.
Métro Square-Victoria.
If there's a big game on, then
head to this branch of a
province-wide sports bar
chain for a pitcher of beer
and popcorn while watching
one of the dozens of TVs
surrounded by baseball
pennants and portraits of
hockey players. Don't come
hungry, though – the food is
mediocre at best.

Le Jardin Nelson
Map 4, G3. 407 Place
Jacques-Cartier ⓣ861-5731.
Métro Place-d'Armes or
Champ-de-Mars.
Most come here to enjoy a
glass of wine on one of the
finest terraces on Place
Jacques-Cartier, but there are
decent crepes and light meals
as well. A classical trio plays
at noon daily, and there's a
jazz ensemble Sunday to
Thursday evenings.

Modavie
Map 4, E4. 1 rue St-Paul O
ⓣ287-9582.
Métro Place-d'Armes.
Although they serve pizzas,
pasta and grilled fish, the
focal point of this bistro is the
huge bar at its centre, popular
with bureaucrats from nearby
city hall who come to puff
on a stogie while sipping
scotch or port.

Pub McGill
Map 4, A4. 431 rue McGill
ⓣ844-4330.
Métro Square-Victoria.
This old-time pub has been
drawing regulars for decades,
along with an influx of
tourists in the summer
months, for draft Guinness
and Sleemans to go along
with the burgers, pizza and
sandwiches.

Pub St-Paul
Map 4, F4. 124 rue St-Paul E
ⓣ874-0485.
Métro Place-d'Armes.
A friendly pub with decent
grub and a good range of
suds on tap. Its atmospheric
location amid the stone
buildings of one of Vieux-

Montréal's prettiest cobblestone streets assures that it's typically packed.

Union

Map 4, A7. 600 rue d'Youville O ⓣ286-9851.

Métro Square-Victoria.

By far the most buzzing bar in Vieux-Montréal, *Union* draws late-twenty-something multimedia types for its *5 à 7* and stays jam-packed all night. In summer, the action busts out onto the huge terrace, where a DJ keeps things buzzing.

DOWNTOWN AND THE GOLDEN SQUARE MILE

- - - - - - - - - - - - - - - - - - - -

Alexandre

Map 3, E5. 1454 rue Peel ⓣ288-5105.

Métro Peel.

A Parisian café, bistro and brasserie rolled into one, replete with marble-topped tables and rattan chairs facing the street where you can pose with the rest of the *beau monde*, while quaffing one of the dozen wines by the glass.

Brutopia

Map 3, D6. 1219 rue Crescent ⓣ393-9277.

Métro Peel or Guy-Concordia.

A quiet and cosy pub with exposed-brick walls serving up a great selection of tasty ales, porters and stouts brewing away in the vats next to where you can chat or play board games. Live music towards the end of the week, but no cover charge.

Cock n' Bull Pub

Map 3, A6. 1944 rue Ste-Catherine O ⓣ933-4556.

Métro Guy-Concordia.

There's a good mix of crusty, old regulars and fresh-faced Concordia students at this unpretentious watering hole at the western end of downtown. The cheap tap beers keep many of them rooted until closing.

Hurley's Irish Pub

Map 3, D6. 1225 rue Crescent ⓣ861-4111.

Métro Peel or Guy-Concordia.

A little south of the rue Crescent carnival, *Hurley's* is one of the city's best Irish pubs, with friendly regulars downing pints of Guinness hoping that it'll improve their dart-tossing skills. There's a nice selection of single malts and good pub food served from noon until just after the live bands start up at 9.30pm.

Jimbo's Pub

Map 3, C6. 1238 rue Bishop ☎398-9661.

Métro Guy-Concordia.

A dark and smoky local with a friendly Anglophone crowd that surges before and after the comedy and improv shows at *Comedyworks* upstairs (see p.174). There's karaoke on the main floor whenever the owner is in the mood.

Luba Lounge

Map 3, I5. 2109 rue de Bleury ☎288-5822.

Métro Place-des-Arts.

Chilled out lounge near Place des Arts that attracts a trendy twenty- and thirty-something set. DJs and occasional live bands play against a backdrop of cushy old sofas and red-velvet curtains.

Madhatter Library Pub

Map 3, D5. 1230 boul de Maisonneuve O ☎987-9988.

Métro Peel.

Although popular with students from nearby Concordia, the main studies in this rumpled campus pub involve who can down a glass of Rousse the fastest, especially on extra-cheap Wednesday nights.

Peel Pub

Map 3, E6. 1107 rue Ste-Catherine O ☎844-6769.

Métro Peel.

A pilgrimage spot for first-year McGill students who come for the cheap pitchers of draft and largely forgettable food (try the cheap rib steak if pressed) in a mess-hall atmosphere. You can come back to pay for your sins the next morning – $1.99 fry-ups are available from 8am.

Café Sarajevo

Map 3, K4. 2080 rue Clark ☎284-5629.

Métro Saint-Laurent.

Fitted out like someone's cosy rec-room, *Café Sarajevo* is a great place to hang out and

listen to occasional bands –
Rufus Wainwright often
played the piano here before
hitting it big – and there's a
lovely garden out back to
boot.

Sharx

Map 3, C6. 1606 rue Ste-
Catherine ☎934-3105.
Métro Guy-Concordia.
Popular and stylish pool hall
in the Faubourg Ste-
Catherine that draws a mix of
young downtown workers to
its 36 tables ($9/hr for two
players, $11/hr for four). You
can chill out in the cigar
lounge as well, or give one of
the ten bowling lanes a try
($20/hr for two, $30/hr for
three or more; $10 deposit
for shoes).

Sherlock's

Map 3, F6. 1010 rue Ste-
Catherine O ☎878-0088.
Métro Peel.
Upstairs inside the Square
Dominion Building, the
British pub-style decor
provides an appropriate
backdrop to the dozen or so
pool tables ($10/hr)
frequented by a thirty-

something after-work crowd.
There's a small dance floor
and cigar lounge as well.
Closed Sun.

Sir Winston Churchill Pub (Winnie's)

Map 3, D5. 1459 rue Crescent
☎288-3414.
Métro Peel or Guy-Concordia.
A prime pick-up joint, this
English-style pub attracts an
older crowd of local and
visiting Anglophone
professionals. Though there
are pool tables, a small dance
floor, and a wine bar upstairs,
the real action is on the front
terrace, *the* place to be seen
on the Crescent strip.

Stogies

Map 3, D5. 2015 rue Crescent
☎848-0069.
Métro Peel or Guy-Concordia.
Swanky cigar lounge where
you can puff away on a *cubano*
while sipping a martini
($7.50), or get down on the
dance floor where a DJ spins
jazz and R&B. Popular with
businessmen.

Le Vieux Dublin Pub & Restaurant

Map 3, G6. 1219A rue University ⊤861-4448.

Métro Bonaventure or McGill.

Don't let the windowless facade put you off – there's a warm glow inside the *Old Dublin* (as it's better known) furnished by back-lit stained-glass panels, polished wood and the best pint of Guinness in town. Irish bands create a rollicking mood by cramming onto the corner stage nightly.

QUARTIER LATIN

- -

Le Cheval Blanc

Map 3, N4. 809 rue Ontario E ⊤522-9205.

Métro Berri-UQAM.

Old-style Montréal pub, with the same Art Deco decor as when it opened in the 1940s, that's popular with a fun Francophone crowd. The bar brews its own beer, and it's really good – try one of the seasonal varieties or choose from five types of ale.

L'Île Noire

Map 3, M4. 342 rue Ontario E ⊤982-0866.

Métro Berri-UQAM.

Named after the book where Tintin travels to Scotland (*The Black Island*, in English), this pub attempts to do the same, with cushy, dark-green booths set against dark wood-panelled walls. They certainly succeed on the Scotch front, with an amazing selection of single-malt whiskeys, which you can chase with a pint of Tartan, bitter or stout.

L'Ours Qui Fume

Map 3, M4. 2019 rue St-Denis ⊤845-6998.

Métro Berri-UQAM.

Drawing *habitués* of all ages with its faded charm, this small brasserie feels like it could be in Paris. Go when there's a blues band playing (Wed–Sun 10.30pm) and you'll find a loud, boisterous crowd.

Le P'tit Bar

Map 3, M3. 3451 rue St-Denis ⊤281-9124.

Métro Sherbrooke.

Though technically on the

Plateau (it's just north of rue Sherbrooke), this *boîte à chanson* has more in common with the Quartier Latin scene. French singers play daily except Thursday, when you'll have to content yourself with checking out the cartoon-strewn walls.

Pub Quartier Latin
Map 3, M4. 318 rue Ontario E ⓣ845-3301.
Métro Berri-UQAM.
Stylish pub that attracts thirtyish professionals for the *5 à 7*, followed by students chilling out later in the evening. Bands play anything from funk to electronica on Friday nights ($5), with DJ sets the rest of the week ($3 cover on Sat). For something different, check out the Thursday screenings of old films with a DJ spinning along with it.

Le Saint-Sulpice
Map 3, M4. 1680 rue St-Denis ⓣ844-9458.
Métro Berri-UQAM.
The lively terrace in front is a good place to watch the human traffic on rue St-

Denis, but it's even more fun out back in the boisterous garden. The warren of rooms inside the three-storey greystone house fill nearly as quickly.

Le Ste-Élisabeth
Map 3, L6. 1412 rue Ste-Élisabeth ⓣ286-4302.
Métro Berri-UQAM.
Boxed in by high brick walls, the ivy-covered courtyard terrace is one of Montréal's finest – but if it's full, a window seat on the upper floor is the next best thing. In winter, an open fire keeps things cosy for knocking back a scotch or imported beer along with the low-key but friendly crowd of UQAM regulars.

PLATEAU MONT-ROYAL

Bacci
Map 5, G4. 4205 rue St-Denis ⓣ844-3929.
Métro Mont-Royal.
You shouldn't have a problem scoring a table – there are 26 of them – in this large pool

hall, plus there are table-hockey and -football games for the cueless. If you're a fan of loud Top 40, you'll feel right at home. A second branch at 3553 boul St-Laurent (Ⓣ287-9331; Map 5, E7) has a flashier clientele, with house, R&B and hip-hop backing the clank of the pool balls. Both charge $11.50/hr for two players.

Bar St-Laurent

Map 5, E5. 3874 boul St-Laurent Ⓣ844-4717. Bus #55 or Métro Sherbrooke or Mont-Royal.

A dark bar popular among punks and young slackers playing everything from punk to ska to rockabilly as long as it's loud; live bands ($3–5) replace the DJ on some nights. Large bottles of Molson Ex and Blue Dry are a cheap $4.50.

Bières & Compagnie

Map 5, F3. 4350 rue St-Denis Ⓣ844-0394.
Métro Mont-Royal.

A stylish restaurant/bar with large booths and dim lighting, serving up platters of mussels, sausages, burgers and pasta. It should rank high on any beer fanatic's list as there are 115 types of brews to choose from, including a wide selection from Belgium.

Bifteck St-Laurent

Map 5, E6. 3702 boul St-Laurent Ⓣ844-6211.
Métro Sherbrooke or Saint-Laurent.

A loyal crowd of students and ex-students frequent this tavern to drink pitchers of Boréale Rousse between sets of pool. The stereo blasts anything from hip-hop to hard rock, and band members occasionally drop in (Melissa Auf der Maur, who played bass for both Hole and Smashing Pumpkins, once worked here).

Bily Kun

Map 5, F3. 354 av du Mont-Royal E Ⓣ845-5392.
Métro Mont-Royal.

Tiled walls lend an Eastern European feel to this hopping Plateau bar, where stuffed ostrich heads look down on a mixed Anglo/Franco crowd. The music's too loud to really worry what language someone's speaking anyway, and the range of microbrews from mother bar *Le Cheval Blanc* (see p.162) provide more than adequate distraction.

Blizzarts

Map 5, E5. 3956A boul St-Laurent ⓣ843-4860.

Bus #55 or Métro Sherbrooke or Mont-Royal.

Funked-out lounge with retro furnishings, Sputnik-lighting, and exhibitions by local artists on the walls. The tiny dance floor gets packed every night – there's a $5 cover charge on Fridays, but it's free other nights, including a great drum'n'bass set on Saturdays and a sampling of downtempo, breaks and hip-hop on Thursdays. Opens around 9pm.

Copacabana

Map 5, E5. 3910 boul St-Laurent ⓣ982-0880.

Bus #55 or Métro Sherbrooke or Mont-Royal.

Despite the truly awful decor – fake palm trees and surfboards – the *Copa* attracts a loyal following of Anglo hipsters and journalists for a game of pool and lots of cheap beer ($10 for a large pitcher of Boréale Rousse). Though happy hour seems to go on all night, drinks are actually full price from 7–10pm – what the staff calls the "sad hour".

Gogo Lounge

Map 5, E6. 3682 boul St-Laurent ⓣ286-0882.

Métro Sherbrooke or Saint-Laurent.

A long and narrow bar with psychedelic paintings on the walls and a great vibe on the weekends. There are loungey areas at the front and back where you can listen to the funky 60s to 80s tunes playing on the stereo while sitting on red, rounded, plastic chairs reputedly left over from Expo '67.

Laïka

Map 5, E4. 4040 boul St-Laurent ⓣ842-8088.

Bus #55 or Métro Sherbrooke or Mont-Royal.

Hip café by day, trendy

PLATEAU MONT-ROYAL

lounge by night, *Laïka's* urbane decor looks like its been torn from the pages of *Wallpaper* magazine, with comfy suede chairs set against the large colourful tiles on the wall. In summer, the windows slide open letting the sounds of the DJ sets spill onto the street.

Miami

Map 5, E5. 3831 boul St-Laurent ⊤845-2300.

Bus #55 or Métro Sherbrooke. A total dive, but this dingy watering hole for Plateau nihilists and eternal students has cheap beer ($3.50 a pint) and shots (tequila or Jameson's for $2.75) that allows for some serious drinking. The rooftop terrace in back makes for a great escape from the crowded Main.

Sofa

Map 5, G4. 451 rue Rachel E ⊤285-1011.

Métro Mont-Royal. A wonderful little porto and cigar lounge filled with low-slung couches tucked into cosy nooks. The dark-blue

and burgundy interior is a bit gloomy in the day but at night it feels just fine for listening to bands playing soul, funk or even a bit of swing (Wed–Sun 10.30pm; $4–5).

Le Sugar

Map 5, E6. 3616 boul St-Laurent ⊤287-6555.

Métro Sherbrooke or Saint-Laurent. Give the downstairs club a miss and head up the stairs beside the larger-than-life sculptures of a cartoon man and woman to one of the city's coolest terraces – the roof's been removed from the second floor to allow for drinking under the stars.

Le Swimming

Map 5, E6. 3643 boul St-Laurent ⊤282-7665.

Métro Sherbrooke or Saint-Laurent. A bar wearing many hats: while live bands perform on weekends, the dozen or so pool tables in the back are *Le Swimming's* mainstay the rest of the week. There's a great balcony overlooking the

Main in the summertime, and regular drink specials year-long – from 3–8pm you can buy $9 pitchers and two-for-one bottles of beer.

Vol de Nuit

Map 5, E7. 14 rue Prince-Arthur E ⓣ845-6243.

Métro Sherbrooke or Saint-Laurent.

Forgo the unremarkable interior here and nab a table on the pavement. Its location at one of the busiest spots on rue Prince-Arthur's pedestrian strip makes it a mighty fine spot to share a big pitcher of sangria on a sultry summer evening.

El Zaz Bar

Map 5, G4. 4297 rue St-Denis ⓣ288-9798.

Métro Mont-Royal.

The garish piñata-coloured stairs and solarium of this second-floor bar create a festive feel perfect for knocking back margaritas and sangria. The rest of the bar is dark and close, with a dance floor beneath a low ceiling cluttered with giant vines. Live jazz (Thurs–Sat) and gypsy bands (Sun) play to a crowded house. There's a nightly $2–3 cover charge after 9.30pm.

Zinc Bar

Map 5, H3. 1148 av du Mont-Royal E ⓣ523-5432.

Métro Mont-Royal.

A cute and very French little bar with zinc fixtures that draws a young, fun crowd for the *5 à 7* when pints are nearly half-off – a good thing as there are thirty beers on tap, from local Boréale to Belgian Leffe.

MILE END AND OUTREMONT

- -

Dieu du Ciel

Map 5, E1. 29 av Laurier O ⓣ490-9555.

Métro Laurier or bus #55.

Comfortable neighbourhood pub that fills up for the *5 à 7* when the tasty ales and lagers brewed on the premises go for $3.75 a pint. There's a constantly changing beer menu with some thirty brews on tap at any given time.

Fûtenbulle

Map 2, G2. 273 av Bernard O
Ⓣ276-0473.

Métro Outremont or bus
#80 or #535.

One of the largest selections
of beers in Montréal – over
eighty bottled varieties and
another dozen on tap – draws
a noisy crowd of well-off
thirtyish Outremont regulars.

Sergent Recruteur

Map 5, E2. 4650 boul St-
Laurent Ⓣ287-1412.

Métro Laurier or bus #55.

The British-style ales brewed
here include a rich cream ale,
as well as a stout and what
may be the only hand-
pumped bitter in the
province. Live music on some
nights runs the range from
rock to Celtic and folk ($2
cover charge for jazz on
Tuesdays; free other nights),
and if you want to practice
your French check out
the Sunday storytelling
night.

Whisky Café

Map 2, G2. 5800 boul St-
Laurent Ⓣ278-2646.

Métro Outremont or bus #55.

Way up at the corner of
avenue Bernard, this elegantly
decorated bar draws a young
wealthy clientele – the prices
aren't cheap, but then the
liquor's purely top shelf. The
design-conscious approach
even extends to the toilets,
with water cascading down a
zinc wall in the boys', and the
only girl's urinal in Montréal.

Nightlife

Montréal's **nightlife** scene can be quite a spectacle. On weekend nights, the city's main drags are an endless parade of fashionistas dressed in glamorous togs ready to cruise the city's clubscape. Indeed, heading out to **clubs** here is a stylish game – and a great excuse to dress up. The city has long been considered Canada's nightlife capital, and with good reason – dozens of nightclubs pulsate till the wee hours, pumping out music ranging from mainstream Madonna remixes to thumping drum'n'bass with a roster of home-grown and international DJs manning the turntables.

The city's best gay clubs, often the most happening spots in town, are listed on pp.218–220.

Filling out the city's nightlife roster is a wide range of **live music** venues. Montréal's strong **jazz** roots – Frank Sinatra, Louis Armstrong and Sammy Davis Jr all played to sold-out crowds during the Roaring Forties here, and the city produced its own jazz star in Oscar Peterson – are still very much in evidence in the talented groups that play anything from bebop to fusion. But traditional **rock**, **punk** and **ska** bands also take their share of the limelight, and a small **folk** and **spoken word** scene add a pleasantly low-key vibe. When heading out to catch a show, keep in mind that bands usually get off-stage no later than 1am, and some end as early as 11pm. Accordingly, Montrealers treat seeing a band as an evening's primer – not its climax.

Though some live venues close once the show is over, Montréal's clubs serve alcohol until 3am, and even then the party doesn't have to end. The dancefloors at legal **after-hour clubs**, which serve up juice and caffeine laced drinks rather than alcohol, stay packed well past dawn; it's not hard to figure out how the denizens stay up.

CLUBS

On weekends, Montréal's **clubs** are easy to spot – just look for the jostling line-ups spilling out onto the sidewalks either downtown or in the Plateau. **Dance clubs** concentrated in the latter tend to groove to house and techno with some R&B and funk clambering on deck too, while Top 40 generally rules downtown's roost. Most open around 10pm but only really get busy around 1am, and usually apply a cover charge ranging $5–10 no matter what day of the week it is. If you're off to one of the larger clubs, it's a good idea to dress up – you won't be refused entrance, but still may feel a tad out of place if you don't. At most lounges, and the clubs in the Village, though, dress codes are virtually nonexistent. The evening doesn't have to end when the clubs call it a night at 3am, as two excellent **after-hours** spots pick up the slack on weekends, getting started only when the others close shop. To suss out the latest club **flyers**, head to any of the Plateau's record shops, where you can also pick up the current issue of *Night Life Montréal*, a free club guide that's also available on-line at ⓦ*www.nightlifemontreal.com*.

Though Montréal's **comedy** club scene officially blooms during the Just for Laughs Festival (see p.239), a couple of downtown institutions keep patrons entertained year-round. Another form of nightlife "entertainment" is the city's **strip clubs**, their neon signs glowing brightly throughout downtown; see box p.175.

DANCE CLUBS

Angels

Map 5, E6. 3604 boul St-Laurent ☎282-9944.

Bus St-Laurent (#55).

A two-floor Plateau club frequented by university students; the first has the atmosphere of the average common room with pool tables and Top 40 hits, while dark and smoky upstairs resonates with pounding house music all week.

Central Station

Map 5, E3. 4432 boul St-Laurent ☎842-2836.

Métro Mont-Royal.

Though the music consists of pretty mainstream dance music – think Jennifer Lopez remixes, straight-up house and some Latin hits thrown in – this two-level Plateau hotspot draws a big late-twenties crowd to its large palm-tree-lined main dance floor. The downstairs R&B room grooves under chandeliers and tends to get packed to capacity fast.

Club 48

Map 5, E1. 4848 boul St-Laurent, no phone, ⓦ*www.swinginmontreal.com*.

Métro Laurier.

Young Plateau types don two-tone shoes and borsalino hats to swing, hop and jive in an old chandeliered dance hall with occasional live bands. Open Thursdays (7.30pm) and Saturdays (9pm); lessons are available for neophytes.

Club Vatican

Map 3, D6. 1432 rue Crescent ☎845-3922.

Métro Guy-Concordia.

The pope certainly didn't sanctify this rue Crescent club, notable for its gothic-lounge decor of white brick walls and modern stained-glass windows, but the hordes

DANCE CLUBS

of Anglophone twentysomethings that strut their stuff on the dance floor don't seem to mind.

Dôme

Map 3, K6. 32 rue Ste-Catherine O ☎875-5757. Métro St-Laurent.

A massive downtown club with dance floors on two floors and a cast of DJs from Montréal radio stations playing the latest Top 40 singles to a preppy collegiate crowd. When not dancing, they're either shooting pool or lined up at one of 14 bars with frequent beer specials.

Jaï

Map 5, E6. 3603 boul St-Laurent ☎284-1114. Bus St-Laurent (#55).

A sleek hipster Plateau haven led by a rotating retinue of DJs. Deep-house rules on Tuesdays and Fridays, techno takes to the decks Wednesdays, and Saturdays go progressive. Expect a good-looking crowd any night of the week. Sectional sofas add a cozy feel.

Jingxi

Map 5, G4. 410 rue Rachel E ☎985-5464. Métro Sherbrooke or Mont-Royal.

Submarine travel is the motif at this trendy Plateau nightspot. Porthole windows, straight-backed chairs and two bars keep the stylish crowd entertained when they're not dancing to house, drum'n'bass, and techno on the smallish dance floor. DJ Ram's Tuesday nights are especially good.

Kokino

Map 5, E7. 3556 boul St-Laurent ☎485-0957. Bus St-Laurent (#55).

A swanky nightclub on The Main decked out in early Sixties decor – brass light fixtures, puffy barstools, and circular bars lined with red vinyl – under a canopy of billowing white sheets. Very popular with fashionable young things who dance to hip-hop, R&B, latino, funk or house depending on the night of the week.

DANCE CLUBS

Living

Map 5, E2. 4521 boul St-Laurent ⓣ286-9986.
Métro Mont-Royal.

Living took an old Plateau bank building, kept its classical facade, and turned the interior into a three-floor club frequented by under-35 yuppies and ruled by a musical output ranging from salsa to deep house. The ground-floor bar with its lofty ceiling and snug sitting areas is the best spot to scope out the action. Sundays with Luc Raymond bring on smoothed-out house.

Passeport

Map 5, G4. 4156 rue St-Denis ⓣ842-6063. Métro Sherbrooke or Mont-Royal.

An intimate bar-club that's right out of the polished 1980s era – spot lighting cuts through the black atmosphere, booze is served from a burnished wood-and-steel bar, and the smallish dance floor gleams with stainless steel. Not surprisingly, 80s music is the norm. Dress in black and you'll fit right in.

Tokyo

Map 5, E6. 3709 boul St-Laurent ⓣ842-6838.
Bus St-Laurent (#55).

A busy club in the thick of the Main attracting a mixed ethnic crowd to its main room decked out with Japanese lanterns, plush and intimate booths, and tunes of the R&B and Top 40 variety. A smaller room off to the left known as the Blue Room spins house and techno to scenesters lounging on sunken oval sofas. There's a smashing rooftop deck in summer.

Wax Lounge

Map 5, E7. 3481 boul St-Laurent ⓣ282-0919.
Métro Sherbrooke or Saint-Laurent.

Situated on the Main's flashiest block, this lounge is decorated with antique chandeliers and fringed lamps that create an air of faded elegance. The chic 20s and 30s crowd spend as much time dancing to the loud funk and R&B beats as they do chilling on the clusters of sofas and stuffed chairs.

DANCE CLUBS

AFTER HOURS

Sona

Map 3, I5. 1439 rue de Bleury
Ⓣ282-1000,
Ⓦ *www.clubsona.com*.
Métro Place-des-Arts.

A sterile downtown space
where local and international
DJs spin most electronic styles
– Little Louie Vega, Doc
Martin and John Acquaviva
have all graced the turntables.
There's an intimate "before"
hours bar inside as well, open
from 11pm–3am, that usually
plays down-tempo house.
Cover is $25 (even for the
bar) and entrance is usually
based on how you're dressed,
not on how long you've been
waiting at the entrance in the
back of the building; open
Friday and Saturday only.

Stereo

Map 2, H5. 858 rue Ste-
Catherine E Ⓣ282-3307,
Ⓦ *www.clubstereo.com*.
Métro Beaudry.

Founded by local hotshot DJ
Mark Anthony and New
York's DJ David Morales, and
outfitted with a stellar sound

system, the stereo in question
at this Quartier Latin club
blasts techno and house from
2am to 10am. The invited DJ
roster includes local talent
and brilliant out-of-towners
too; New York DJ Danny
Tenaglia, Chicago's Derek
Carter and San Fran's Mark
Farina have headlined here.
Friday and Saturday only;
$20.

COMEDY CLUBS

Comedy Nest

Map 2, D5. 4020 rue Ste-
Catherine O Ⓣ932-6378.
Métro Atwater.

A dinner-comedy venue with
acts Wednesday through
Saturday starting at 8.30pm,
with an 11pm late show on
Friday and Saturday nights.
Out-of-town headliners take
the stage starting Thursday.
$30 gets the *table d'hôte* and
the show; $10 show only.

Comedyworks

Map 3, C6. 1238 rue Bishop
Ⓣ398-9661.
Métro Guy-Concordia.

Montréal's favourite comedy

club stages stand-up every night but Sunday starting at 9pm with late shows on Fridays and Saturdays at 11.15pm. Monday is open-mike night, Tuesdays and Wednesdays belong to the club's in-house improv troupe, and weekends showcase out-of-town talent. Tickets range from $3 (Mondays) to $10 (weekends).

SIN CITY

Though certainly not to everyone's tastes, strip clubs are – and have been since the early part of the twentieth century – an integral part of Montréal's entertainment scene. Back in the old days, dancers like Lili St Cyr were even accorded a sort of mythical status, and even if much of the style (and talent) is absent from today's performances, having been replaced by more than a whiff of sleaze, a few downtown clubs still pack them in.

If you're interested in seeing a "show", expect to encounter typical businessman crowds, alongside some more down-at-the-heel types – entrance after all is free, with a one-drink minimum (the doorman also expects a $2 tip). The classiest of such establishments is the lounge-like Wanda's, 1458 av de la Montagne (☎842-6927; Métro Guy-Concordia), where from the plush chairs you might opt to admire the ornate frescoes on the walls as much as what's happening on stage. Only slightly more downmarket is Chez Paree, 1258 rue Stanley (☎866-0495; Métro Peel), full of gleaming brass fixtures and offering a free lunch buffet. Most popular of all is probably Super Sexe, 696 rue Ste-Catherine O (☎ 861-1507; Métro McGill); you'll hardly fail to notice the massive neon sign, or, once inside, the so-called "erotic bed" on stage.

LIVE-MUSIC CLUBS

Unlike dance clubs, the city's **live music** venues are well spread throughout the city. **Jazz** spots are the most numerous, but **spoken-word**, **rock**, **punk** and **ska** also have a good hold on the performance scene. Many of the locales do double duty as wateringholes or dance clubs, but when there is a performance on, it typically begins around 9pm, with headliners taking the stage around 11pm. Big-ticket bands play in the city's **large venues**, most of which are located in or around the Quartier Latin. None has a favourite genre, and instead book whomever can fill the place.

Cover ranges from $3 on weekdays to upwards of $25 on the weekends, with freebie shows occasionally thrown in during the week. For up-to-the-minute show listings, consult the *Mirror* (ⓦ*www.montrealmirror.com*) and *Hour* (ⓦ*www.afterhour.com*), two free English weeklies available in stores and on newspaper stands everywhere. *The Montreal Gazette*, an English-language daily, also carries comprehensive listings; its Friday weekend guide is best.

JAZZ, WORLDBEAT AND FOLK

L'Air du Temps

Map 4, C5. 191 rue St-Paul O
ⓣ842-2003.

Métro Place-d'Armes.

Montréal's most famous jazz spot is right in the heart of Vieux-Montréal and decked out with an ornate antique interior and a small stage. Live acts start at 10pm, but get there early to get a seat. Cover in the $10 range.

Aux Deux Pierrots

Map 4, F4. 104 rue St-Paul O
ⓣ861-1686.

Métro Champ-de-Mars.

Québécois folk singers are the mainstay of this Vieux-Montréal club where everyone sings along. There's usually a good crowd, but don't expect to understand a word unless your French is excellent. There's an outside terrace in the summer.

Balattou

Map 5, E3. 4372 boul St-Laurent ⊤845-5447.
Bus St-Laurent (#55).
The city's only African nightclub has been around so long that it's nearing institution status. The dark and smoky establishment attracts a mostly older crowd out to the Plateau for weekends of salsa, souk and lambada; Tuesdays and Wednesdays usually showcase live worldbeat acts from just about anywhere.

Barfly

Map 5, E4. 4062A boul St-Laurent ⊤993-5154.
Bus St-Laurent (#55).
This Plateau hole-in-the-wall is the city's least pretentious showcase for local folksy and alternative bands. The beer is cheap, there's a pool table to while away the time and the odd time a cover applies, it's usually next to nothing.

Biddles

Map 3, H5. 2060 rue Aylmer ⊤842-8656. Métro Peel.
Downtown *Biddles* offers up a sampling of jazz with a side order of ribs, but for a paltry $2.50 cover charge, you can skip the meat and tuck into a pint at the bar while being serenaded by Charles Biddle's grooving double bass and his in-house band from 8pm–midnight.

Casa del Popolo

Map 5, E2. 4873 boul St-Laurent ⊤284-3804.
Bus St-Laurent (#55).
"The House of the People" is a sofa-strewn, low-key Plateau spot where high-calibre spoken-word and folk bands perform for a marginal fee. A good spot to mingle with the locals.

Jello Bar

Map 3, L4. 151 rue Ontario E ⊤285-2621. Métro St-Laurent.
Live acid jazz, blues and funk acts frequently take to the tiny stage at this Quartier Latin bar-cum-lounge furnished with 1960s and 1970s novelties like lava lamps

LIVE-MUSIC CLUBS

and loveseats. Superb martinis, too.

Upstairs

Map 3, C6. 1254 rue Mackay ⓣ931-6808.

Métro Guy-Concordia.

Upstairs is actually downstairs in a half-basement ensconced between walls of exposed rock and wood. It's certainly the city's most easy-going jazz spot, with fresh jazz and blues on tap most weeknights in a wonderfully attitude-free atmosphere. There's also a pleasant outdoor terrace come summertime. Admission charges on Friday and Saturday are between $10 and $25.

ROCK, PUNK AND SKA

- - - - - - - - - - - - - - - - - - - -

Café Campus

Map 5, F6. 57 rue Prince-Arthur E ⓣ844-1010.

Métro St-Laurent.

A low-frills venue with two stages showcasing local bands ranging the gamut from rock to pop, and a DJ that keeps things humming when there's no band in the house. Best visited when a live act is playing.

Foufounes Électriques

Map 3, L6. 87 rue Ste-Catherine E ⓣ844-5539.

Métro St-Laurent.

Don't let the bizarre name (The Electric Buttocks) throw you; this venue on the Quartier Latin's western outskirt is the best place in Québec to catch punk and ska acts. There's a huge outside terrace perfect for summer evenings and inside there's usually a punter or two involved in some form of body painting. Admission is free when no band is booked and the pitchers of beer are nice and cheap.

Jailhouse Rock Café

Map 5, E3. 30 av du Mont-Royal O ⓣ844-9696.

Métro Mont-Royal.

An eclectic roster of punk, ska and rockabilly bands get booked at this gritty Plateau bar with a small stage and sparse furnishings. Some spoken-word too.

LARGE VENUES

- - - - - - - - - - - - - - - - - -

Cabaret

Map 3, K4. 2111 boul St-Laurent ⊤845-2014.
Métro St-Laurent.
A cosy spot with high ceilings and a wraproundmezzanine lined with bistro tables that's hosted the likes of The The and Ninja Tune's Amon Tobin. Get there early if you want a seat, as the main floor is usually standing room only. Entrance is through the front doors to the defunct Musée Juste Pour Rire.

Centre Molson

Map 3, D8 & E8. 1260 rue de la Gauchetière O ⊤932-2582.
Métro Bonaventure.
Jams out to mainstream stadium rock and pop like U2 and the Rolling Stones.

Club Soda

Map 3, K6. 1225 boul St-Laurent ⊤286-1010.
Métro St-Laurent.
Small enough to remain intimate, but attracts quality acts like French DJ Laurent Garnier and the Thievery Corporation. It's especially popular during the Jazz Festival. Nonsmoking.

- -

Tickets for big shows are available through the Admission network (⊤790-1245 or 1-800/678-5440, Ⓦ*www.admission.com*) and at each venue's box office.

- -

Métropolis

Map 3, K6. 59 rue Ste-Catherine E ⊤861-5851, Métro St-Laurent.
Hosts bands with big pretty large followings like Björk and The Chemical Brothers in run-down surroundings that evoke the venue's earliest days as a vaudeville theatre.

Spectrum

Map 3, I6. 318 rue Ste-Catherine O ⊤861-5851. Métro Place-des-Arts.
Excellent acoustics, hundreds of candlelit tables, and an upstairs balcony with great views of the stage. You should get there early to get a seat. Drum'n'bass star Roni

LARGE VENUES

Size has played here as has Brazil's Bebel Gilberto. Nonsmoking.

Stade Olympique

Map 2, M3. 4141 av Pierre-de-Courbertin ☏252-8687, Métro Pie-IX.

Hosts blowout parties like *Black and Blue* (see p.240) and raves with impressive house and jungle DJ rosters in cavernous chambers beneath the Expos' baseball diamond. There's a moratorium on above-ground concerts till the roof is fixed.

Performing Arts and Film

Montréal offers a richly varied cultural scene, from highbrow **classical music** – led by the world-renowned Orchestre Symphonique de Montréal – to excellent avant garde **dance** companies like the explosive LaLaLa Human Steps. Still, the city's best known cultural attraction is undoubtedly the **Cirque du Soleil**, who've wowed audiences with their kaleidoscopic performances in more than 100 cities around the world; see box p.188.

The city is blessed with a major performing-arts complex right downtown: **Place des Arts** is home to the OSM and Les Grands Ballets Canadiens as well as opera, theatre and a host of chamber-music ensembles. It's also centre stage for the city's big **festivals** – notably the Festival International de Jazz de Montréal and Les FrancoFolies festival of French music – with stages festooned about the large plaza and the closed-off streets nearby.

For info on these festivals, see Chapter 18.

MULTIDISCIPLINARY VENUES

A number of Montréal's larger venues provide a range of pro-gramming throughout the year. The major companies performing at these spots are detailed individually in this chapter, but the multidisciplinary venues you're likely to catch them at are:

Place des Arts ☏285-4200, tickets: ☏842-2112, Ⓦ*www.PdArts.com*. Montréal's premier performing-arts venue is home to the city's flagship orchestra, opera and ballet com-panies. The two largest halls are the **Salle Wilfrid Pelletier**, which seats 3000, and the **Théâtre Maisonneuve**, about half that size. Tickets for events here can also be purchased from the main concourse box office (Mon–Sat noon–9pm; Sun one hour before showtime only).

Salles du Gesù 1200 rue de Bleury ☏861-4036. Located below the Èglise du Gesù (Jesuit Church), hosts theatre, come-dy and classical music, as well as jazz acts during the festival.

Théâtre St-Denis 1594 rue St-Denis ☏849-4211. The biggest names in comedy play here during the Just For Laughs festival (see p.239), while concerts and touring Broadway-style pro-ductions fill it up the rest of the year.

Le Théâtre de Verdure ☏872-2237. The open-air theatre in Parc Lafontaine has the most eclectic scheduling in the city, with Shakespeare, contemporary dance, world music and cin-ema interspersed with appearances by the city's major ballet, symphony and chamber companies. Best of all, the perfor-mances are free.

By comparison, English **theatre** is a bit of a letdown, and it pales next to what's on offer in the French theatre scene. You won't have a problem finding decent English-language **film**, though – in addition to the mainstream movie theatres there's a clutch of repertory cinemas showing fairly diverse programmes and the city hosts dozens of film festivals year-round.

Information on cultural events is available from the main concourse of Place des Arts, as well as in the *Montreal Gazette* and the free alternative weekly papers, *Hour* and the *Mirror*. You can also pick up a list of special events and festivals from the Infotouriste office. Most companies or venues sell **tickets** directly, as well as through the Admission Network (℡790-1245 or 1-800/361-4595, ⓦ*www.admission.com*), which adds a service charge of around $4.

CLASSICAL MUSIC AND OPERA

Montréal's main **symphony** and **chamber** groups perform in the various halls at Place des Arts throughout the autumn–spring season, spreading out to other venues like the outdoor Théâtre de Verdure and the Basilique Notre-Dame in the summer. Other ensembles play at a number of smaller venues, particularly at the universities.

There are also frequent lunchtime concerts in Montréal's churches, as well as in city parks in the summertime. St James United Church, 463 rue Ste-Catherine O (℡384-8179), and Christ Church Cathedral, 635 rue Ste-Catherine O (℡843-6577), both offer weekly concerts, while the Oratoire St-Joseph, 3800 chemin Queen-Mary, provides a suitably grand venue for the annual **Organ Festival** held on Wednesdays throughout the summer (℡526-4261 or 733-8211).

COMPANIES AND VENUES

Chants Libres
℡841-2642, ⓦ*www.chantslibres.org*. Although they only perform one or two operas a year, this company is known for pushing the boundaries of the genre, with anything from

techno music to multimedia spectacles accompanying the lyrical singers.

I Musici de Montréal
☏982-6038,
Ⓦ*www.imusici.com.*
From September to April, this celebrated chamber orchestra plays everything from Baroque classics to present-day compositions, under the direction of cellist Yuli Turovsky. Although you can catch them at McGill's Pollack Concert Hall or the Théâtre Maisonneuve for $25, the daytime concerts in the Tudor Hall on the fifth floor of the Ogilvy department store (see p.205) are much more intimate – and will only set you back $17.

Orchestre Métropolitain
Map 3, J5. Théâtre Maisonneuve, Place des Arts
☏598-0870.
Métro Place-des-Arts.
Though overshadowed somewhat by the OSM, the Orchestre Métropolitain still turns out a decent range of concerts at, surprise, the

Place des Arts along with other venues across the city. Tickets for the PdA shows start at $18.70, and the best seats cost a mere $36.

L'Opéra de Montréal
Map 3, J5. Salle Wilfrid-Pelletier, Place des Arts
☏282-6737 or 985-2258,
Ⓦ*www.operademontreal.qc.ca.*
Métro Place-des-Arts.
L'Opéra de Montréal stages an impressive number of performances each year, and of the half dozen or so annual shows at least two are house premieres. The backbone of the schedule is chosen from the European lyrical repertory, but twentieth-century composers like Debussy and Janacek are often on the programme. English and French subtitles are projected above the stage. Tickets range from $38 to $105.

Orchestre Symphonique de Montréal (OSM)
Map 3, J5. Salle Wilfrid-Pelletier, Place des Arts
☏842-9951, Ⓦ*www.osm.ca*
Métro Place-des-Arts.

The OSM, the granddaddy of the city's classical scene, is led by the energetic Charles Dutoit, who runs a gruelling schedule of concert series built around guest artists, composers and nations, as well as crossover and contemporary performances. The symphony also manages to squeeze in Sunday afternoon shows and Wednesday morning matinees, and sell-out Christmas and Easter performances in the Basilique Notre-Dame. Tickets for most shows start at $16 and run to $74 or more for a box seat.

Pollack Concert Hall

Map 3, H4. 555 rue Sherbrooke O, McGill University
ⓣ398-4547 or 398-5145,
ⓦ*www.music.mcgill.ca.*
Métro McGill.

Located in McGill's Faculty of Music building, this modern venue offers the up-and-coming generation of musicians a chance to perform. Everything from recitals and chamber groups to symphony and opera are heard here, oftentimes for free.

Pro Musica

Map 3, J5. Place des Arts
ⓣ845-0532.
ⓦ*www.promusica.gc.ca*
Métro Place-des-Arts.

Every year, Pro Musica lines up a strong international selection of small chamber groups to perform in the Place des Arts during the October to March season. Tickets are normally $20–25.

Redpath Hall

Map 3, F4. 3461 rue McTavish, McGill University Main Campus
ⓣ398-4547 or 398-5145,
ⓦ*www.music.mcgill.ca.*
Métro Peel.

The more traditional of McGill's two main classical-music venues, Redpath Hall likewise gives students a chance to shine. The warm wood of the interior adds to the ambience of the many chamber and early-music concerts performed here, several of which are taped for broadcast by CBC Radio.

CLASSICAL MUSIC AND OPERA

185

DANCE

Montréal has a justifiably strong reputation in the world of **dance**, based not just on its well-regarded **ballet** and **jazz dance** companies – Les Grands Ballets Canadiens de Montréal and Les Ballets Jazz de Montréal – but on the huge variety of **experimental and contemporary dance**. Dancers and choreographers like Marie Chouinard, Margie Gillis, and Édouard Lock and Louise Lecavalier of LaLaLa Human Steps have been blazing an international reputation for the city – though unfortunately this means they're often out of town. Other companies to look out for are Montréal Danse, O Vertigo and PPS Danse. In addition to the local talent, Montréal hosts North America's premier dance festival, the **Festival International de Nouveau Danse**, held at various city locations biennially from late September to early October (see p.240).

DANCE TROUPES AND VENUES

L'Agora de la danse
Map 5, G6. 840 rue Cherrier
☎525-1500.
Métro Sherbrooke.
This four-storey building is ground-zero for contemporary dance – it's Montréal's main venue and a number of companies have their studios here.

Les Ballets Jazz de Montréal
☎982-6771,
ⓦ www.bjm.qc.ca.
For a quarter of a century, this company has been touring the world and showing off a brilliant fusion of dance and jazz. You might be able to catch them at Espace GO in spring, or Théâtre de Verdure in the summer.

Les Grands Ballets Canadiens de Montréal
Map 3, J5. Théâtre Maisonneuve and Salle Wilfrid-

Pelletier, Place des Arts
ⓣ849-8681 or 849-0269,
ⓦ*www.grandsballets.qc.ca*.
Métro Place-des-Arts.
Under the tutelage of
Gradimir Pankov, Les Grands
Ballets present a season of
classical ballet and more
contemporary works,
collaborating with some of
the biggest names in the
dance world. Tickets are
normally $19–56, but they
jack the price of the best seats
up to $99 for seasonal
favourite, *The Nutcracker*.

THEATRE

While Montréal may be largely bilingual on the streets, that
rarely carries over to **theatre** productions, and most troupes
perform in either French or English only – although when
Les Misérables came to town, the same actors performed in
English one night and French the next. While on the
whole the finest theatres perform in French, there are a few
worthwhile English options in the city; the rest are scattered about the Anglophone bastion of the Eastern
Townships (see p.287). We've noted a few of the finest
Francophone theatres below also, only worthwhile if you're
language skills are up to the task.

   In addition to the local theatre productions, bigger
Broadway-style shows play at Place des Arts and Théâtre St-
Denis (see box on p.182). Festivals also supplement the reg-
ular September to May theatre season – the biennial
Festival de Théâtre des Amériques is the best of the
lot.

Expect to pay around $15–40
for a regular-price theatre ticket.

CIRQUE DU SOLEIL

Begun by a group of youthful street performers in 1984, the Cirque du Soleil (☏722-2324 or 1-800/678-2119, ⓦ*www.cirquedusoleil.com*) has grown into Montréal's most famous cultural export. With a mix of street-theatre whimsy and big-top drama – without the animals – this human circus relies on acrobatic performers, colourful costumes and atmospheric lighting and music to keep your attention. And they do, as evidenced by sell-out shows throughout the world, including permanent residencies in Las Vegas and Orlando.

Not only were each of the Cirque's thirteen different productions (so far) created and produced in Montréal, but each new touring show premieres in the city and often returns between tours. When in town, they perform at Place du Chapiteau ("The Big Top") at their international headquarters in the northeastern suburb of St-Michel.

ENGLISH THEATRE

Centaur Theatre

Map 4, C4. 453 rue St-François-Xavier ☏288-3161, ⓦ*www.centaurtheatre.com*. Métro Place-d'Armes.
The old Stock Exchange Building that houses the Centaur's two stages is a fitting setting for Montréal's most established English-language theatre company. Both modern and contemporary plays make up the half-dozen productions in the season, which runs from late September to early June. Tickets cost $26–36.

Monument National

Map 3, K6. 1182 boul St-Laurent ☏871-2224 or Admission ☏790-1245. Métro St-Laurent.
Renovated by the top-calibre National Theatre School, this venue has three stages and still features plays put on by the students, at least a couple of which are in English. The rest of the year, smaller

THEATRE

theatre companies and individual performers rent out the venue.

The Other Theatre

Map 5, G1. 5115 rue St-Denis
Ⓣ279-4853,
Ⓦ*www.cam.org/~other.*
Métro Laurier.

For the past decade, The Other Theatre has striven to develop alternative and experimental theatre in the city, in both English and French, with excellent results.

Players' Theatre

Map 5, F4. 3480 rue McTavish
Ⓣ398-6813,
Ⓦ*www.cam.org/~other.*
Métro Peel.

Hidden up on the third floor of the William Shatner University Centre, this small black-box theatre sees half a dozen low-budget productions a year, put on by the entirely student-run resident company, with an emphasis on contemporary Canadian plays. Tickets are a snip at $8.

Saidye Bronfman Centre for the Arts

Map 2, B3. 5170 chemin de la Côte Ste-Catherine
Ⓣ739-2301,
Ⓦ*www.thesaidye.org.*
Métro Côte-Ste-Catherine.

This multimedia centre's Leanor and Alvin Segal Theatre is home to the Yiddish Theatre, the only one of its kind in North America (translation in English is available). The centre's English Theatre also stages three productions a year, and guest companies occasionally appear.

FRENCH THEATRE

Théâtre d'Aujourd'hui

Map 5, F5. 3900 rue St-Denis
Ⓣ282-3900,
Ⓦ*www.theatredaujourdhui.qc.ca.*
Métro Sherbrooke.

As the name suggests, "today's theatre" is the focus, and this company has been *au courant* for three decades now. Théâtre d'Aujourd'hui specializes in the work of Quebec playwrights and often stage premieres of their plays.

THEATRE

189

Théâtre du Nouveau Monde

Map 3, J6. 84 rue Ste-Catherine O
ⓣ866-8668,
ⓦ*www.tnm.qc.ca.*
Métro St-Laurent.

At the time this French theatre company was formed in 1951, the theatre it now occupies was the Gayety Burlesque Theatre (where the famous stripper Lili St Cyr performed – see p.175). Recent architectural interventions have brought the venue up to date, but the company itself focuses on large-scale mainstream fare, staging French repertory standards like Molière as well as translations of Shakespeare and European works.

Théâtre Espace GO

Map 5, E1. 4890 boul St-Laurent ⓣ845-5455
or tickets: 845-4890,
ⓦ*www.espacego.com.*
Bus #55.

Innovative and contemporary still, despite having been around long enough to be considered an established theatre, they cram in 9 shows between early September and the very start of June, though half are outside productions. Regular price for tickets is $25.

Usine C

Map 5, I7. 1345 rue Lalonde
ⓣ521-4493.
Métro Beaudry.

This old warehouse was converted into a superb performance space by Carbone 14, a company known for pushing the bounds of theatre with their innovative, multimedia productions (their show *Le Dortoir* toured internationally and won an Emmy Award). It's also used by a number of emerging and experimental companies.

THEATRE

FILM

Like any large North American city, Montréal has a glut of multiplex cinemas showing the latest Hollywood releases and the odd independent or foreign film, though a spate of cinema closures in early 2001 has – at least temporarily – reduced the amount of choice downtown.

To find out what cinemas are open and what's playing, listings are readily available in daily newspapers as well as the free weekly papers *Hour* (ⓦ*www.afterhour.com*) and the *Mirror* (ⓦ*www.montrealmirror.com*). In addition to the repertory houses listed below, cultural centres such as the Goethe-Institut at 418 rue Sherbrooke E (☎499-0149) and the Centre Canadien d'Architecture at 1920 rue Baile (☎939-7026) screen special series of films, and provide venues for festivals.

Cinemas show either French or English versions, rarely both. If in doubt, ask before you buy your ticket.

The average ticket price for a movie is $9.75, though matinées and Tuesday-night screenings are cheaper.

CINEMAS

Centre Eaton
Map 3, G6. 705 rue Ste-Catherine O
☎866-0111.
Métro McGill.
Tucked away on the top floor of the Centre Eaton, little about this six-screen cinema to invites lingering – people just come for the mainstream first-run films shown in English here.

Cinéma du Parc
Map 3, I3. 3575 av du Parc
☎281-1900.
Bus #80 or #129.
This student standby, in the mall under the intersection of rue Prince-Arthur and avenue du Parc, stages

FILM

week-long runs of worthy independents and a repertory programme of second-run and classic films on the other two screens.

Cinéma Impérial

Map 3, I6. 1430 rue Bleury
T 848-0300.

Métro Place-des-Arts.

The grandest of Montréal's film palaces was once *the* place to see a premiere, although these days it offers $3, second-run films as well as the popular FantAsia film festival (W*www.fantasiafest.com*) every July.

Cinémathèque Québécoise

Map 3, M5. 335 boul de Maisonneuve E
T 842-9768,
W*www.cinematheque.qc.ca*.

Métro Berri-UQAM.

Founded over thirty years ago to preserve and promote film and television, the Cinémathèque has a collection of over 50,000 films and videos. Their programme features everything from retrospectives to animation festivals, by

Québécois as well as international auteurs. Facilities include the "mediathèque" documentation centre (Tues 1–6pm, Wed–Fri 1–8pm), exhibition galleries (Wed–Sun 3–6pm; $5. Wed 6–8.30pm; free) and a boutique.

Ex-Centris

Map 3, K3; Map 5, E7. 3536 boul St-Laurent
T 847-3536,
W*www.ex-centris.com*.

Bus #55.

This sleek art-house theatre has three screens and one very trendy café. A mix of thoughtfully chosen independent films are shown in either English or French (but mostly the latter), supplemented by experimental works – the New Media Film Festival is held here annually. Purchasing the $8 tickets at the high-tech kiosks is an experience in itself.

FILM

Famous Players Paramount – Montréal

Map 3, F6. 977 rue Ste-Catherine O

ⓣ842-5828.

Métro Peel or McGill.

Taking up a good chunk of the old Simpson department store, the Paramount was the first cinema in Montréal to offer stadium-style tiered seating – and increased prices ($12; matinees and cheap nights $7) to match. It's got the best "event" feel of the downtown cinemas, with throngs of people in the lobbies – there's nearly four thousand seats shared among a dozen large floor-to-ceiling screens, along with an IMAX cinema.

IMAX Old Port

Map 4, E5–F7. Near rue de la Commune and boul St-Laurent

ⓣ496-IMAX (4629),

ⓦwww.imaxoldport.com.

Métro Place-d'Armes.

The big screen on Quai King-Edward offers the usual 2D and 3D IMAX fare, but its location provides a welcome escape if you are touring the Vieux-Port and the weather turns ugly. French and English versions of the same productions alternate throughout the day. The 40-minute films will set you back $9.95.

NFB Cinema (Cinéma ONF)

Map 3, M5. 1564 rue St-Denis

ⓣ496-6895,

ⓦwww.nfb.ca.

Métro Berri-UQAM.

The National Film Board of Canada showcases their own films – they have nine Oscars to their name – here, as well as other Canadian productions. There are comfy seats in the cinema and video-screening theatre, but for a novel experience try the individual "CineScopes" ($3/hr), where viewers can select films and freeze the frame or fast-forward as the whim strikes. They're run by the unique "CineRobotheque", a central robot that dishes out one of the 5000 available videodiscs like a 21st-century jukebox.

FILM

Shopping

While Montréal has its share of chain stores, the city's reputation as a stylish shopping centre stems from the smart trove of boutiques, most of which are clustered in neighbourhoods outside of downtown. In them, you can find pretty much anything at any price, though the city's real strength is designer and streetwear threads – and politically incorrect furs too. More recently, Montréal has also become a hotspot for twentieth-century design collectors and a great source of house-heavy records.

The best part of shopping in Montréal is the atmosphere on the streets themselves, as some of the best boutiques are wedged in beside cafés with terraces giving off great vibes. Nowhere blends shopping and drinking better than the Plateau's two main drags: **rue St-Denis** forte is Québec-designer boutiques along with sleek home-decor shops and funky accessory outlets. In contrast, affordable-clubby chic is the mainstay of **boulevard St-Laurent**, which also has the city's most concentrated selection of techno-driven record shops.

On the Village's western border, **rue Amherst** is tops for twentieth-century design, while more traditional antiques are found along **rue Notre-Dame ouest** in St-Henri. Nearby, a different sort of feast awaits at the **Marché Atwater**, where farmers sell their wares outside and some

SHOPPING CATEGORIES

Antiques and twentieth-century design	p.195
Books	p.196
Clothing	p.199
Department stores and malls	p.204
Food and drink	p.206
Galleries	p.209
Music	p.210
Specialty shops	p.211
Sporting goods	p.212

of the city's best butchers and *fromageries* ply their trade along the interior arcade. Otherwise most of the action takes place downtown along **rue Ste-Catherine**. Most chains have their flagship stores here, but the real standout is **Simons**, a Québec City original with highly affordable contemporary garb and upmarket designer threads to boot. Shopping **malls** are also found here, the best being the **Cours Mont-Royal**, a former hotel that now hosts dozens of fashionable boutiques in a swanky setting. For art dealing, head to the **Golden Square Mile**, home to the city's finest commercial galleries.

Unless otherwise specified, opening hours are
Mon–Wed 10am–6pm; Thurs–Fri 10am–9pm;
Sat 11am–5pm; Sun noon–5pm.

ANTIQUES AND TWENTIETH-CENTURY DESIGN

Cité Déco
Map 2, I5. 1761 rue Amherst.
Mon–Sat 11am–4pm, Sun
1–4pm. ☎528-0659.

Métro Beaudry.
Head to the back room for retro martini shakers, blenders, juicers and toasters;

the smart leather chairs in the front are made in-house and sell for a tidy sum – around $1500 a piece.

Couleurs Meubles & Objets du 20ème Siècle
Map 5, G5. 3901 rue St-Denis ⓣ282-4141.
Métro Sherbrooke.
A twentieth-century design boutique tucked in a half-basement and full of pristine early-1960s Scandinavian teak tables and chairs, and exotic 1930s pottery pieces. Some knick-knacks cost as little as $7.

Grand Central
Map 2, E6. 2448 rue Notre-Dame O ⓣ935-1467.

Métro Lionel-Groulx.
The classiest shop on the rue Notre-Dame strip, Grand Central stocks first-rate eighteenth-and nineteenth-century antiques. Superbly crafted chandeliers sway over a collection of dining tables, sculptures and gleaming gold-leaf candelabras.

Milord
Map 2, E6. 1870 rue Notre-Dame O ⓣ933-2433.
Métro Lionel-Groulx.
The emphasis at this attractive shop is European arts and furniture, and its showroom floor is laden with ornately carved writing desks, marble busts, and Rococo gilt mirrors.

BOOKS

NEW

Bella Books
Map 5, E5. 3968 boul St-Laurent ⓣ282-7730.
Bus St-Laurent (#55).
While there's a section of carefully chosen fiction on sale, the best reason for hitting up this shop is their ecclectic collection of comics and 'zines.

Champigny
Map 5, G3. 4380 rue St-Denis.
Daily 9am–midnight. ⓣ844-2587. Métro Mont-Royal.

One of the finest French bookstores in town, located in a lofty, wood-toned space, Champigny stocks everything from CDs to cookbooks to go along with large kids' and literature sections.

Chapters
Map 3, E6. 1171 rue Ste-Catherine O. Mon–Thurs 10am–10pm; Fri and Sat till 11pm; Sun 11am–9pm. ℡849-8825. Métro Peel. The biggest English-language bookstore in town, where people tend to linger a while in the comfortable armchairs scattered amidst the four-and-a-half floors. There's also a café and regular readings and book-signings; 30 per cent off best sellers.

Indigo Books, Music and Café
Map 3, F6. Place Montréal Trust, 1500 av McGill College. Daily 9am–11pm. ℡281-5549. Métro McGill. This bright and airy two-storey bookstore stocks fashion, cooking, architecture, art books, fiction, travel and music on

the second floor, where a discounted book table frequently turns up great finds for under $10. Housewares as well as new English and some French texts are found on the main floor.

Nicholas Hoare
Map 2, D5. 1366 av Greene. ℡933-4201. Métro Atwater. A superb array of books – ranging from fiction to children's to travel – adorn the shelves in an atmosphere reminiscent of an old boys' club, wood-panelled walls included. The top floor also stocks a selection of CDs, mostly classical and jazz. There's a second outlet in Ogilvy (see p.205).

Paragraphe
Map 3, G5. 2220 av McGill-College. Mon–Fri 7am–11pm, Sat & Sun 9am–11pm. ℡845-5811. Métro McGill. Though it became part of the Québécor chain a few years back, this bookshop has maintained an independent attitude and boasts a carefully chosen selection that's good

BOOKS

for fiction, philosophy, and art. Frequent readings too.

SECONDHAND BOOKSTORES

Footnotes
Map 3, C5. 1454 rue Mackay ⊤938-0859.

Métro Guy-Concordia.

A hole-in-the-wall spot whose shelves are filled by nearby Concordia University students trading in their texts. The fiction is hit-and-miss, but there's a good selection of philosophy and history.

Sam Welch
Map 5, E5. 3878 boul St-Laurent ⊤848-9358.

Bus St-Laurent (#55).

On sunny days there's a bargain bin out in front, while inside there's always a good selection of modern fiction, sci-fi, and art books, guarded by the requisite bookstore cat.

The Word
Map 5, D7. 469 rue Milton ⊤845-5640.

Métro McGill.

Aside from being the textbook dumping ground for nearby McGill University students, there's usually a good collection of out-of-date publications bought from estate sales.

GAY AND LESBIAN BOOKS

L'Androgyne
⊤842-4765.

Open since 1973, L'Androgyne is a mainstay of the local gay community and acts as an info centre as well as a bookstore. The thrust of the collection is specifically gay, lesbian and feminist writings, but they make room for all kinds of literature as well. Definitely worth a browse if you're looking for works that are both intelligent and controversial. Note that at the time of writing, L'Androgyne was in the midst of moving; call ahead for their new address.

TRAVEL BOOKS

Librairie du Voyage Ulysse
Map 5, G4. 4176 rue St-Denis
Ⓣ843-9447.
Métro Sherbrooke or
Mont-Royal.
The city's main shop devoted

to selling travel guides and
travel-related accessories has a
great selection of items like
neck pillows, money belts
and voltage converters, along
with plenty of French and
English guidebooks. Also at
560 av du Président-
Kennedy.

CLOTHING

DESIGNER BOUTIQUES

Dubuc Mode de Vie
Map 5, G3. 4451 rue St-Denis
Ⓣ282-1465.
Métro Mont-Royal.
Dubuc's flair for finely cut
suits, ties and shirts produces
sharp, sexy and *très* chic men's
attire – and the occasional
sarong too. Suits from $700.

Marie St-Pierre
Map 3, D5. 2081 av de la
Montagne Ⓣ281-5547.
Métro Peel.
Quebecers in the know can
spot this designer's works
from a mile away. The items

on sale here are completely
original, with exquisite hand-
painted silks, crinkly chiffon
and high-tech fabrics like
polyamide in innovative cuts
that easily pass for *haute
couture*. Expect to pay at least
$400 for a dress.

Nadya Toto
Map 3, D5. 2057 av de la
Montagne Ⓣ350-9090.
Métro Peel.
Her clothing caters to the late
20s and early 30s set with
comfortable, sporty threads
and feminine skirts and
dresses with a predilection for
low necklines and clingy
fabrics. Prices start around
$150.

CLOTHING

Revenge

Map 5, G5. 3852 rue St-Denis
☎843-4379.

Métro Sherbrooke.

Revenge used to house only
Quebec designers but has
since gone cross-Canada in
scope, carrying Vancouver's
Ron et Norman line in
addition to Quebecers like
Nadya Toto (see overleaf).
The selection caters mostly to
an older, moneyed crowd,
but the occasional trendy
outfit for the younger set can
be found.

Rugby North America

Map 5, E7. 3526 boul St-
Laurent ☎849-9759.

Bus St-Laurent (#55).

Montrealers with a leather
fetish tend to head for
Rugby, where skirts, pants,
and halters come in modern
styles and fashionable colours.
Be sure to check the
newspapers to see if a
warehouse sale is taking place.
If so, go – the prices are
fantastic.

Scandale

Map 5, E6. 3639 boul St-
Laurent ☎842-4707.

Bus St-Laurent (#55).

Designer Georges Lévesque's
fashion sense matches fluid
retro-styled knits and jersey
with wild and bright colour
combinations. Not the place
to pick up the perfect little
black dress, but an excellent
stop for something no one
else will have back home.

UOMO

Map 3, E6. 1452 rue Peel
☎844-1008.

Métro Peel.

The clothes here ooze quiet
elegance – sedate grey and
black tints abound – in labels
like Kiton, Nino Cerruti,
Giorgio Armani, and
Valentino. The service is
exceptional – no wonder
Mick Jagger, Eric Clapton
and Michael Jackson shop
here when in town. Suits
start around $1000.

CHAIN STORES

Club Monaco

Map 3, F5. Cours Mont-Royal,
1455 rue Peel ☎499-0959.

Métro Peel.

Once designed by Toronto-

CLOTHING

born Alfred Sung, the clothes have lost some of their spark after being bought out by Ralph Lauren a couple of years ago. But while the line is decidedly more beige and conservative than it once was, it's still exemplary for clean lines and a modernist look.

Harry Rosen

Map 3, F5. Cours Mont-Royal, 1455 rue Peel ⓣ284-3315.
Métro Peel.

Making and tailoring fine clothes for the white-collar professional – read high-powered-high-salaried CEO – is Harry Rosen's mantra. His annual Boxing Day sale, where everything is marked down a minimum of fifty percent, has men lined up outside the front doors before they open.

Parasuco Santana Jeans

Map 3, D6. 1414 rue Crescent ⓣ284-2288.
Métro Guy-Concordia.

The jeans in the brand's name are some of the sexiest denim on the market, made to hug every curve and then some. The stock also includes slinky sweaters and halter-tops.

Roots

Map 3, F6. 1035 rue Ste-Catherine O ⓣ845-7995.
Métro Peel.

Although founded by two Americans, Canadians treat Roots as a made-in-Canada phenomenon. The chain's hallmark leather jackets, bags and cotton sweatshirts have a classically preppy sense about them that never goes out of style.

FURS

Haricana

Map 3, K5. 10 rue Ontario O, suite 208 ⓣ287-6517.
Métro St-Laurent.

Local designer Mariouche takes old fur coats and recycles them into new, fashion-forward threads and accessories – boot covers, sleeveless vests, handbags and pillow cases are among the standouts. Handbags start around $150, pillow cases $75 to $400. Call for an appointment.

CLOTHING

CLUB WEAR

- - - - - - - - - - - - - - - - - - - -

Juan and Juanita

Map 3, F5. Cours Mont-Royal, 1455 rue Peel ☎847-2292.
Métro Peel.

A veritable rave emporium featuring some of the best club gear in town: heaps of fun fur, phat pants and baby T-shirts – ravers will think they've died and gone to ecstasy heaven.

Mosquito

Map 3, F5. Cours Mont Royal, 1455 rue Peel ☎286-5244.
Métro Peel.

Most of the stock sports France's Kookaï label, but Montréal gets the label's high-quality line – not the shoddy knock-offs the brand is known for back home. Clean lines, crisp colours and affordable, stylish items. Another location at 3521 boul St-Laurent.

Mousseline

Map 3, E6. 1180 rue Ste-Catherine O ☎878-0661.
Métro Peel.

Seriously funky high-street clothes for both men and women imported from France, with Paris-based Bill Tournade's line getting top rack space for its blend of classic lines with clubby fabrics. Some boots and shoes as well.

Zara

Map 3, F6. Place Montréal Trust, 1500 av McGill-College ☎868-1516.
Métro McGill.

Decent quality knock-offs of Euro fashions arrive here even before the pieces they're modeled on hit stores. The stock is hip and unbelievably cheap – and produced so quickly you'll be lucky if it lasts an entire season. But by then it's nearly out of style anyway.

VINTAGE AND CONSIGNMENT SHOPS

- - - - - - - - - - - - - - - - - - - -

Boutique Encore

Map 3, D5. 2165 rue Crescent.
Tues–Fri 10am–6pm, Sat 10am–5pm, closed Sun & Mon.
☎849-0092. Métro Peel.

Tucked away in this second-floor shop is a gold mine of designer names at cut-rate prices – you'll find Helmut Lang and Costume Nationale skirts for $200 and Christian Lacroix coats at $1200, some of which have never been worn.

Energy X Change
Map 3, F5. Cours Mont-Royal, 1455 rue Peel ☎282-0912. Métro Peel.
If you're looking for a pair of dated pants by the likes of Jean-Paul Gaultier, this is where to find them. Two-year-old designer stock, including Versace and Dolce & Gabbana, is dumped here for sale at bargain prices.

Retro Raggz Friperie
Map 5, F3. 171 av du Mont-Royal E. Mon–Wed and Sat noon-6pm, Thurs–Fri noon–9pm, Sun noon–5pm. ☎849-6181. Métro Mont-Royal.
The mostly raver-style clothes here are in excellent condition, not to mention highly affordable; jeans retail for $10. But the best merchandise are the campy

T-shirts emblazoned with Wonder Woman, Superman and Star Wars decals that cost about $25.

Twist Encore
Map 5, E5. 3972 boul St-Laurent ☎842-1308. Bus St-Laurent (#55).
Good retro shoes, original jewellery (including a spectacular array of chunky cufflinks) and a wicked used-coat selection are the hallmarks here, although there's also a fairly good in-house clothing line, Jong.

Village des Valeurs
Map 2, L4. 2033 boul Pie-IX ☎528-8604. Métro Pie-IX.
When out by the Stade Olympique (see p.81), drop into this massive store to browse among dozens of racks rammed to the hilt with bargain-basement used threads. Of the five Value Villages in Montréal, this outlet is the best for decorative scarves, shoes and fur coats that often go for as low as $35.

CLOTHING

ACCESSORIES

Agatha
Map 5, D1. 1054 av Laurier O
☏272-9313.
Bus du Parc (#80).

Québec women's-fashion
magazines favour this
jewellery shop over all others
when it comes to
accessorizing their models.
Hundreds of spectacular
pieces of costume, silver and
gold jewellery, mostly
imported from France, are
crammed into a space the size
of a shoebox.

Kamikaze Curiosités
Map 5, G4. 4156 rue St-Denis
☏848-0728.

Métro Sherbrooke or Mont-
Royal.

By night, this eclectic shop
transforms into the nightclub
Le Passeport (see p.173). You'd
never know it by day though,
when they somehow clear
out the smoke before
covering the walls and floor
with hair accessories, hats,
leggings, socks and nylons of
all stripes and shades.

Voyeur
Map 5, G5. 3844 rue St-Denis
Closed Mon. ☏288-6556.
Métro Sherbrooke.

An impressive collection of
handcrafted silver jewellery
for both men and women, as
well as some imported pieces
like Boy London watches.

DEPARTMENT STORES AND MALLS

DEPARTMENT STORES

La Baie
Map 3, H6. 585 rue Ste-
Catherine O ☏281-4422.
Métro McGill or Place-des-Arts.
With Eaton's out of the way,

the Bay has regained its
former status as Canada's
flagship department store.
Though it's shortened its
name from the Hudson's Bay
Company, it still stocks the
trademark striped blankets
that began as bartering fodder
in the fur-trading days. The

rest of the stock is quite contemporary.

Holt Renfrew

Map 3, D5. 1300 rue Sherbrooke O ⓣ842-5111. Métro Guy-Concordia.

Head here for your Chanel, Prada, Gucci and Calvin Klein fix. The in-house Studio line, found on the third floor, offers chic styles at more affordable prices.

La Maison Simons

Map 3, F6. 977 rue Ste-Catherine O ⓣ282-1840. Métro Peel.

Simons' house-lines Twik and Trente-et-Un promise good-quality clothing for both men and women at very reasonable prices, and fashion snobs will be happy here as well; designer labels like Gaultier, Dolce & Gabbana, Calvin Klein and Tommy Hilfiger are on hand, occasionally at reduced prices.

Ogilvy

Map 3, D6. 1307 rue Ste-Catherine O ⓣ842-7711. Métro Peel.

Stocks upscale fashions, including a Louis Vuitton boutique, in an atmosphere true to the original department-store concept. Chandeliers hang overhead as you browse along oak counters and a bagpiper serenades the place during the lunch hour.

MALLS

Centre Eaton

Map 3, G6. 705 rue Ste-Catherine O. Mon–Fri 10am–9pm, Sat 10am–5pm, Sun noon–5pm. ⓣ288-3708. Métro McGill.

This large mall covers an area roughly the size of a city block with close to 200 shops on four floors. It's the best place to shop if you're short on time since virtually every major chain store has an outlet here. The high-end shops are on the second floor, mid-range gear is on the main floor, and cheapie togs and accessories dominate the lower levels. The basement has a food court; the top has cinemas.

DEPARTMENT STORES AND MALLS

Cours Mont-Royal

Map 3, F5 & F6. 1455 rue Peel Ⓣ842-7777. Métro Peel. Three floors of high fashion – the dozen odd shops on the mall's second floor cater to the young, hip, clubby set, while the third floor goes way upmarket with Donna Karan and Giorgio Armani. The basement level is oriented towards budget shoppers.

Place Montréal Trust

Map 3, F6 & G6. 1500 av McGill-College Ⓣ843-8000. Métro McGill.
Perhaps the most conservative mall in the city, Place Montréal Trust has gained some points by adding an excellent bookstore, Indigo (see p.197), and the high-street fashion vixen, Zara (see p.202) to its ground-floor offerings.

FOOD AND DRINK

GOURMET FOOD AND WINE SHOPS

- - - - - - - - - - - - - - - - - - - -

Au Festin De Babette

Map 5, G4. 4118 rue St-Denis Ⓣ849-0214. Métro Sherbrooke. A small gourmet shop selling rich delicacies like glazed duck gizzards, foie gras and Russian caviar, along with sweeter items like dark chocolates and rich and creamy ice cream.

Première Moisson

Map 3, C5. 1490 rue Sherbrooke O Ⓣ931-6540. Métro Guy-Concordia.
A mouthwatering gourmet shop selling delectable patés, cheeses and pastries. If you're on a diet, stay far away. There's a second location in the Marché Atwater (see p.208).

Pierre-Yves Chaput

Map 2, G2. 1218 rue Bernard O Ⓣ279-9376. Métro Outremont.
Though off the beaten path, this shop is undoubtedly the best *fromagerie* in the entire

province. Close to thirty unpasteurized cheeses are on offer here, with chèvre (goat's cheese) in the starring role. Five cheeses are made locally by Pierre-Yves Chaput himself, a star in his own right as he's the only *maître affineur* in North America. As an extra bonus, you don't buy without tasting first.

SAQ Express

Map 5, G5. 4053 rue St-Denis ⊤845-5200. Métro Sherbrooke. Good for grabbing a bottle before heading to an *apportez votre vin* joint, this liquor outlet is conveniently located right at the corner of av Duluth and the busiest BYO restaurant strip in town; appropriately, they keep a wide range of whites and rosés perpetually chilled.

SAQ Signature

Map 3, F5. Cours Mont-Royal, 1455 rue Peel ⊤282-9445. Métro Peel. There's no cheap plonk at this liquor store – instead you'll find an exemplary port, spirit and rare-wine selection.

BAKERIES AND SWEETS

- -

Bilboquet

Map 2, G2. 1311 rue Bernard O ⊤276-0414. Métro Outremont. Delectable home-made ice cream is the reason to visit this popular spot. The banana ice cream is loaded with real chunks, and the seasonal specialties, like the Maple Taffy flavour, are brilliantly original. Closed late October to mid-March.

Fairmount Bagel Bakery

Map 2, G3. 74 av Fairmount O ⊤272-0667. 24hr. Métro Laurier. The granddaddy of Montréal bagel shops, opened in 1951, produces nearly 2000 bagels an hour (the most popular are poppy and sesame seed, best when still warm). The line-ups on the weekend stretch outside the door, even in the middle of winter.

Mr Felix et Mr Norton

Map 3, C6. Faubourg

FOOD AND DRINK

207

Ste-Catherine, 1616 rue Ste-Catherine O ☎939-3207. Métro Guy-Concordia.
This basic counter shop serves the most decadent cookies in town. The headliner, the *mènage à trois*, is a heady combination of dark, milk and white chocolates in one soft cookie.

Patisserie de la Gascogne
Map 5, D1. 237 av Laurier O ☎490-0235. Métro Laurier.
The French term for window-shopping is *lèche vitrine* (window licking), which is exactly what you'll want to do before the array of rich cakes and sweet tarts displayed behind the glass.

HEALTH-FOOD STORES

Optimum
Map 3, H5. 630 rue Sherbrooke O ☎845-1015. Métro McGill.
A one-stop downtown health shop selling all the alternative health gear you'd expect and some natural beauty products

(soap and body washes) to boot.

Tau
Map 5, G4. 4238 rue St-Denis ☎843-4420. Métro Sherbrooke.
If you're looking for vitamin-enriched fruit juices, herbal medicines, soy milk and other organic foodstuffs, this small and helpful Plateau shop is bound to have it.

MARKETS

Marché Atwater
Map 2, D6. 138 av Atwater ☎937-7754.
Métro Lionel-Groulx.
A wonderfully atmospheric 1930s Art Deco market with an interior arcade home to 40-odd gourmet butchers, bakers and cheese makers who often proffer bite-sized samples to passing customers.

Marché Jean-Talon
Map 2, H1. 7075 rue Casgrain ☎277-1588. Métro Jean-Talon.
Little Italy's market buzzes with shoppers year-round as dozens of stalls display superb fresh produce, flowers and

baked goods in a plaza lined with gourmet cheese and meat shops; worth checking out for the palette of colours

alone, but great for loading up on snacks or picnic supplies too.

GALLERIES

Galerie Claude Lafitte
Map 3, D5. 1270 rue Sherbrooke O. Mon–Sat 10.30am–5pm, Sun noon–5pm. ⊤842-1270. Métro Peel.
The ritziest gallery in the city – indeed, it's located in the *Ritz Carlton* – dealing in European, Canadian and American masters. Works by Chagall, Picasso and Renoir have all made appearances.

Guilde Canadienne des métiers d'art
Map 3, F5. 2025 rue Peel ⊤849-6091. Métro Peel.
This nonprofit gallery sells a wide selection of native crafts, including sterling Inuit soapstone and West Coast Haida prints and carvings. The top floor has a free permanent collection of predominantly Inuit artworks.

Oboro
Map 5, G5. 4001 rue Berri. Wed–Sun noon–5pm. ⊤844-3250, Ⓦ*www.oboro.net*. Métro Sherbrooke.
A happening Plateau gallery with a penchant for multidisciplinary works from local artists. Installations commonly showcase video, radio and Internet projects.

Zeke's
Map 5, E5. 3955 boul St-Laurent ⊤288-2233. Bus St-Laurent (#55).
A quirky Plateau gallery devoted exclusively to showcasing first-time artists' works, a bent that gets some innovative output like *Montreal Mirror* restaurant critic Spanky Horowitz's photographs of what he ate for six months. Call for hours.

GALLERIES

MUSIC

NEW

Archambault
Map 3, N6. 500 rue Ste-Catherine E ⓣ849-6201. Métro Berri-UQAM.
This music superstore seemingly has every French artist who ever recorded. It has also got one of the best electronica sections in town and a passable jazz and world music selection too. As an extra bonus, you can listen to any of the CDs before buying.

HMV
Map 3, F6. 1020 rue Ste-Catherine O ⓣ875-0765. Métro Peel.
Sure it's mammoth and impersonal, but it's also practical. Listening booths abound, and with three floors packed with all musical styles, HMV is sure to have what you're looking for.

Noize
Map 5, E6. 3697 boul St-Laurent ⓣ985-9989.
Bus St-Laurent (#55).
Offering new vinyl of the house, techno and hip-hop variety; the shop also does duty as a gallery of sorts and showcases local artists' works on the walls.

Sam the Record Man
Map 3, I6. 399 rue Ste-Catherine O ⓣ281-9877. Métro Place-des-Arts.
Sam's is rather grubby and lacking polish but its three vast floors are well stocked with tapes and CDs – upstairs finds jazz, world and rock, while the downstairs' electronica section is better than HMV's, and often less expensive too.

USED

Cheap Thrills
Map 3, F5. 2044 rue Metcalfe ⓣ844-8988. Métro Peel.
The stock is dictated by the musical tastes of Concordia University students. You'll

find an eclectic mix of jazz, rock, world, soul, reggae and electronica here as well as a reasonable collection of used books.

Disquivel

Map 3, K5. 1587 boul St-Laurent ⓣ 842-1607. Métro Saint-Laurent.
Electronica and lounge are the norm here, as well as some dance/club music, mostly on vinyl, though CDs are becoming more prevalent.

Primitive

Map 5, G5. 3828 rue St-Denis ⓣ 845-6017. Métro Sherbrooke.
A good stop for rock, psychobilly, punk, garage and Francophone vinyl, as well as some jazz and soul.

Le Rayon Laser

Map 5, E6. 3656 boul St-Laurent ⓣ 848-6300. Métro Saint-Laurent.
World music, Francophone and rock show up used alongside small jazz and techno sections that deal more in new imports.

SPECIALTY SHOPS

Condom du Fun

Map 3, D5. 2015 rue Crescent ⓣ 847-9297. Métro Guy-Concordia.
Looking for fruity or glow-in-the-dark condoms? Then head to this tiny half-basement boutique where jars of tropical-flavoured rubbers are displayed like candy and sell for $1.50 a pop. There's an assortment of other sex toys too, including inflatable

sheep – in case you left yours at home.

Curio Cité

Map 5, G5. 3870 rue St-Denis ⓣ 286-0737. Métro Sherbrooke
One of Montreal's best-kept secrets, this little shop is tucked under a set of stairs and packed to the hilt with knick-knacks of a predominantly Asian-influence. The sushi plates,

posters, cushions and handbags are all exquisite and, best of all, affordable.

Davidoff

Map 3, C5. 1458 rue Sherbrooke O ⓣ289-9118. Métro Guy-Concordia.

An unabashedly posh tobacco emporium selling swanky smoking accoutrements, fine cigarettes, and all manner of cigars – *the* place to get your Cubans.

Essence du Papier

Map 5, G4. 4160 rue St-Denis ⓣ288-9691. Métro Sherbrooke.

The store could easily be called the essence of writing – elegant gift cards, notepaper and pens are on offer, along with luxurious wrapping paper.

Priape

Map 2, I5. 1311 rue Ste-Catherine E ⓣ521-8451. Métro Beaudry.

This has been Montréal's gay department store since 1974, with all sorts of gifts, clothing, calendars, magazines, books and videos, and a more hard-core collection of leather gear and accessories downstairs. It's also a good spot to pick up event tickets and community info.

Tallulah

Map 2, C5. 4919B rue Sherbrooke O ⓣ481-6950. Métro Vendôme.

The aroma emitted by this body-product shop is enticing enough, but it's the packaging that seals the deal. Fanciful hand soaps shaped like Victorian shoes and polka-dotted canisters containing fruity suds are just some of the fun stuff.

SPORTING GOODS

Inukshuk

Map 3, F5. 1472 rue Peel ⓣ288-8010. Métro Peel.

A friendly budget-traveller boutique with great rates on camping rentals; you can get all the necessary gear for around $35/day, including tent, sleeping bag, backpack, mattress and stove. Of course, you can buy the stuff too.

Sports Experts

Map 3, F6. 930 rue Ste-Catherine O ☎866-1914. Métro McGill.

A one-stop-all-season, sporting-goods superstore – if you can't find what you're looking for here, then it probably doesn't exist. Also does ski and snowboard tune-ups for around $25.

For bicycle and rollerblading shops see "Sports and outdoor activities", p.226.

SPORTING GOODS

Gay and Lesbian

Montréal is one of the most open and tolerant cities in the world, and the province of Québec was one of the first jurisdictions anywhere to begin recognising the rights of same-sex couples. Things haven't always been so rosy, though. Until the mid-1970s, the gay centre was located around rue Stanley, but in an effort to present a cleaner image of Montréal for the Olympic Games, city authorities harassed bar owners out of the area. They relocated to the run-down Centre-Sud neighbourhood where the **Village** has since developed along the dozen or so blocks of rue Ste-Catherine between rues Amherst and Papineau, and you'll find the majority of the city's gay services, **accommodation** and **nightlife** here.

The city tourist board heavily promotes Montréal as a top gay destination, and with good reason. From the extravagant **circuit parties** and huge **pride celebrations** to a wealth of cafés, restaurants, shops, saunas, bars and nightclubs that are hopping throughout the year, the possibilities are there for leather boys, drag queens and even sedate, long-term partners.

INFORMATION AND RESOURCES

It's pretty hard to find **information** about gay and lesbian life written in English in Montréal, although you should be able to decipher the **listings** in the free French-language magazines found in bars and cafés if you know even a bit of French. The monthly *Fugues* (ⓦ *www.fugues.com*) is best, with a comprehensive directory of gay resources and event listings – their bilingual *Rainbow Guide*, published in May and October, is especially useful. The English weeklies *Mirror* and *Hour* (see p.12), though, may also have some info to get you started. If you have access to a **radio**, catch the weekly *Queercorps* show of gay news and features on CKUT 90.3FM (Mon 6–7pm), followed by *Dykes on Mykes* the second and fourth Monday of the month. Still, your best bet is the **Internet**: there are separate pages for lesbians and gay men at ⓦ *www.directiongayquebec.com*, while ⓦ *www.tourism-montreal.org/gay/index.html* has a good list of links.

In the Village itself, the **tourist information centre** at 1260 rue Ste-Catherine E, Suite 209 (late June to early Sept Sun–Wed 10am–6pm, Thurs–Sat 10am–7.30pm; early Sept to late June Mon–Fri and weekends during major events 9am–5pm; ☎522-1885 or 1-888/595-8110), can help with queries about accommodation, services and entertainment. The city's main queer **resource centre** is the Centre Communautaire des Gais et Lesbiennes de Montréal, Suite 101, 2075 rue Plessis (call ahead to confirm opening hours and location – they may be moving: ☎528-8424, ⓦ *www.ccglm.qc.ca*), who have information on community groups and a well-stocked library. Information on HIV and AIDS is available from Info Sida (☎521-7432). Community bulletin boards and event information can be found at the stores L'Androgyne (see p.198) and Priape (see p.212), who also sell event tickets.

For details on Montréal's gay pride celebrations and Black & Blue circuit party, see Chapter 18, "Festivals". Info on other circuit parties is available at ⓦ *www.bbcm.org*.

ACCOMMODATION

Although you shouldn't have a problem staying in any of the accommodations listed in Chapter 9, there is a decent range of options for visitors wanting to stay in a specifically gay **hotel**, **guesthouse** or **B&B**. Note that if you're arriving in the summer or for one of the major annual events, it's best to book way ahead.

For accommodation price codes see p.110.

Auberge Cosy

Map 2, I5. 1274 rue Ste-Catherine E ⓣ525-2151, ⓦ*www.aubergecosy.com*. Métro Beaudry.

A tastefully furnished hotel in the heart of the Village, whose fourteen simple rooms come with air conditioning and TV. There's a jacuzzi for relaxing in as well. ❹

Aux Berges

Map 3, C7. 1070 rue Mackay ⓣ938-9393 or 1-800/668-6253, ⓦ*www.auxberges.ca*. Métro Lucien-l'Allier.

Billing itself as "Canada's Finest All Male Hotel", this recently spruced up 42-room downtown hotel has been around since 1967. Most rooms have private bath,

though the spa facilities – sauna, steam room and jacuzzi – are definitely shared. The small bar has an ivy-covered terrace or you can sun yourself on the clothing-optional roof deck. ❹

Bed & Breakfast du Village

Map 2, I5. 1279 rue Montcalm ⓣ522-4771 or 1-888/228-8455, ⓦ*www.bbv.qc.ca*. Métro Beaudry.

Clean and cosy B&B in the Village with eight rooms spread over two floors, and a jacuzzi out on the secluded terrace. Parking is included. ❹

Hotel Bourbon

Map 2, I5. 1574 rue Ste-Catherine E ⓣ523-4679

THE SAUNA SCENE

Montréal's cruisey reputation is no doubt helped by the dozen or so saunas (bathhouses) scattered about town. Prices and clientele at each establishment tend to differ depending on the time of day but most are open 24hr and busiest for *cinq à sept* (5–7pm) and around the time the clubs close. All offer rooms and lockers, and most include a steam room, jacuzzi and sauna, as well as secluded corners and somewhere to watch videos. The saunas with the best reputations are *Oasis Spa*, 1390 rue Ste-Catherine E (Ⓣ521-0785, Ⓦ*www.thebest spa.com*) and *Le 456*, 456 rue de la Gauchetière ouest (Ⓣ871-8341, Ⓦ*www.le456.ca*), which also has a gym. A complete list of the city's saunas is available in *Fugues* and online at Ⓦ*www.fugues.com/guide/mtl_sauna.html*.

or 1-800/268-4679, Ⓦ*www.bourbon.qc.ca*. Métro Beaudry. The ever-expanding *Complexe Bourbon* includes a sauna, restaurants and *La Track* nightclub (see p.220), which is good if you want to be in the centre of things. The hotel itself has 30 rooms and 5 suites, the largest of which has two bedrooms, a lounge and a jacuzzi. ❹

La Conciergerie Guest House

Map 2, I6. 1019 rue St-Hubert Ⓣ289-9297, Ⓦ*www.laconciergerie.ca*.

Métro Berri-UQAM. A Victorian town house with duvet-covered queen-sized beds in 17 comfortable air-conditioned rooms, half of which have private bath. There's also a rooftop terrace, indoor jacuzzi and an exercise room. ❹

Le House Boy

Map 2, I5. 1281 rue Beaudry Ⓣ525-1459, Ⓦ*www.geocities.com/ lehouseboybb*. Métro Beaudry. A friendly B&B with a quiet garden and large breakfasts. The five brightly painted

ACCOMMODATION

rooms have contemporary IKEA-style furnishings, and the bathrooms are shared. ❹

NIGHTLIFE

Montréal has a fabulous **bar** and **club** scene for gay men. But with nightspots forever renovating or closing down, it's best to ask around or check one of the listings magazines (see p.215) for the latest hotspot. The city is notoriously fickle when it comes to entertainment for **lesbians** – bars and clubs open every year just to close down again after a few months – and at press time, *Sisters* was the only venue catering primarily for women, though *Le Drugstore* is a popular mixed hangout. The larger dance clubs usually have **cover charge** of around $6 at the weekend, but cost only a couple of dollars or are even free on quieter nights.

For cafés and restaurants in the Village, see Chapter 10, "Eating". More bars and lounges – many of them gay friendly – are covered in Chapter 11, "Drinking".

Aigle Noir (Black Eagle)
Map 2, I5. 1315 rue Ste-Catherine ⊤529-0040.
Métro Beaudry.
A favourite haunt of leathermen, there's nowhere in this dark and narrow bar you can stand without seeing a television showing music videos or porn films. Men only.

Cabaret L'Entre-Peau
Map 2, I5. 1115 rue Ste-Catherine E ⊤525-7566.
Métro Beaudry.
The drag shows here attract a large number of straight people as well as a loud and appreciative gay contingent.

Campus
Map 2, I5. 1111 rue Ste-Catherine E ⊤526-3616, Ⓦwww.campusmtl.com.

Métro Beaudry.

The best known of the Village's four strip joints, it's as cheesy as you'd expect here with mirrored walls and young men baring it on the stage or at your table. Women allowed on Sundays after 8pm.

Club Date

Map 2, I5. 1218 rue Ste-Catherine E ⊤521-1242.

Métro Beaudry.

Most younger gay men walk right past this piano bar, though the karaoke every night can be a lot of fun if you're able to leave your attitude at the door. Open from 8am.

Le Drugstore

Map 2, I5. 1366 rue Ste-Catherine E ⊤524-1960.

Métro Beaudry.

A central stairwell lit up like Times Square connects the many levels of this gay and lesbian entertainment complex. If you don't fancy drinking or dancing, you can grab a bite to eat or even get your hair cut here. In summer, the roof terrace is the place to be.

Q-Zone

Map 3, C6. 1401 rue Mackay ⊤841-3131.

Métro Guy-Concordia.

Downtown bar frequented by businessmen complemented by a few students from nearby Concordia University. Comfy sofas and pool tables keep things relaxed.

Sisters

Map 2, I5. 1333 rue Ste-Catherine ⊤522-4717.

Métro Beaudry.

The only spot in Montréal that's just for lesbians, there's a good vibe on the dance floor, especially for the Sunday T-dance. Tuesdays draw a mixed crowd for "Men's Night".

Sky

Map 2, I5. 1474 rue Ste-Catherine E ⊤529-6969.

Métro Beaudry.

Before *Unity* opened, this was *the* place to go, and almost annual facelifts keep people coming back. The ground-floor bar opens onto the street and attracts an after-work and pre-clubbing crowd, while upstairs you can

NIGHTLIFE

choose from two dance floors – retro pop hits or house and techno – as well as loungey chill-out rooms.

Stud

Map 2, I5. 1812 rue Ste-Catherine E ⓣ598-8243, ⓦ*www.studbar.com*. Métro Papineau.

As the name suggests, you're more likely to find beefy boys than precious young things here, but the atmosphere is more friendly than intimidating and you can dance to a mix of 80s and techno on the small dance floor. Men only except Wednesday nights.

La Track

Map 2, I5. 1584 rue Ste-Catherine E ⓣ523-4679. Métro Papineau or Beaudry.

Up-for-it men come for the sweaty dance floor and cheap beer specials (Sun & Wed) at this longtime dance club. There's a series of side bars for a quieter drink and a rooftop terrace in summer. Part of the *Hotel Bourbon* complex (see p.216).

Unity

Map 2, I5. 1171 rue Ste-Catherine E ⓣ523-4429, ⓦ*www.unity-surf.com*. Métro Beaudry.

A young and outgoing crowd fill the large ground-floor pub, broken up by a pair of semicircular bars, though the most coveted seats are by the windows open to the street. On Tuesday evenings it becomes the fun "Cabaret Marleen" ($4), with chanteuses singing classics and gay anthems. The club upstairs packs them in, with a large dance floor, bars off to the sides and a smaller retro dance floor another level up.

Sports and Outdoor Activities

Montrealers are among the continent's most fickle sports fans, and in recent years their attitudes towards their **major league teams** could best be described as dejected. There are constant rumours of baseball's Expos leaving town, and hockey's pride, the Canadiens, have left their glory days well behind. Indeed the only professional sports that get a passionate response nowadays are Canadian football – the Alouettes are one of the league's best teams – and boxing, which has made a strong comeback in the last few years.

Tickets to sporting events can be purchased through the Admission network (℡790-1245 or 1-800/678-5440, Ⓦ*www.admission.com*), or at individual stadium box offices.

Though professional sports may be on a downturn, Montrealers continue to thrive on **recreational** sporting activities, especially during the winter months when cross-country skiing, ice-skating and even snowshoeing provide excellent antidotes to the winter blues. But the city is also blessed with warm summers and residents take full advantage of them by bicycling and in-line skating along the many bike paths at their disposal. The city's waterways also get full use come summer as boating and white-water rafting outfits cast-off for wet and thrilling excursions. To find any public facility and enquire about opening hours and fees, call **Accès Montréal**, the city's frontline information centre (Mon–Fri 8.30am–5pm; ☎872-1111).

HOCKEY

The **Montréal Canadiens** are the most fabled hockey team in the National Hockey League (NHL). Some of the league's greatest stars – Ken Dryden, Guy Lafleur and Maurice "Rocket" Richard – have donned the classic blue and red uniforms, helping the team win an astounding total of 24 Stanley Cups, professional hockey's ultimate trophy. Still, even with their storied history, the Habs, as they're familiarly known, have lost some polish in recent years – the team hasn't won a Stanley Cup since 1993 and has been on a perpetual losing streak. Some claim the move from the hallowed Forum – their former digs – into the Centre Molson in 1996 put a curse on the team's game. A perhaps even more damaging blow to their aura came when an American businessman bought a controlling interest in the team in January 2001. The NHL's regular season runs from October to April, and the playoffs can carry on into June. Home-game schedules are posted on ⓦ*www.canadiens.com*; **tickets** vary between $17.25 and $135 and are pretty easy to get, even on a game day.

BASEBALL

The **Expos**, Montréal's major-league **baseball** team, have an uncertain future. Since the franchise was created in

1968 (and named after Expo '67), it's been dogged by two major handicaps: a poor stadium in which to play baseball (the Stade Olympique, see p.81), and insufficient funds to compete salary-wise with major-market teams. And it's debatable whether the team will stay at all – promises to give them a downtown stadium were dashed in 2000 when investors let their lease expire on land earmarked for the team. The good news, though, is that **tickets** to a game are the cheapest in the league, starting at $8 – the most expensive cost a paltry $36 – and good seats abound since so few people actually attend the games. The season runs from April to October; check Ⓦ*www.expos.mlb.com* for schedules.

FOOTBALL

Canadian **football**, though lacking the panache of its American counterpart, is still good fun: played on a longer and wider field than its southern version, with twelve rather than eleven players on each team and three rather than four downs to advance the ball in ten-yard increments. The result is a faster-paced, arguably more dramatic game that the home team, the **Alouettes**, excel at. Indeed, they barely lost the league's Grey Cup final game in 2000 and have sold out every game since 1998. You'll need to buy tickets well in advance if you want to see them play. The season runs from August to November, culminating with the Grey Cup playoffs, and the games are played at McGill University's Percival-Molson Stadium, at 475 av des Pins O; catch bus #144 from either Sherbrooke or Atwater Métro stations. **Tickets** cost $15 to $47 for regular games, but go up to $100 for playoffs. Home-game schedules are posted on Ⓦ*www.canoe.ca/Alouettes*.

FOOTBALL

BOXING

Montréal ranks among the most popular **boxing** venues in North America. One reason for this is because four locals, Otis Grant, Arturo Gatti, and brothers Davey Jr and Matthew Hilton (part of the Fighting Hiltons clan), have held world titles in recent years, and the last three are still getting into the ring to defend them. Add to this the city's rather unique drawing point – its long-standing French–English rivalry – and things get very interesting when Anglophone boxers square off against Francophone rivals. If Stéphane Ouellet and Davey Hilton Jr are headlining, expect a real show, especially from Hilton, who fans the linguistic flames by entering the ring to the strain of bagpipes. Up to six fights a year are held at the Centre Molson (see p.41) and, depending who's on the card, attendance can peak at 15,000. **Tickets** range from $20 to $125; upcoming bouts are posted at ⓦ*www.interbox.ca.*

CROSS-COUNTRY SKIING

After a heavy snowfall, city residents often treat main streets as **cross–country ski** trails. During the rest of the winter, they tote their skis to the numerous trails located around town, though by far the most popular are the well-groomed paths winding around Mont Royal. The other hotspots, the Lachine Canal path and Île Ste-Hélène, aren't groomed, but they are far more serene than the heavily used mountain. Otherwise, the wintry flora and fauna of the Jardin Botanique can also be cruised on skis. Information on additional paths and ski conditions is available through the **Parcs Nature** network (ⓣ280-7272, ⓦ*www.cum.qc.ca/parcs-nature*); your best option for ski **rentals** is Mont Royal's Pavillon du Lac aux Castors ($5/hr, $15/day; ⓣ843-8240), which also rents **snowshoes** for stomping the trails ($5/3hr).

During the summer months, the same paths used for
cross-country skiing make great jogging trails.

ICE-SKATING

A mind-boggling 168 public **skating rinks** are open from
late December to late February in the city's parks, used for
figure skating, "shinny" (informal hockey matches) and just
plain goofing off. The best of the lot are Mont Royal's Lac
aux Castors and Parc Lafontaine's ponds, though a much
less crowded option is the Olympic Rowing Basin on Île
Notre-Dame. The city-run sports and recreational service
keeps daily tabs on rink conditions (Mon–Fri 9am–noon &
1–6pm; ℡872-2644), which vary greatly as nearly all are
naturally frozen and exist at the whim of the temperature.
Montréal's only artificial outdoor rink is the privately run
Bassin Bonsecours down in the Vieux-Port (10am–10pm;
$2; ℡283-6141) and it's always in top shape since Zamboni
machines keep it smooth and polished. If you're looking to
go **indoors**, head downtown to the year-round rink in the
Bell Ampithéatre, 1000 rue de la Gauchetière O
(Sun–Thurs 11.30am–9pm, Fri & Sat 11.30am–7pm; $5;
℡395-0555); there's also a DJ night for the over-16 crowd
on Friday and Saturday nights from 7pm til midnight.

For a quick blast of winter fun, head to the slides
at the top of Mont Royal, which are frozen over for
inner-tubing weather permitting (Mon–Fri 10am–5pm,
Sat 10am–8pm, Sun 10am–6pm; $7.50 including
inner tube at the Pavillon du Lac aux Castors).

ICE-SKATING

CYCLING

Montréal gets high marks for its **bicycle**-friendly attitude, and boasts 400km of trails throughout the city streets and parklands. You'll find bike stands on most major streets, and some thoroughfares also have two-way lanes and traffic lights specifically for cyclists – look for the sections marked off by waist-high metal posts. Still, the most popular routes are those immune to car traffic, with the path alongside the Lachine Canal among the most picturesque. The circuitous roads that traverse Île Notre-Dame and Île Ste-Hélène are also well travelled, while the nearby 2.4km Circuit Gilles-Villeneuve teems with cyclists when it's not in use by Formula One drivers.

The city's best **cycling resource** is the Maison des Cyclistes, 1251 rue Rachel E (℡521-8356, Ⓦ*www.velo.qc.ca*), an outfit that organizes guided bike tours (see p.15) and publishes *Cycling in Montreal*, a detailed cycling guide with maps; they also **rent** bikes ($8/hr, $25/24hr). To cycle along the Lachine Canal paths, you can hire wheels from the Vieux-Port's Vélocité, 99 rue de la Commune E (℡876-3660; $9/hr, $30/24hr). Note that bicycles are subject to the same rules of the road as cars, though the city doesn't mandate that cyclists wear protective helmets. Bikes are also allowed in the Métro when it's not rush hour, but only in the first car (Mon–Fri 10am–3pm & 7pm–close; all-day Sat, Sun & holidays).

SKATEBOARDING AND IN-LINE SKATING

Most Montrealers show no regard whatsoever for the law banning **in-line skates** and **skateboards** from the streets of the city – though there are perfectly legal ways to partake of both activities. As with biking and cross-country skiing, the Lachine Canal and the Formula One racetrack get most of the action, but Parc Lafontaine draws its share of 'bladers too. Though the city's public squares get high traffic from boarders, especially after nightfall, neither the authorities nor the locals look favourably on the activity. There is a good outlet for skateboarders however, in the outdoor skate-park of Parc Jarry. Though it's a bit out of the way, in the area northwest of Little Italy, the place is equipped with brilliant ramps and half-pipes and, best of all, access is free (Daily 6am–midnight; ☎872-1111). Several shops **rent** blades (along with wrist and kneepads): the Plateau's Cycle Pop, 1000 rue Rachel E (☎526-2525); the Vieux-Port's Vélocité, 99 rue de la Commune E (☎876-3660); and nearby Ça Roule, 27 rue de la Commune E (☎866-0633); to all offer similar rates ranging from $7/hr to $30/24hr.

WHITE-WATER RAFTING, JET-BOATING AND CRUISES

The Lachine Rapids that once prohibited ships from travelling between Montréal and Lachine get ample **boating** action nowadays in the form of inflatable zodiacs and jet-boats that **raft** the current. Two quality outfits run 2hr trips down the choppy waters; you're guaranteed to get wet, so bring along a change of clothing. Lachine Rapids Tours departs from the Vieux-Port's Quai de l'Horloge (May to mid-Oct every 2hr 10am–6pm; $49; ☎284-9607, ⓦ*www.jetboatingmontreal.com*). Further afield, Les Descentes sur le St-Laurent casts off from 8912 boul LaSalle (May–Sept daily 9am–6pm, times vary; $42; ☎767-2230 or 1-800/324-7238, ⓦ*www.raftingmontreal.com*) – the best way to get there is via the shuttle bus service provided from the Centre Infotouriste at 1001 Square Dorchester. Reservations are strongly recommended for both.

Less energetic, but a great way to see the city, are the meandering 2hr river **cruises** on glassed-in Bateaux-Mouches that depart from the Quai Jacques Quartier (☎849-9952, Ⓦ*www.bateau-mouche.com*; mid-May to mid-Oct daily every 2hr 10am–4pm; $19.75; dinner cruises 7–10.30pm; $65.25–$112). More unusual is the amphibious **Amphi-bus** (see p.15) that sails on water and drives along the streets of Vieux-Montréal.

WHITE-WATER RAFTING, JET-BOATING AND CRUISES

Kids' Montréal

lthough at first glance Montréal may not appear to be a child's city, those with tots in tow can rest assured that there are plenty of activities tailor-made to keep kids anything but bored. The many **outdoor parks**, notably Mont Royal, Parc Lafontaine and Parc Jean-Drapeau – where you can picnic and ride pedal-boats along the waterways – are ideal for spending an afternoon simply playing and lounging about. **Boat trips** on the St Lawrence (see opposite) are another favourite pastime and a fun way to see the city – the same goes for the **cable car** ride up the leaning tower above the Stade Olympique (see p.81). And there are also a number of exceptionally kid-friendly museums, listed and cross-referenced below.

MUSEUMS AND SIGHTS

Perhaps nowhere better stresses the fun side of learning than the **Biosphère**, where exhibits on water ecology include squirt-guns and water drums (see p.93). The **Jardin Botanique de Montréal**'s lush gardens, especially the Chinese and Japanese pavilions, are equally captivating (see p.83). The **Insectarium** (see p.87), with its creepy-crawly bugs, and the **Centre iSci** (see p.35), filled with interactive science displays, are obvious places to let the kids loose; both appeal to the curious-minded, not to mention the gross-out factor many adolescents crave. Though further afield, both the **Centre-de-Commerce-de-la-Fourrure-à Lachine** (see p.105) and the **Maison St-Gabriel** (see p.102) provide good Sunday diversions with costumed performances that bring the city's history to life. For animal sightings, head to the **Biodôme**, where monkeys and sloths frolic amidst the greenery (see p.83). And finally, for sheer thrills, the city's **amusement park** (see p.96) can't be beat, though it will probably sap a great deal of energy on your part.

Be sure to ask about family rates before purchasing tickets for any of the attractions listed in this chapter.

ACTIVITIES

For a less-informative, but no less fun, kind of entertainment, you can visit one of the arcades along rue Ste-Catherine ouest, though your best bet for one-stop recreation is the **Paramount** (see p.193); it's got video games, movie theatres decked out with comfy armchairs and an IMAX screen. Otherwise, any of the options listed below should prove to be worthwhile distractions. Your best resource for additional activities is the "Family" section in the *Montreal Gazette*'s daily What's On listings.

Céramic Café Studio
Map 5, G4. 4201-B rue St-Denis. Mon–Wed 11am–11pm, Thurs 11am–midnight, Fri & Sat 11am–1am, Sun 11am–10pm. ⓣ848-1119. Métro Sherbrooke or Mont-Royal.

Children explore their creative sides by painting on ceramic mugs, bowls and plates, any of which make a unique keepsake. Just note that you'll need to go back and pick up the piece the following day after it's dried. Prices start at $8 for a mug, with $7 hourly fees added to the total to cover the paint and glazing.

Laser Quest

Map 3, E6. 1226 rue Ste-Catherine O. Mon–Thurs 6–10pm, Fri 5pm–midnight, Sat 10am–midnight, Sun noon–10pm. ⓣ393-3000. Métro Peel.

A video game brought to life as players armed with lasers chase each other through a dark maze, along catwalks, and up various ramps while sound effects echo around them. Each game lasts twenty minutes and costs $7 each.

Métaforia Centre

Map 3, G6. 698 rue Ste-Catherine O. Mon–Wed 11am–11pm; Thurs 10am–midnight; Fri 10am–1am; Sat 9am–1am; Sun 9am–11pm; $16–30 adults, $12–25 children under-16. ⓣ878-6382, ⓦwww.metaforia.com. Mètro McGill.

The main draw here is a twenty-minute virtual-reality "journey" to the watery depths of an imaginary kingdom complete with 3D projections, elaborate stage sets and IMAX-style cinematography. Dozens of state-of-the-art video games and a climbing wall provide further distraction.

Planétarium de Montréal

Map 3, E9. 1000 rue St-Jacques. Daily screenings late June to early Sept; early Sept to late June Tues–Sun; $6.50 adults, $3.25 under-17s. ⓣ872–4530. Métro Bonaventure.

Documentaries about the solar system are projected onto the Planetarium's domed ceiling while you lie back in reclined chairs; the stars and planets swooshing above produce a fun out-of-body experience, and sneak in some education also.

For information on outdoor activities, see Chapter 16, beginning on p.221.

ACTIVITIES

SHOPS

When the kids get tired of pushing buttons – both yours and the exhibits – you can always get lost in one of Montréal's **malls** (see p.205). You won't find the best **children's stores** in the malls, though; they tend to be a bit more scattered about. We've listed a few of the best below.

Chez Farfelu
Map 5, G3. 843 av du Mont-Royal E ⓣ528-6251.
Métro Mont-Royal.
The name means scatterbrained – and it's meant in the best way possible. The shop's shelves are chock full of amusing gimmicks and squishy toys. A second location across the street, at no. 838, brims with kid-friendly accessories like cartoon-decorated cups and saucers and colourful shower curtains.

Citrouille
Map 5, D1. 206 rue Laurier O ⓣ948-0555.
Métro Place-des-Arts and bus #80.
This small Mile-End boutique is the place to shop for original wooden toys like trains, building blocks and string puppets. Most are imported from Europe and are of excellent quality.

Crazy Suzie
Map 2, C5. 4917 rue Sherbrooke O ⓣ483-6262.
Métro Vendôme.
A tiny shop on the western edge of Westmount is jam-packed with games, books, stuffed animals, pillows and girlish cosmetics. You'll find scads of Hello Kitty, Curious George, Madeleine, Tintin and Loony Tunes paraphernalia as well.

Franc Jeu
Map 5, F5. 4152 rue St-Denis ⓣ849-9253. Métro Sherbrooke.
Franc Jeu's shelves stock everything from board games to wooden toys and stickers to complete any collector's book. Be sure to check the language of the game you buy though – they come in

SHOPS

both French and English at this Plateau store.

Oink Oink

Map 2, D5. 1343 av Greene ☎939-2634. Métro Atwater. The ground floor of this Westmount boutique is devoted to selling heaps of Hello Kitty gear alongside girly accessories like rhinestone headbands, fanciful make-up and feathery boas. Boys can have fun too – though the focus is much less on them – with model building sets, plastic figurines and board games. Upstairs is gender neutral, with clothing of all kinds on sale.

Scarlett O'Hara Jr

Map 5, F3. 256 av du Mont-Royal E ☎842-6336. Métro Mont-Royal.

There aren't many used children's-clothing stores in Montréal to begin with, and there definitely isn't one to match Scarlett O'Hara Jr, where the focus is on quality brand names like Le Petit Bateau, Osh Kosh and Deux par Deux in sizes from 0–12 for both boys and girls.

Uni Foods

Map 3, K7. 1029 boul St-Laurent ☎866-9889. Métro Place-d'Armes. Don't let the bland name put you off; Uni Foods is the most original candy store in town. Its Chinatown location gives it an exotic edge, and kids will go crazy over the Hello Kitty strawberry-flavoured pretzel sticks and candy boxes embossed with various Pokémon characters.

Most Montréal shops keep longer hours in the summer than in the winter, but the rule of thumb that generally applies is Mon–Wed 10am–6pm, Thurs–Fri 10am–9pm, Sat 11am–5pm & Sun noon–5pm.

SHOPS

THEATRE AND PUPPET SHOWS

While there are several children's theatre troupes in Montréal, none of them have their own stages. Your best chance of seeing one perform is at the **Centaur**, 453 rue St-François-Xavier (℡288-3161), which hosts a Saturday Morning Children's Series. The performances of children's classics are generally of high quality, and a few educational pieces are thrown into the programme too; show time is 10.30am, tickets cost $5 adults, $3 children, and they sell out fast. The **Maison du Théâtre**, at 245 rue Ontario est (℡288-7211) stages mostly Francophone plays, but occasionally puts on silent puppet shows. The curtain rises at 3pm Sat & Sun and tickets cost $15.85 adults, $11.85 children.

Festivals

Perhaps as a reaction to the harsh winters, Montréal's social calendar is booked solid throughout the warmer months, with one or more big **festivals** happening nearly every week. Folks take to the blocked-off streets in the thousands for huge international events like the jazz and film festivals, where a wonderfully exuberant atmosphere pervades. In the cooler months the regular performing-arts season is supplemented by a host of smaller film festivals, and there's a variety of ethnic celebrations on offer all year long. Québec City's main festivals – including the famous Carnaval – are described on p.276.

While the selection of events below can give you a general idea of what's on, it's worth asking for the quarterly *What to do in Montréal* guide put out by **Tourisme Montréal** (see pp.9–12).

JANUARY

La Fête des Neiges
Île Ste-Hélène becomes a winter playground for three straight weekends beginning in late January. There's a massive snow-castle to explore, ice-skating trails and tobogganing hills to romp around on, as well as horse- and dog-sled rides (℡872-4537 or 1-800/797-4537, ⓦ*www.fetedesneiges.com*).

FEBRUARY

Le Festival Montréal en Lumière

The mid-February Montreal High Lights Festival gives artists free reign to illuminate the sides of buildings and urban spaces any way they'd like – and the results are often spectacular; theatre, music and dance performances round out the festival (☎288-9955 or 1-888/477-9955, ⓦ*www.montrealhighlights.com*).

MARCH

St Patrick's Day Parade

It seems like everyone in Montréal sports green for one of the largest and longest-running – the first parade was in 1824 – celebrations of all things Irish. The parade is always on the Sunday nearest March 17 and rolls down rue Ste-Catherine (☎645-3880 or 993-7997).

APRIL

Metropolis Bleu

The five-day Blue Metropolis literary festival brings Québécois and international writers (such as Margaret Drabble and Norman Mailer) together in the middle of April for multilingual readings, signings, panel discussions and a "translation slam" (☎932-1112, ⓦ*www.blue-met-bleu.com*).

MAY

Tour de l'Île de Montréal

Late May to early June. Billed as the world's largest bicycle race – the 70km spin around the island attracts 45,000 participants annually – this happening caps off a week of cycling events under the Montréal Bike Fest banner. Advance registration required (☎521-8687 or 1-888/899-1111, ⓦ*www.velo.qc.ca*).

JUNE

First People's Festival

A celebration of Québec's First Nations takes over Place Émilie-Gamelin for a mid-June weekend of concerts, traditional dance and exhibitions of aboriginal sculpture and painting; a mini film festival runs concurrently at the NFB and the Cinémathèque Québécoise (☎278-4040, ⓦ www.nativelynx.qc.ca).

Festival de Fringe de Montréal

With tickets priced at $9 or less, the mid-June Fringe Festival brings affordable theatre to venues around the Main. The quality of productions varies wildly, so head to the beer tent first to catch the buzz on what the must-see shows are (☎849-FEST, ⓦ www.montrealfringe.ca).

Air Canada Grand Prix

Mid-June. For one weekend every June, Formula One cars battle it out on the Circuit Gilles-Villeneuve on Île Notre-Dame. If you don't want to shell out the $50-and-up ticket price, at least check out the entertainment on rue Crescent and boul St-Laurent (☎350-0000, ⓦ www.grandprix.ca).

Beer Mundial/Mondial de la Bière

In mid- to late June, the Quai Jacques-Cartier in the Vieux Port turns into a giant booze can, with more than 250 varieties of beer, scotch and whiskey on offer. There are various forms of entertainment, but testing one's limits of inebriation seems to be the main draw (☎722-9640, ⓦ www.festivalmondialbiere.qc.ca).

Montreal International Fireworks Competition

From the middle of June to late July, Sunday evenings (as well as a couple of Wed nights) feature fantastic half-hour fireworks displays. Although you can pay to hear an orchestra accompany the pyrotechnics at La Ronde ($31.50–42), most

JUNE

Montrealers watch from the Pont Jacques-Cartier, the Vieux-Port or whatever rooftop terrace they can find (☎872-4537 or 1-800/797-4537, ⓦ *www.parcjeandrapeau.com*).

Fête Nationale du Québec

The provincial holiday – St-Jean-Baptiste Day – sees thousands parading down the street on June 24th, proudly waving the blue-and-white *fleur-de-lis* of the Québec flag. Many events take place the evening before, with fireworks, concerts and loads of neighbourhood block parties throughout the city (☎849-2560, ⓦ *www.cfn.org*).

Festival International de Jazz de Montréal

Late June to early July. During the world's best jazz festival, the streets around Place des Arts are shut down for hundreds of free concerts on a dozen or so stages; the major show, held the middle of the festival's second week, draws an audience of 200,000 good-humoured revellers.

There's usually a range of other genres, from salsa to hip-hop, to check out if jazz isn't your bag (☎871-1881, 1-888/515-0515, ⓦ *www.montrealjazzfest.com*).

JULY

Canada Day

While there's a parade along with fireworks and festivities in the Vieux-Port (☎866-9164), Canada Day (July 1) is better known to most Montrealers as "moving day". A large percentage of leases end on July 1, and it's hilarious to watch the scramble as thousands try to move house on the same day.

Carifiesta

It's too cold in February for a Caribbean-style Carnival, so the colourful parade along boul René-Lévesque takes place in early July instead. The calypso music and dancers move on to the big party at Champ de Mars afterwards, where you can, of course, tuck into some spicy Caribbean cooking (☎735-2232,

Ⓦ *www.black-studies.org/carnival/welcome.htm*).

Festival International Nuits d'Afrique

Mid- to late July. African and Caribbean music festival best attended during the three days of outdoor concerts in Place Émilie-Gamelin (Ⓣ 499-FINA, Ⓦ *www.festnuitafric.com*).

Juste pour rire (Just for Laughs Festival)

Mid-July. Over a thousand free shows in the Quartier Latin and hundreds more at venues around the city comprise one of the world's largest comedy festivals. The best acts are always at the "Gala" shows at Théâtre St-Denis (Ⓣ 790-4242, Ⓦ *www.hahaha.com*).

Les FrancoFolies de Montréal

Late July to early August. Hot on the heels of the jazz festival, rue Ste-Catherine is again closed for this celebration of French song and music from around the world. Indoor shows at various city venues supplement more than a hundred free outdoor shows ranging from traditional *chansons* to hip-hop (Ⓣ 876-8989, Ⓦ *www.francofolies.com*).

AUGUST

- - - - - - - - - - - - - - - - -

Divers/Cité

On the first Sunday in August, the biggest event of the year for Montréal's queer community takes place with a massive parade from downtown to the Village, full of colourful and outrageous costumes, cheered on by more than half a million spectators. A week-long series of parties, concerts and events in celebration of gay and lesbian pride precedes the main event (Ⓣ 285-4011, Ⓦ *www.diverscite.org*).

Rogers AT&T Canada Cup/ Tennis Masters Series

The brightest stars in the tennis universe descend on Parc Jarry (northwest of Little Italy) in early August for an international tournament,

AUGUST

239

with women playing even-numbered years and men the odd. The best seats are usually sold out half a year in advance (℡273-1515, Ⓦ*www.tenniscanada.com*).

Les Fêtes Gourmandes

Early to mid-August. City chefs and restaurateurs take over Île Notre-Dame for this gourmet-foods festival, where you can sample dozens of different cuisines, even the elusive Québécois variety (℡861-8241, Ⓦ*www.lesfetesgourmandes.com*).

Festival des Films du Monde Montréal

Although Toronto's higher-profile festival tends to nab more premières, you still might catch a few stars at the Montreal World Film Festival from late-August through early September. Even if you don't, there's plenty happening, including films on the outdoor screen in front of Place des Arts (℡848-3883, Ⓦ*www.ffm-montreal.org*).

SEPTEMBER

Festival International de Nouvelle Danse (FIND)

Late Sept to late Oct; odd-numbered years. One of the world's best gatherings for energetic contemporary dance companies is centred at the Agora de la Danse (see p.136); in addition to home-grown talent, the festival pays tribute to dancers of an invited country (℡287-1423, Ⓦ*www.festivalnouvelledanse.ca*).

OCTOBER

Black & Blue Festival

A festival of cultural events, sports and club nights fills the week leading up to Thanksgiving weekend in early October, when the Black & Blue, a huge gay circuit party and AIDS fundraiser, fills the Olympic Stadium with some 18,000 all-night revellers (℡875-7026, Ⓦ*www.bbcm.org*).

Festival International Nouveau Cinéma Nouveau Médias

Mid-Oct. Given the strength of the city's multimedia industry, it's fitting that the International Festival of New Cinema and New Media, showcasing cutting-edge works in cinema, video and digital media is held in the Plateau's suitably high-tech Ex-Centris cinema (☎847-9272, ⓦ www.fcmm.com).

NOVEMBER

Santa Claus Parade

Late November. The big guy in red draws over a quarter of a million spectators to rue Ste-Catherine, though for many Montrealers it's the unveiling of the Christmas display in the Ogilvy department-store window that marks the start of the holiday season.

DECEMBER

Salon des métiers d'art du Québec

Hundreds of mostly Québécois artisans display their creations for sale in the lead up to Christmas at Place Bonaventure (☎861-2787, ⓦ www.metiers-d-art.qc.ca).

New Year's Eve

December 31. In addition to the wide array of parties thrown in the city's clubs and bars, you can see in the new year under the stars at the Place Jacques-Cartier Formal Ball's heated outdoor dance area (☎871-1873).

NOVEMBER • DECEMBER

City Directory

AIRLINES Air Canada, Air Alliance, Air Nova and Air Ontario, 2020 rue University (☎ 393-3333 or 1-888/247-2262); Air France (☎ 847-1106 or 1-800/667-2747); Air Transat (☎ 1-877/872-6728); American Airlines (☎ 397-9635 or 1-800/433-7300); British Airways (☎ 287-9161 or 1-800/247-9297); Canada 3000 (Dorval: ☎ 633-6090; Mirabel: ☎ 450/476-9500 or 1-888/CAN-3000); Continental Airlines (☎ 1-800/231-0856); Delta Air Lines (☎ 337-5520 or 1-800/361-1970); KLM/Northwest Airlines (☎ 939-4040 or 1-800/361-5073); Royal Aviation (☎ 450/476-3800 or 1-800/667-7692); Swissair (☎ 879-9154 or 1-800/267-9477); United Airlines (☎ 1-800/241-6522).

AREA CODES Montréal ☎ 514; off-island suburbs, Lower Laurentians and western areas of the Eastern Townships ☎ 450; Upper Laurentians and rest of Eastern Townships ☎ 819; Québec City ☎ 418.

BANKS AND ATMS Banks are widespread and almost all have ATMs, which accept Plus and/or Cirrus networked cards. The major banks are Banque Royale, Banque de Montréal, CIBC, Banque TD, Banque Scotia and Banque Laurentienne.

CAR RENTAL Avis, 1225 rue Metcalfe (☎ 866-7906); Budget, 1240 rue Guy (☎ 938-1000); Discount, 607 boul de Maisonneuve O (☎ 286-1554);

Hertz Canada, 1073 rue Drummond (☎938-1717); Thrifty, 800 boul de Maisonneuve E (☎845-5954); Via Route, 1255 rue Mackay (☎871-1166), which charges a bit less than the majors.

CITY INFORMATION Accès Montréal (☎872-2237) has recorded information on all manner of municipal services, from tennis courts to parking tickets.

CONSULATES France, 1 Place Ville Marie (☎878-4385); Germany, 1250 boul René-Lévesque O (☎931-2277); Italy, 3489 rue Drummond (☎849-8351); Japan, 600 rue de la Gauchetière O (☎866-3429); Netherlands, 1002 rue Sherbrooke O (☎849-4247); South Africa, 1 Place Ville Marie (☎878-9217); UK, 1000 rue de la Gauchetière O (☎866-5863); US, 1155 rue St-Alexandre (☎398-9695). For the following countries, contact the embassy in Ottawa: Australia (☎613/236-0841); Ireland (☎613/233-6281); New Zealand (☎613/238-5991).

CURRENCY EXCHANGE Most large downtown banks will change currency and traveller's cheques. American Express, 1141 boul de Maisonneuve O (☎284-3300); Bureau de Change de Vieux-Montréal, 230 rue St-Jacques; Downtown Currency Exchange, 2000 av McGill College; Thomas Cook, 777 rue de la Gauchetière O.

DENTISTS 24hr dental clinic, 3546 av Van-Horne (☎342-4444); Walk-in Clinic, Montreal General Hospital, 1650 av Cedar (Mon–Fri 8.30am–4.30pm ☎934-8397; after-hours call ☎934-8075).

DISABILITY Kéroul (☎252-3104, ⓦ*www.keroul.qc.ca*) provides information on, and publishes the *Accessible Québec* ($10) guide to, attractions around the province.

ELECTRICITY Voltage (110V) and plug types are the same as in the US.

EMERGENCIES ☎911 for fire, police and ambulance.

CITY INFORMATION—EMERGENCIES

HOSPITALS Central English-language hospitals are the Montreal General Hospital, 1650 av Cedar (☏937-6011), on the mountain's slope above the Golden Square Mile; and Royal Victoria Hospital, 687 av des Pins O (☏842-1231) up the hill from McGill University.

INTERNET The cheapest access is often at photocopy shops, such as Allô Copie, 928 av du Mont-Royal E (10¢/min or $5/hr; ☏523-2488). Dedicated Internet cafés include *Le Café Électronique*, 1425 boul René-Lévesque O ($5.50/30min; ☏871-0307); *Cyberground Café Internet*, 3672 boul St-Laurent ($8/hr; ☏842-1726); *Network Café*, 5120 chemin Queen-Mary ($8/hr; ☏344-0959).

LAUNDRY Net-Net, 310 av Duluth E, will wash, dry and fold your clothes in neat bags for you within 24 hours for 69¢/pound; doing it yourself works out to around $4. Most hotels have laundry service as well.

LEFT LUGGAGE There are $2 lockers at the main train and bus terminals.

PHARMACIES Jean Coutu and Pharmaprix are the major chains with branches all over the city. The Pharmaprix near the Oratoire St-Joseph at 5122 chemin de la Côte des Neiges (☏738-8464) is open 24hr. Closer to the centre and open until midnight are Jean Coutu, 501 av du Mont-Royal E (☏521-3481), and the Pharmaprix on 901 rue Ste-Catherine E (☏842-4915) and 1500 rue Ste-Catherine O (☏933-4744).

POLICE ☏280-2222.

POST OFFICES The main downtown branch is at 1250 rue University (Mon–Fri 8am–5.45pm, Sat 8am–noon). Poste restante can be picked up at Station A, 285 rue St-Antoine O (same hours).

PUBLIC HOLIDAYS New Year's Day (January 1), Good Friday, Easter Monday, Fête de Dollard/Victoria Day (Mon preceding May 25), Fête

Nationale du Québec/St-Jean-Baptiste Day (June 24), Canada Day (July 1), Labour Day (1st Mon in Sept), Thanksgiving (2nd Mon in Oct), Christmas Day (Dec 25), Boxing Day (Dec 26).

RAPE CRISIS Bilingual rape crisis line (T934-4504).

RIDESHARING Allô-Stop, 4317 rue St-Denis (T985-3032 or 985-3044, W*www.allo-stop.com*), is a carpool service that matches drivers with passengers for destinations within Québec. Membership costs $6 per year, and you pay for your share of petrol. Québec City also has a branch, located at 665 rue St-Jean (T418/522-0056).

SKI/SNOW REPORTS T493-1810, W*www.quebecskisurf.com*.

TAX Two taxes are applied to just about every purchase: the 7 percent GST (TPS in French) and the 7.5 percent QST (TVQ in French). You can claim a rebate on the GST for items you take outside of Canada, as well as on short-term accommodation: the total pre-tax value must exceed $200, with each individual receipt being at least $50. Several private companies process claims for a fee, only worthwhile if you want your refund right away – Maple Leaf Tax Refunds, on the fourth level of Centre Eaton, 705 rue Ste-Catherine O (T847-0982) charges a fee of 18 percent (minimum $9). You're better off applying directly to the Canada Customs and Revenue Agency (T902/432-5608 or 1-800/668-4748) – forms are available at the Centre Infotouriste, at the airport, and at duty-free shops on the US/Canada border.

TELEPHONES Local calls cost 25¢ at a payphone; more if you pay by credit card. Prepaid cards are available from Bell-Canada outlets, newsagents and the Centre Infotouriste. Dial T411 for information, T0 to reach the operator. Toll-free (freephone) numbers begin with 1-800, 1-877 or 1-888.

TICKETS The Admission network sells tickets for almost

RAPE CRISIS

everything (☏790-1245 or 1-800/361-4595, Ⓦ www.admission.com).

TIME Montréal is on Eastern Standard Time (EST), five hours behind GMT. Daylight Savings Time runs from the first Sunday in April to the last Sunday in October.

TIPPING It's customary to tip 15 percent of the total before taxes to waiters, bar staff and taxi drivers. Note that "TPS" or "GST" which appear on the bill are not abbreviations for "tips" or "Good Service Tip" – these are taxes (see overleaf).

TRAVEL AGENTS Tourisme Jeunesse Boutique, 4008 rue St-Denis (☏844-0287) and Tourbec, 595 boul de Maisonneuve O (☏288-4455) are both excellent sources for budget travellers. Voyages Campus, 1455 boul de Maisonneuve O (☏288-1130), 3480 rue McTavish (☏398-0647), 225 av du Président-Kennedy (☏281-6662) and 1613 rue St-Denis (☏843-8511), books travel primarily for students with an International Student Identification Card (ISIC).

WEATHER AND ROAD CONDITIONS ☏283-3010 or 1-900/565-MÉTÉO (charged at premium rates) for info on weather and winter road conditions; ☏284-2363 for roadworks.

OUT OF THE CITY

20	Québec City	249
21	Les Laurentides	278
22	Les Cantons-de-l'Est	287

Québec City

I f Montréal is French-speaking Canada at its most dynamic, **Québec City**, some 250km away, more truly captures the religious and colonial legacy of New France. Spread over Cap Diamant and the banks of the St Lawrence, Québec City is Canada's most beautifully located and historic city. At its centre stands **Vieux-Québec**, the only walled city in North America, a fact that prompted UNESCO to classify it as a World Heritage Site in 1985. In both parts of the old city – Haute and Basse (Upper and Lower) – the winding cobbled streets are flanked by seventeenth- and eighteenth-century stone houses and churches, graceful parks and squares, and countless monuments.

This is an authentically and profoundly French city: 95 percent of its 600,000 population are French-speaking and though not as bilingual as Montréal, the people are friendlier and most in the tourist trade speak some English. When arriving from Montréal, you'll be immediately struck by the differences between the province's two main cities. While Montréal feels international, Québec City is more than a shade provincial, often seeming too bound up with its religious and military past – a residue of the days when the city was the bastion of the Catholic Church in Canada. The Church, though, can claim much of the credit for the creation and preservation of the finest buildings, from the quaint Église Notre-Dame-des-Victoires to the opulent Basilique Notre-Dame de Québec and the vast Séminaire. Austere defensive structures, like the massive Citadelle, reveal the military pedigree of a city dubbed by Churchill as the "Gibraltar of North America".

The area code for Québec City is ☎ 418.

Some history

For centuries the clifftop site on which Québec City sits was occupied by the Iroquois village of Stadacona. Permanent European settlement did not begin until 1608, when Samuel de Champlain established a fur-trading post in what is now Place Royale. To protect the rapidly developing inland trade gateway, the settlement shifted to the clifftop in 1620. Québec's steady expansion was noted in London, and in 1629 Champlain was starved out of the fort by the British, an occupation that lasted just three years. Before the century was out, the long-brewing struggles between England and France spilled over into the colony again, prompting the Comte de Frontenac, known as the "fighting governor", to replace Champlain's Fort St-Louis with Château St-Louis, and begin work on the now famous fortifications that ring Vieux-Québec.

In September 1759, during the Seven Years War, the most significant battle in Canada's history took place here, between the British under General James Wolfe and Louis Joseph, Marquis de Montcalm. The city had already been under siege from the opposite shore for three months and Montcalm had carefully protected the city from any approach by water. Finally, Wolfe and his 4500 troops heard of an unguarded track, scaled the cliff of Cap Diamant and crept up on the unprepared French regiment.

The twenty-minute battle on the Plaines d'Abraham left both leaders mortally wounded and the city of Québec in the hands of the English, a state of affairs confirmed by the Treaty of Paris in 1763.

In 1775, the town was attacked again, this time by the Americans, who had already captured Montréal. The battle was won by the British and for the next century the city quietly earned its livelihood as the centre of a timber-trade and shipbuilding industry. By the time it was declared the provincial capital of Lower Canada in 1840, though, the accessible supplies of timber had run out. Ceasing to be a busy seaport, the city declined into a centre of small industry and local government, its way of life still largely determined by the Catholic Church until the Quiet Revolution in the 1960s and the rise of Québec nationalism. Québec City has since grown with the upsurge in the economy, developing a suburbia of shopping malls and convention centres as slick as any in the country.

Arrival

Québec City is easy enough to get to from Montréal, with excellent air, rail and road links. You won't save much time by flying once you've tacked transport and airport formalities onto the fifty-minute flying time, but if you do you'll arrive at **Aéroport Jean-Lesage**, 20km west of the city. A shuttle connects the airport with several downtown hotels (8.45am–10.20pm; 7–8 daily; $9 to Vieux-Québec). The twenty-minute trip by taxi is a fixed rate of $24.50.

VIA Rail **trains** from Montréal take three hours to arrive at the central Gare du Palais (☎692-3940 or 1-800/361-5390) in Basse-Ville. **Buses** are cheaper, and the regular express buses just as fast as the train, arriving at the main bus terminal, 320 rue Abraham-Martin (℡ 525-3000), adjoining the Gare du Palais.

A ridesharing service between Montréal and Québec City is available through Allô-Stop – see p.245 for details.

If you come by **car**, there's a choice of two *autoroutes* for the two-and-a-half-hour journey from Montréal: Hwy 40 follows the north shore of the St Lawrence and Hwy 20 the south, the latter being marginally more interesting. **Parking** within the city walls can be a pain and it's best to leave your vehicle outside the centre, at the car park near the tourist office on avenue Wilfrid-Laurier outside Porte St-Louis or at the long-term car park opposite the bus terminal. Note that motorcycles are not permitted in Vieux-Québec.

Information and getting around

Québec City's main **information centre**, which also offers an accommodation service, is located beside the Voltigeurs de Québec armoury at 835 av Wilfrid-Laurier (daily: late June to mid-Oct 8.30am–7.30pm; mid-Oct to late June Mon–Thurs & Sat 9am–5pm, Fri 9am–6pm, Sun 10am–4pm; ℡ 649-2608, ⓦ *www.quebecregion.com*). More information is available at the **Centre Infotouriste** on the opposite side of Place d'Armes from the *Château Frontenac* at 12 rue Ste-Anne (similar hours; ℡ 1-877/266-5687, ⓦ *www.bonjourquebec.com*). Grab the free booklet *Greater*

Québec Area from either for a detailed map.

Québec City's sights and hotels are packed into a small area, so **walking** is the most practical and pleasurable way to get around. For sights further out, like the Musée du Québec, STCUQ **local buses** (℡627-2511) are efficient and run from around 6am to 1am (certain routes run until 3am Fri & Sat). Fares are a standard $1.75 per journey by prepaid ticket, available at newsstands and grocery stores across town, as are one-day passes ($4.70); the cash fare per journey is $2.25, exact fare only. **Taxis** are available from Taxi Coop (℡525-5191) and Taxi Québec (℡525-8123).

Accommodation

There's a wealth of **accommodation** in Québec City, with dozens of hotels in Vieux-Québec alone. There are also two **youth hostels** within the walls of the old city – the one on rue Ste-Ursule is surrounded by **budget hotels**. Always try to reserve in advance, particularly during the summer months and the Carnaval in February.

Accommodation price codes are listed on p.110.

HOTELS

Auberge St-Antoine
Map p.257, G3. 10 rue St-Antoine ℡692-2211
or 1-888/692-2211,
ⓦ*www.saint-antoine.com*.

Close to the Musée de la Civilisation, this cosy hotel is divided into two buildings. The stone walls and chunky wood posts and beams in the lofty reception hall are replicated in a number of the rooms, while others are a playful medley of colours and styles, some with views of the river. ❽

Auberge St-Louis

Map p.257, C5. 48 rue St-Louis Ⓣ692-2424 or 1-888/692-4105, Ⓦ*www.quebecweb.com/ aubergestlouis*.

The cheapest two-star inn along rue St-Louis is ideally located and comprises two three-storey houses dating from the 1830s whose rooms have basic furnishings but are comfy nonetheless. Cheaper rooms have shared bath. ❷–❹

Hôtel Cap-Diamant

Map p.257, D6. 39 av Ste-Geneviève Ⓣ694-0313, Ⓦ*www.hcapdiamant.qc.ca*.

Two-star, nine-bedroom guesthouse dating from 1826 with Victorian furnishings located on a quiet street near the Jardin des Gouverneurs. All rooms are en-suite, and have air-conditioning and tvs. In summer, you can take your

continental breakfast into the peaceful courtyard garden. ❸

Le Château Frontenac

Map p.257, F5. 1 rue des Carrières Ⓣ692-3861 or 1-800/441-1414, Ⓦ*www.fairmont.com*.

This opulent Victorian "castle" opened in 1893, and has accommodated such dignitaries as Churchill, Roosevelt, Madame Chiang Kai-shek and Queen Elizabeth II. It's the most expensive place in town and has magnificent views, elegant dining halls, a tiled swimming pool and impeccably well-furnished rooms. If you can't afford to stay, you can still take a guided tour (see p.258). ❽

Hôtel Le Clos St-Louis

Map p.257, C5. 69 rue St-Louis Ⓣ694-1311 or 1-800/461-1311, Ⓦ*www.quebecweb.com/ clos_saint-louis*.

Three-star hotel in two interconnected 1840s houses with decor to match – Victorian stuffed chairs and settees, four-poster beds in

some of the rooms, gilt mirrors and lots of antiques.
⑤

Hôtel Dominion 1912

Map p.257, G2. 126 rue St-Pierre Ⓣ692-2224 or 1-888/833-5253, Ⓦ*www.hoteldominion.com*.
Fabulous boutique hotel with all the touches – feather pillows and duvets, subdued lighting, stylish modern decor and cool frosted-glass sinks lit from below. Windows run the lengths of the rooms offering terrific views of the St Lawrence or Vieux-Québec. ⑦

Maison historique James Thompson

Map p.257, C5. 47 rue Ste-Ursule Ⓣ694-9042, ⓌNwww.bedandbreakfast quebec.com*.
One of the few B&Bs in Vieux-Québec, this historic 1793 house is surprisingly bright and bestrewn with antiques; there are sleigh beds in two of the three bedrooms.
③

Hôtel Manoir d'Auteuil

Map p.257, B5. 49 rue d'Auteuil ⓉN694-1173, ⓌNwww.quebecweb .com/dauteuil*.
Lavish 1835 town house by the city walls, refurbished a century later with 16 Art Deco rooms. Friendly service and a free continental breakfast is included. ⑥

HOSTELS

Auberge de la Paix

Map p.257, C3. 31 rue Couillard ⓉN694-0735.
Situated just off rue St-Jean, this is by far the better of Québec City's two youth hostels, with a friendly staff and a large courtyard to hang out in. Rates – $19 whether in dorms or one of the two private rooms – include a do-it-yourself breakfast. It fills up fast, so book ahead.

HOSTELS

Centre International de Séjour de Québec
Map p.257, B4. 19 rue Ste-Ursule ⓣ 694-0755 or 1-800/461-8585, ⓦ *www.cisq.org*.
The official youth hostel, in a former hospice run by nuns, is impersonal and fills up quickly despite offering 245 beds in dormitories ($17 for members, $21 for non-members), large shared rooms ($18/$22) and doubles ($46/$50 for the room). It's well kitted-out for budget travellers, though, with laundry facilities, Internet access ($2 for 20min) and luggage lockers. No curfew, but you'll need to be buzzed in after 11pm. Discounts for week-long stays and children under 12.

The City

Québec City spreads from its historic heart into a bland suburbia, but the highlights lie beside the St Lawrence, with main attractions being evenly distributed between the upper and lower portions of **Vieux-Québec** (Old Québec). Perched atop Cap Diamant and encircled by the city walls, **Haute-Ville** (Upper Town) forms the Québec City of tourist brochures, dominated appropriately enough by a hotel – the towering *Château Frontenac*. Its stupendous clifftop location accounts for part of its allure, and the wide boardwalk of the Terrasse Dufferin running along the front allows anyone to enjoy the same views over the St Lawrence River and **Basse-Ville** (Lower Town). Steep stairs and a funicular provide access to Basse-Ville, the site of some of the city's oldest and best-preserved buildings as well as the worthwhile Musée de la Civilisation. Back away from the cliff edge, amid the jumble of streets in the middle of Haute-Ville, are a number of museums and the city's most

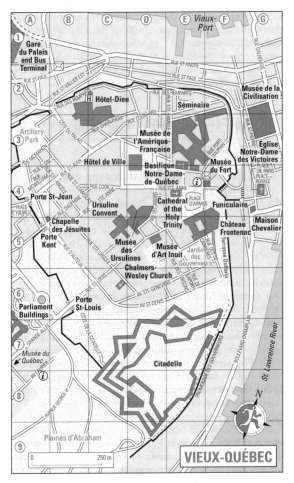

Gare du Palais and Bus Terminal

RUE ST-PAUL

RUE ST-VALLIER EST

RUE ST-PAUL

RUE ST-ANDRÉ

RUE ST-PAUL

Vieux-Port

RUE DALHOUSIE

Musée de la Civilisation

Hôtel-Dieu

RUE DES REMPARTS

RUE DES REMPARTS

RUE COUILLARD

Séminaire

RUE ST-FLAVIEN

RUE STE-FAMILLE

Artillery Park

CÔTE DU PALAIS

RUE CHARLEVOIX

RUE FERLAND

RUE ST-PIERRE

Musée de l'Amérique-Française

Église Notre-Dame des Victoires

RUE ST-JEAN

Hôtel de Ville

RUE COOK

Basilique Notre-Dame-de-Québec

RUE PORT DAUPHIN

Musée du Fort

PLACE DE PARIS

PLACE-ROYALE

Porte St-Jean

RUE ELGIN

RUE ST-JEAN

RUE STANISLAS

RUE STE-ANNE

RUE STE-ANNE

Cathedral of the Holy Trinity

PLACE D'ARMES

Funiculaire

RUE McWILLIAM

RUE ST-ANGÈLE

RUE DAUPHINE

PLACE D'YOUVILLE

Ursuline Convent

Château Frontenac

Maison Chevalier

Chapelle des Jésuites

RUE D'AUTEUIL

RUE STE-URSULE

Musée des Ursulines

Musée d'Art Inuit

Jardins des Gouverneurs

Porte Kent

Chalmers-Wesley Church

AV STE-GENEVIÈVE

Terrasse Dufferin

RUE DES CARRIÈRES

RUE DU PARLOIR

RUE DES GRISONS

RUE HALDIMAND

Parliament Buildings

Porte St-Louis

RUE ST-LOUIS

AV ST-DENIS

Musée du Québec

GRANDE ALLÉE

CÔTE DE LA CITADELLE

Citadelle

PROMENADE DES GOUVERNEURS

BOULEVARD CHAMPLAIN

St. Lawrence River

AVENUE GEORGE VI

N

Plaines d'Abraham

0   250 m

VIEUX-QUÉBEC

THE CITY

257

dramatic churches, while the fortifications are best seen at the western end of Vieux-Québec. You can follow them along to the star-shaped Citadelle, protecting the city from attack across the Plaines d'Abraham, although the only clashes there now are the bold colours of modernist paintings in the Musée du Québec at the far end of the former battlefield.

THE CHÂTEAU FRONTENAC AND AROUND

Map p.257, E4–F5.

Champlain established his first fort in 1620 on the site now occupied by the gigantic **Château Frontenac**, probably Canada's most photographed building. New York architect Bruce Price drew upon the French-Canadian style of the surroundings to produce a pseudomedieval, red-brick pile crowned with a copper roof. Although the hotel he designed was inaugurated by the Canadian Pacific Railway in 1893, its distinctive main tower was only added in the early 1920s – during which time the hotel never closed – resulting in an over-the-top design that makes the most of the extreme location atop Cap Diamant. Numerous celebrities, including Queen Elizabeth II, have stayed here, and the hotel has hosted one pair or more of newlyweds every night since it opened. If you can't afford to stay (see p.254), there are fifty-minute guided tours departing on the hour from the lower level (May to mid-Oct daily 10am–6pm; mid-Oct to April Sat & Sun noon–5pm; $6.50; reservations preferable ℡691-2166).

Place d'Armes

Map p.257, E4.

The main square fronting the *Château*, **Place d'Armes**, with a central fountain topped by a monument to the

Récollet missionaries who arrived here in 1615, is surrounded by a number of historic buildings. One of the finest, to the right of the *Château* at 17 rue St-Louis, is the **Maison Maillou**, which houses the Québec chamber of commerce. Dating from 1736, this grey-limestone house, with metal shutters for insulation and a steeply slanting roof, displays the chief elements of the climate-adapted architecture brought over by the Norman settlers.

Among the hotels and restaurants on the square's north side is the entrance to the narrow alley of **rue du Trésor**, where French settlers paid their taxes to the Royal Treasury; nowadays it's a touristy artists' market with vendors hawking saccharine cityscapes. You're better to visit the courtyard just west of Place d'Armes between rue Ste-Anne and the Cathedral of the Holy Trinity, where Québec-based artisans operate small crafts and clothes stalls. To the east of the alley, the former Union Hotel, built in 1803, houses the **Infotouriste** office (see p.252).

Terrasse Dufferin

Map p.257, E5–F4.

The east side of Place d'Armes merges into the wide cliff-top boardwalk of the **Terrasse Dufferin**, which overlooks the narrowing of the river that was known to the natives as the *kebec* – the source of the province's name. At the beginning of the walkway stands a romantic statue of **Champlain** and, beside it, a modern sculpture symbolizing Québec's status as a UNESCO World Heritage Site. Beyond the Charles Baillairgé-designed open-air pavilions and streetlamps, first electrified in 1885, the boardwalk ends where the cape rises to the Citadelle (see p.268).

THE CHÂTEAU FRONTENAC AND AROUND

Beyond the Terrasse Dufferin, you can follow
the Promenade des Gouverneurs, perched
precariously between the Citadelle and the cliff face,
to the Plaines d'Abraham (see p.268).

BASSE-VILLE

Map p.257, F5–G2.

The birthplace of Québec City, **Basse-Ville** (Lower Town), can be reached from Terrasse Dufferin by the funicular opposite Place d'Armes, but you're better saving that for the weary journey back up. Instead, take the stairs at the north end of the terrace down to Porte Prescott, where a path continues across the top of the gate to **Parc Montmorency**, the meeting place of Québec's first legislature in 1694. Descend the steps before crossing the gate, though, to reach the winding Côte de la Montagne from where the steep **escalier casse-cou** (Breakneck Stairs) leads to lively rue du Petit-Champlain (see p.263) and another few metres along an unassuming staircase leads down to Place Royale. The latter offers perhaps the best introduction to Basse-Ville, opening onto a lovely square of seventeenth-century stone buildings.

Place Royale

Map p.257, G4.

Champlain built New France's first permanent settlement at **Place Royale** in 1608, to begin trading fur with the native peoples. The square remained the focal point of Canadian commerce until 1759, and after the fall of Québec the British continued using the area as a lumber market, vital for shipbuilding during the Napoleonic Wars. After 1860

Place Royale was left to fall into disrepair, a situation reversed as recently as the 1970s, when the scruffy area was renovated. Its pristine stone houses, most of which date from around 1685, are undeniably photogenic, with their steep metal roofs, numerous chimneys and pastel-coloured shutters, but it's a Legoland townscape, devoid of the scars of history. Fortunately the atmosphere is enlivened in summer by entertainment from classical orchestras to juggling clowns, and by the Fêtes de la Nouvelle-France (see box, p.276), when everyone dresses in period costume and it once again becomes a chaotic marketplace.

In Maison Hazeur, a seventeenth-century merchant's house, the **interpretation centre** at 27 rue Notre-Dame (late June to mid-Oct daily 10am–5.30pm; mid-Oct to late June Tues–Sun 10am–5pm; $3), outlines the stormy past of Place Royale. Domestic objects and arrowheads are exhibited on the upper floors, while the vaulted cellars have modern-looking displays of 1800s domestic scenes; kids will enjoy trying on the period costumes.

The **Église Notre-Dame-des-Victoires** (daily 9am–4.30pm), on the west side of the square, was instigated by Laval (see p.264) in 1688 but has been completely restored twice – after being destroyed by shellfire in 1759 and after a fire in 1969. Inside, the fortress-shaped altar alludes to the two French victories over the British navy that gave the church its name: the destruction of Admiral Phipp's fleet by Frontenac in 1690 and the sinking of Sir Hovenden Walker's fleet in 1711. Above the altar, paintings depicting these events hang by copies of religious paintings by Van Dyck, Van Loo and Boyermans, gifts from early settlers to give thanks for a safe passage.

BASSE-VILLE

Musée de la Civilisation

Map p.257, G3. **85 rue Dalhousie.** Late June to early Sept daily
9.30am–6.30pm; early Sept to late June Tues–Sun 10am–5pm; $7,
free on Tues Sept–June; ⓦ*www.mcq.org*.

Place Royale leads to **Place de Paris**, where a geometric
black-granite and white marble sculpture called *Dialogue
with History* marks the disembarkation place of the first settlers from France. To the east, you can see the promenade
along the St Lawrence that passes the restaurants and attractions of the **Vieux-Port de Québec**, while a walk north
along rue Dalhousie brings you to one of Québec City's
most impressive museums, the **Musée de la Civilisation**.

Concentrating primarily on Canada but also diversifying
into a wider perspective, the museum presents worthwhile
temporary exhibitions ranging from soap operas to a recent,
comprehensive showing of Syrian antiquities. Other than
the foyer sculpture, Astri Reusch's *La Débâcle*, which sym-
bolizes the break-up of the ice in the spring thaw, there are
two permanent exhibitions. "Memories" is a labyrinth that
expertly displays life in Québec from the early days of the
settlers to the present. "Encounter with the First Nations",
set up in consultation with all eleven of the First Nations of
Québec, presents the history and culture of these earlier
residents using artefacts and videotaped oral histories; the
larger items – including a *rabaska*, a large birch-bark canoe
– were crafted in recent years.

Quartier du Petit-Champlain

Map p.257, F5–G4.

From the rear exit of the museum, rue St-Pierre leads south
through the heart of the former financial district past Place
Royale to the **Batterie Royal**, used to defend the city during the siege of 1759. Any of the small passageways along

boulevard Champlain south of here will bring you to the narrow, cobbled **rue du Petit-Champlain**. Dating back to 1685, this is the city's oldest street, and the surrounding area – known as the **Quartier du Petit-Champlain** – is the oldest shopping area in North America. The boutiques and art shops in the quaint seventeenth- and eighteenth-century houses are not as overpriced as you'd think and offer an array of excellent crafts, from weird and wonderful ceramics to Inuit carvings. At the north end of the street, near the base of the *escalier casse-cou*, the 1683 Maison Louis-Jolliet was built for the retired discoverer of the Mississippi, Louis Jolliet. It now houses the base station for the **funicular** (daily 7.30am–11pm, until midnight in summer; $1.25) – the least taxing way to scale the cliff back up to Terrasse Dufferin and Place d'Armes in Haute-Ville.

BASILIQUE NOTRE-DAME DE QUÉBEC

Map p.257, E4. Mon–Fri 9am–2pm, Sat & Sun 9am–5pm and between shows (see below); free. Multimedia show: May to mid-Oct Mon–Fri 4–5 shows daily from 3.30pm, Sat & Sun 2–3 shows daily from 6.30pm; 45min; $7.50.

From Place d'Armes, rue du Trésor points directly towards the impressive bulk of the **Basilique Notre-Dame de Québec**. The oldest parish north of Mexico, the church was burnt to the ground in 1922 – one of many fires it has suffered – and was rebuilt to the original plans of 1647. Absolute silence within the cathedral heightens the impressiveness of the Rococo-inspired interior, culminating in a painted ceiling of blue sky and billowy clouds. The silver chancel lamp, beside the main altar, was a gift from Louis XIV and is one of the few treasures to survive the fire. In the crypt more than nine hundred bodies, including three governors and most of Québec's bishops, are interred. Champlain is also rumoured to be buried here, though

BASILIQUE NOTRE-DAME DE QUÉBEC

archeologists are still trying to work out which body is his. Access to the cathedral is limited to half an hour at a time in the afternoons unless you pay for the worthwhile *Act of Faith*, a multimedia presentation telling the church's history and spotlighting architectural features in the pitch-black basilica to wondrous effect.

Opposite the basilica, Côte de la Fabrique leads down to rue St-Jean, filled with shops and restaurants.

SÉMINAIRE DE QUÉBEC

Map p.257, E3–F3.

The wrought-iron gates beside the basilica lead into a large courtyard flanked by austere white buildings with handsome mansard roofs, where the vast **Séminaire de Québec** – founded by the aggressive and autocratic Monseigneur François de Laval-Montmorency in 1663 – spreads out to the north. In the three decades of his incumbency, Laval secured more power than the governor and intendant put together, and any officer dispatched from France found himself on the next boat home if Laval did not care for him. Laval retired early due to ill health, brought on by a religious fervour that denied him blankets and proper food. Death finally came after his feet froze on the stone floor of the chapel during his morning prayer session.

The seminary was the finest collection of buildings the city had seen, leaving Governor Frontenac muttering that the bishop was now housed better than he. Primarily a college for priests, the seminary was also open to young men who wanted to follow other professions, and in 1852 it became Laval University, the country's first Francophone Catholic university.

Musée de l'Amérique Française

Map p.257, E3. Late June to early Sept daily 9.30am–5pm; late Sept to early June Tues–Sun 10am–5pm; $4, free on Tues Sept–June; Ⓦ *www.mcq.org*.

The Séminaire's main areas of interest – and the departure point for one-hour guided tours of the seminary – can be found in the ever-expanding **Musée de l'Amérique Française**, whose main entrance is in the **Maison du Coin** on your left as you face the main gate. The Maison du Coin houses a small upstairs exhibition on the early colonists and adjoins the Roman-style chapel, whose Second Empire interior holds Canada's largest collection of relics, such as bones, ashes and locks of hair – a few of which are on display. Laval's memorial chapel contains his ornate marble tomb, but not his remains, which were moved to the basilica when the chapel was deconsecrated in 1993. The whole interior is a bit of a sham, though – fed up with rebuilding after the chapel burnt down yet again in 1888, the church authorities decided to construct the pillars and coffered ceilings out of tin and paint over them; the stained-glass windows have been painted on single panes of glass and even the tapestries are the result of some deft brushwork.

From the chapel, an underground corridor runs to the **Pavillon Jérôme-Demers**, which displays mostly well-presented, historical exhibitions. On show are only a tiny sample of the eclectic items gathered by Québec's bishops and the academics at Laval: scientific instruments, an Egyptian mummy, a diverting collection of European and Canadian paintings assembled by the art historians, as well as silverware and some of Laval's personal belongings.

MUSÉE DE L'AMÉRIQUE FRANÇAISE

COUVENT DES URSULINES

Map p.257, D5.

Heading south from the basilica along rue des Jardins brings you to narrow rue Donnacona, where a sculpted hand holding a quill – a monument to the women who, since 1639, have dedicated their lives to teaching Québec's young – rests on a pedestal. It seems to point the way to the **Couvent des Ursulines**, built by a tiny group of Ursuline nuns who arrived in Québec in 1639 calling themselves "the Amazons of God in Canada". Their task was to bring religion to the natives and later to the daughters of the settlers, a mission carried out in the classrooms of North America's first girls' school – the buildings still house a private school.

The remains of the Ursulines' first mother superior, **Marie Guyart de l'Incarnation**, are entombed in the oratory but public access is limited to the adjoining **chapel** (May–Oct Tues–Sat 10–11.30am & 1.30–4.30pm, Sun 1.30–4.30pm; free). Rebuilt in 1902, it retains the sumptuous early eighteenth-century interior by sculptor Pierre-Noël Levasseur and a collection of seventeenth and eighteenth-century paintings acquired from France in the 1820s. A plaque indicates General Montcalm's resting place below the chapel, though only his skull is buried there.

RUE ST-LOUIS

Map p.257, B6–E5.

On the corner of rue des Jardins and rue St-Louis – the main restaurant strip in Vieux-Québec – stands **Maison Jacquet**, occupied by the restaurant *Aux Anciens Canadiens*. The name comes from Québec's first novel, whose author, Philippe Aubert de Gaspé, lived here for a while in the middle of the nineteenth century. Dating from 1677, the house is another good example of seventeenth-century New France architecture, as is the blue-and-white **Maison Kent** at no. 25 on the other side of rue St-Louis, which was built in 1649. Once home of Queen Victoria's father, the Duke of Kent, it's best known as the place where the capitulation of Québec was signed in 1759.

It's well worth checking out the excellent Musée d'Art Inuit Brousseau (see below) located between the two historic houses before continuing on rue St-Louis to the **Porte St-Louis**, one of the four gates in the city wall. It's surrounded by **Parc de l'Esplanade**, the main site for the Carnaval de Québec, and departure point for the city's smart horse-drawn calèches and a good spot to begin the 4.5-kilometre stroll around the fortifications ringing the city.

Musée d'Art Inuit Brousseau

Map p.257, D5. 39 rue St-Louis. Daily 9.30am–5.30pm; $6.

The delightful **Musée d'Art Inuit Brousseau** traces the development of Inuit art from the naive works of the mid-twentieth century to the highly narrative and intricately carved sculptures by contemporary artists. The few ancient items are from the Dorset and Thulé cultures, nomadic peoples who worked in small easy-to-carry pieces of ivory. Stone sculpture really only began in the 1940s, replacing the declining fur and hunting industries as a source of income – the Inuit artists used aspects of the everyday, like animals and hunting, for inspiration, but would also carve an ashtray if they thought they could sell it to a traveller passing through. The museum groups sculptures by region so that you can see the legends and daily rituals of the different Inuit cultures.

MUSÉE D'ART INUIT BROUSSEAU

THE CITADELLE AND THE PLAINES D'ABRAHAM

Map p.257, C8–E7. Daily: April 10am–4pm; May & June 9am–5pm; July & Aug 9am–6pm; Sept 9am–4pm; Oct 10am–3pm; $6; ⓦ www.lacitadelle.qc.ca.

Towering over the southern section of Vieux-Québec, the massive star-shaped **Citadelle** is the tour de force of Québec City's fortifications. Occupying the highest point of Cap Diamant, 100m above the St Lawrence, the site was first built on by the French, but most of the buildings were constructed by the British under orders from the Duke of Wellington, who was anxious about American attack after the War of 1812.

The complex of 25 buildings covers forty acres and is the largest North American fort still occupied by troops – it's home to the Royal 22nd Regiment, Canada's only French-speaking regiment. Around the parade ground are ranged various monuments to the campaigns of the celebrated "Van-Doos" (*vingt-deux*), as well as the summer residence of Canada's governor general and two buildings dating back to the French period: the 1750 powder magazine, now a mundane museum of military artefacts, and the Cap Diamant Redoubt, built in 1693 and thus one of the oldest parts of the Citadelle.

In addition to entertaining hour-long **guided tours** around the Citadelle, other activities include the colourful **Changing of the Guard** (mid-June to early Sept daily 10am) and the **Beating of the Retreat** tattoo (July & Aug Wed–Sat 6pm).

The Parc des Champs-de-Bataille

Westward of the Citadelle are the rolling grasslands of the **Parc des Champs-de-Bataille** (National Battlefields Park), a sizeable chunk of land stretching along the cliffs above the St Lawrence. The park encompasses the historic **Plaines d'Abraham**, which were named after Abraham Martin, the first pilot of the St Lawrence River in 1620, and were the site on which Canada's history was rewritten (see pp.250–251). Standing out amid the landscaped gardens, scenic drives and jogging paths of the wooded parklands designed by Frederick G. Todd in the 1930s is the **Martello Tower 1**, built in 1808 for protection against the Americans and today containing an unmemorable exhibition. A better bet is the park's **Discovery Pavilion**, below the tourist office at 835 av Wilfrid-Laurier E (May–Aug daily 11am–5.30pm; Sept–Oct Tues–Sun 11am–5.30pm), with maps, information panels and a short film on the site's history.

HÔTEL DU PARLEMENT

Map p.257, A7. Late June to early Sept Mon–Fri 9am–4.30pm, Sat & Sun 10am–4.30pm; early Sept to late June Mon–Fri 9am–4.30pm; Ⓦ *www.assnat.qc.ca*.

Sweeping out from Porte St-Louis and flanked by grand Victorian mansions, the tree-lined boulevard of **Grande-Allée** bustles with restaurants, hotels and bars. At its eastern end stand the stately buildings of the **Hôtel du Parlement**, designed by Eugène-Étienne Taché in 1877 using the Louvre for inspiration. Inside, finely chiselled and gilded walnut panels in the entrance hall depict important moments in Québec's history. From here the corridor of the President's Gallery, lined with portraits of all the Legislative Assembly's speakers and presidents, leads to the Chamber of the National Assembly, where the 125 provincial representatives meet for debate.

MUSÉE DU QUÉBEC

June to early Sept Mon–Tues & Thurs–Sun 10am–6pm, Wed 10am–9pm; early Sept to May Tues & Thurs–Sun 10am–5pm, Wed 10am–9pm; $7, free on Wed Sept–May only; ⓦ *www.mdq.org*. Bus #11.

Canadian art had its quiet beginnings in Québec City and the full panoply of this output can be found on the western edge of Parc des Champs-de-Bataille in the **Musée du Québec**, whose 20,000-strong collection is displayed in two buildings – one, the Neoclassical **Pavillon Gérard-Morisset**, the museum's original home, and the other a renovated Victorian prison, renamed the **Pavillon Charles-Baillairgé**.

In addition to excellent touring exhibitions, a good survey of Québécois art up to 1945 can be found on the top level of the Pavillon Gérard-Morisset. The first gallery here covers the period from the beginnings of Québécois art in the early seventeenth century until the end of the nineteenth century. Most of the earliest works are **religious art**, including the output of **Frère Luc**, represented here by *The Guardian Angel*, depicting the story of Tobias and the archangel Raphael.

Under the British, art in Québec saw a broadening in subject matter, and the bourgeoisie's penchant for portraiture can be seen in favoured painter **Antoine Plamondon**'s poised *Madame Tourangeau*. The first artist to depict Canadian landscapes was the Québec-born **Joseph Légaré**; his *View of the Fire in the Saint-Jean District of Quebec City, Looking West* powerfully records a local tragedy that left thousands homeless.

The adjacent gallery covers the **modernist period** of Québécois art. The European influence made itself felt in sculpture throughout this period, largely due to Rodin, as evidenced in **Alfred Laliberté**'s bronzes and the plaster works of **Marc-Aurèle de Foy Suzor-Côte**. The latter is perhaps better known for his paintings, which also have a Parisian influence: *Cartier Meets the Indians at Stadacona* was painted shortly after his return, and the contrast between impressionistic style and traditional subject is emblematic of the entire exhibition.

The only permanent **contemporary** exhibition is a room devoted to the abstract painter **Jean-Paul Riopelle** on the ground floor, the centrepiece of which is *L'Hommage à Rosa Luxemburg* (1992), a 40m-long triptych in thirty segments.

In the **Pavillon Charles-Baillairgé**, the red brick interior walls of the former jail have been spruced up, creating a warm atmosphere surprisingly conducive to displaying art. Vaillancourt's *Tree on rue Durocher* sweeps up into the atrium, which leads to the temporary galleries and a few of the old prison cells. In the prison's tower, Montréal sculptor David Moore has created a unique two-storey sculpture of bodies scaling walls – just what you might expect in an old prison.

Eating, Drinking and Nightlife

It is when you start **eating** in Québec City that the French ancestry of the Québécois hits all the senses: the city's **restaurants** present a fine array of culinary delights adopted from the mother country, from lovingly presented gourmet dishes to humble baguettes. Vieux-Québec is home to most of the gourmet restaurants and cafés, but other areas – notably along rue St-Jean (quirky and cheaper) and Grande-Allée (generally touristy and expensive), just outside the city walls – have their fair share. Your best bet for good-value mid-price restaurants is to do as the locals do – head for avenue Cartier a kilometre west of the walls near the Musée du Québec, and check out the menus of the numerous terrace-fronted restaurants.

Nightlife in Québec City is far more relaxed than in Montréal: an evening spent in an intimate bar or a jazz or blues soiree is more popular than a big gig or disco. The main bar and nightclub strip is around rue St-Jean.

Restaurant price codes are explained on p.135.

CAFÉS AND RESTAURANTS

Buffet de l'Antiquaire
Map p.257, F2. 95 rue St-Paul ⊺ 692-2661. Inexpensive.
A comfy spot popular with locals for breakfast (served from 6am) and home-cooked comfort food like *poutine*, *ragoût* (pork stew) and *pâté chinois* (shepherd's pie) as well as burgers and club sandwiches.

Café Krieghoff
1089 av Cartier ⊺ 522-3711. Bus #11, #800 or #801. Inexpensive.
A ten-minute walk north of the Musée du Québec stands this French café-bistro, serving up some of the city's best coffee, big breakfasts and light meals like chicken Caesar salad and quiche Lorraine.

Casse-Crêpe Breton
Map p.257, B3. 1136 rue St-Jean ⊺ 692-0438. Inexpensive.
Diner-style restaurant where $5 crepes are made with up to three fillings. Choose from cheese, ham and vegetables for a savoury snack, or fruit and chocolate for something sweeter. There's often a queue, but it moves quickly.

Chez Temporal

Map p.257, D3. 25 rue Couillard ☎ 694-1813.

Inexpensive.

Bowls of steaming *café au lait*, croissants and *chocolatines* make this café, a few doors from the *Auberge de la Paix* hostel, a perfect place for breakfast. Soups and sandwiches are also available until 1.30am.

Cosmos Café

575 Grande-Allée E ☎ 640-0606. Moderate.

By far the best spot on the Grande-Allée due to its cool decor and imaginative menu with specials like trout with blueberries as well as a range of burgers, salads and pizzas. Crowded and lively at lunch and for the *5 à 7* cocktail hour.

La Crémaillère

Map p.257, B3. 21 rue St-Stanislas ☎ 692-2216.

Expensive.

Superior European cuisine in a romantic stone-walled 1829 residence that feels miles away from busy rue St-Jean just beyond the windows. Start with the rabbit terrine with tart glazed cranberries, move on to the *poulet suprême* (tender chicken with risotto and vegetables) and let the white chocolate and raspberry mousse finish you off. Advance booking advised.

Kafe Kookening

565 rue St-Jean ☎ 521-2800.

Inexpensive.

Chilled-out café-bar in the studenty part of rue St-Jean, ten-minutes' walk west of Vieux-Québec, with mismatched furniture, bright walls and board games that makes for a good hideout when the weather's rotten. The eclectic menu features hot dogs, kaiser rolls filled with tandoori chicken, and "tortiazattas" – pizzas on a tortilla base.

La Maison de Serge Bruyère

Map p.257, C3.

1200 rue St-Jean ☎ 694-0618. Three restaurants under one roof: the *Restaurant la Grande Table* is one of the best in the city, serving fresh produce,

CAFÉS AND RESTAURANTS

beautifully prepared and presented. The eight-course *ménu de dégustation* is $85 per person, a classic French extravaganza with dishes like *aiguillettes de canard* (thin strips of duck); reservations are standard. *Chez Livernois Bistro*, downstairs, is more affordable, serving the likes of fettucine with portobello mushrooms and roasted chicken. The café is cheaper still, but best for a simple *café au lait* on the terrace.

Le Marie Clarisse
Map p.257, F4. 12 rue du Petit-Champlain ☎ 692-0857.
Expensive–very expensive.
Named after an old schooner, the specialty in this late-seventeenth-century stone house at the foot of the *escalier casse-cou* is seafood. Try the large pan-seared bay scallops, served in a lobster and beet sauce with a touch of saffron or the house *marmite* – a fish stew similar to a bouillabaisse. With only twelve tables, you'll need to make a reservation.

Pizzédélic
1145 av Cartier ☎ 525-5981.
Bus #11, #800 or #801.
Inexpensive–moderate.
A ten-minute walk north of the Musée du Québec, this trendy spot with creative pizzas and pastas has a large, packed terrace – definitely the most fun of those lining the av Cartier strip.

VooDoo Grill
575 Grande-Allée E ☎ 647-2000.
Moderate–expensive.
African masks and sculpture and low-key lighting set the tone at this upstairs restaurant, so it's a bit surprising that the menu is actually a fusion of Thai and Vietnamese flavours applied to grilled steak, duck and satays. The $10 grilled sandwiches are a good lunchtime bet.

CAFÉS AND RESTAURANTS

BARS AND CLUBS

L'Amour Sorcier

789 Côte Ste-Geneviève
⊤ 523-3395.

Popular, intimate lesbian bar with cheap beers and soft music in an exposed-brick interior with a great roof terrace in summer. A ten minute-walk west of the Porte St-Jean.

Chez Son Père

Map p.257, B4. 24 rue St-Stanislas ⊤ 692-5308.
Québécois folk singers keep things humming in this bar just off rue St-Jean in Vieux-Québec. Free admission.

Le Drague

804 rue St-Augustin
⊤ 649-7212.

Similar to Montréal's big gay complexes and located in Québec City's tiny gay district ten minutes west from the Porte St-Jean; inside there's a café, bar and basement nightclub with wraparound mezzanine – the Sunday night drag shows are great fun.

L'Emprise

Map p.257, D4. 57 rue Ste-Anne.

On the main floor of the *Hôtel Clarendon*, the Art Deco surroundings attract a sophisticated touristy crowd to evenings of smooth jazz and blues.

Fourmi Atomik

Map p.257, B4. 33 rue d'Auteuil ⊤ 694-1473.
The best rock bar in Vieux-Québec, with cheap beers, pool tables and loud mainly alt-rock music blasting from the stereo. The terrace facing the city walls fills up early with a lively crowd, many hanging on until the wee hours.

L'Inox

Map p.257, G2. 37 rue St-André ⊤ 692-2877.
The only brewpub in Québec City, the decor's a bit cold, with greys and a metal central bar, but with artisinal cheeses to accompany fine ales such as the brown

QUÉBEC CITY FESTIVALS

Québec City is renowned for its large annual festivals. The Carnaval de Québec (☎626-3716, ⓦ www.carnaval.qc.ca) takes place over eleven freezing days in early February, when large quantities of the warming local brew, Caribou, are consumed amid parades and ice-sculpture competitions.

In early July, the ten-day Festival d'Été (☎529-5200 or 1-888/992-5200, ⓦ www.infofestival.com) is an equally cheery affair. The largest festival of Francophone culture in North America attracts hundreds of performers for this musical celebration.

The Fêtes de la Nouvelle France (☎694-3311, ⓦ www.nouvellefrance.qc.ca), returns Vieux-Québec's Basse-Ville to the seventeenth and eighteenth centuries in early August. It's great fun as thousands of Québécois from around the province dress up in period costume to crowd around the Place Royale's market stalls and engage in street theatre.

Scottiche, Débâcle spruce beer and Trouble-Fête, a Belgian blonde, you won't complain for long.

Maurice
575 Grande-Allée E ☎640-0711.
Happening club with a rotating crew of DJs that attracts a stylish twenties and early thirties crowd. Dress up to get by the selective door policy. The $3 cover also gets you into the more laid-back *Charlotte* upstairs, with couches for chilling out or smoking a cigar.

Sacrilège
447 rue St-Jean ☎649-1985.
Friendly watering hole drawing students and locals, especially for the cheap beer ($4.25 a pint) and popular terrace in back. It's in the Faubourg St-Jean-Baptiste district, less than fifteen minutes west of Place D'Youville.

Le Pub St-Alexandre

Map p.257, B4. 1087 rue St-Jean ⓣ694-0015.

Yuppie English-style pub with a long mahogany bar set against the exposed brick walls. With 40 single malts, 20 beers on tap – including Bass, Tartan and Newcastle Brown – and ten times that many in bottles, it's a good spot to down a few.

Bar St-Laurent

Map p.257, F5. 1 rue des Carrières ⓣ692-3861.

The *Château Frontenac* location may be a bit stuffy, with glasses of wine and pints of beer costing $7 at the polished octagonal bar, but you don't need to dress to the nines and the view from the terrace is stupendous.

BARS AND CLUBS

Les Laurentides

asily reached from Montréal, and a good choice if you want to stretch out a bit in the outdoors and perhaps do some skiing, the **Laurentides** (Laurentians) combines relaxed, somewhat historic towns with a few splendid resorts in its upper reaches. Don't expect dramatic, jagged peaks when exploring the area – five hundred million years of erosion have moulded one of the world's oldest ranges into a rippling landscape of rounded peaks and smooth valleys. Still, the mountains of the **Hautes Laurentides** (Upper Laurentians) extend up to an altitude of nearly 1000m and boast one of the largest concentrations of **ski** resorts in North America, with the fabled **Mont-Tremblant** the biggest draw of all. Immediately north of Montréal, the **Basses Laurentides** (Lower Laurentians), once home to the region's main farmlands, are much flatter and quieter, their landscapes dotted with centuries-old whitewashed cottages and manor houses. Two laid-back towns here, **Oka**, home to one of North America's oldest monasteries, and **St-Eustache**, notable for its battle-scarred historic centre, make for pleasant afternoon detours.

For the accommodation price codes in this chapter, see p.110. For restaurant price categories, turn to p.135.

HITTING THE SLOPES

The ski resorts around Montréal start under an hour's drive away via either Autoroute des Laurentides (Hwy 15) or the slower Hwy 117, lined with a number of antique shops en route. Limocar Laurentides (☎ 514/842-2281) offers regular service from the Station Centrale d'Autobus to most of the towns for around $38.50 return.

As the region's towns are little more than après-ski spots, accommodation is pricey, though a smattering of B&Bs, motels and a couple of hostels do offer hope for those on a tight budget. Check with travel agents in Montréal before heading out as weekend packages can be a bargain, or try the free accommodation service for the region (☎ 1-800/561-6673, ⓦ www.laurentides.com). Keep in mind, though, that staying overnight need not be a priority if you're willing to leave early and come back late the same day.

For up-to-date ski conditions visit ⓦ www.quebecski surf.com or call ☎ 514/493-1810.

ST-EUSTACHE

Map 1, C4.

At the centre of sprawling **St-Eustache**, forty minutes northwest of Montréal along Hwy 13 or 15 north to Hwy 640 west, lies tiny **Vieux–St-Eustache**, whose historic interest is clustered along two narrow streets. The silver twin bell-towered **Église de St-Eustache** at 123 rue St-Louis looms over the lot, and it was here that a faction of the Patriotes rebellion protesting Francophone oppression under British rule was put down by military detachments in 1837. A third of the 150 men who took refuge in the church were killed after it was blasted by cannon fire, and the church still bears the scars on its soot-licked facade; the interior vault was rebuilt following the battle and shimmers with gold leaf.

British troops went on to raze much of the town, leaving a dozen-odd fieldstone buildings intact, most of which are simply marked with heritage signs. The **Manoir Globensky** at 235 rue St-Eustache postdates the battle and is worth a quick visit if you're interested in the Rebellion's history. Upstairs, the **Musée de St-Eustache et de ses Patriotes** (Tues–Sun 10am–5pm; $3) puts on a hokey multimedia history show and has displays of various tools and weapons; most are reproductions, though a couple of muskets are legitimate articles.

OKA

Map 1, B4.

Some 20km southwest of St-Eustache on Hwy 344 lies the small lakeside town of **Oka**, associated with a controversial armed stand-off between the Mohawks and police in the summer of 1990 (see box, opposite). It's a sleepy spot dotted with apple orchards and you can't miss its most impressive building, the **Abbaye Cistercienne d'Oka**, 1600 chemin d'Oka (daily: 4am–8pm; ☎450/479-8361, ⓦ*pages.infinit. net/trapoka*). Nearly fifty Trappist monks live in the abbey, notable for its century-old bell tower rising amidst enveloping hills. The bright **church** inside has arched ceilings warmly offset by wood panelling on the lower walls, and the nearby monastery shop sells organic Trappist products, including their trademark Oka cheese. Pick up a wedge before heading to the splendid **Parc d'Oka**, at 2020 chemin d'Oka (open year-round; $7.50; ☎450/479-8365 or ☎1-888/727-2652, ⓦ*www.sepaq.com*), a provincial park dotted with 45km of biking and hiking trails. The best of these is the scenic 5.5km **Calvaire d'Oka** trek that ascends to the top of a spectacular viewpoint, passing a unique grouping of seven deserted stone chapels built around 1740 by the Sulpicians en route. The park also has a beach along

STAND-OFF AT OKA

In 1990, Oka became the stage for a confrontation between Mohawk warriors and the provincial government when the town's council decided to expand its golf course onto the former's sacred burial ground. The Mohawks responded by arming themselves and staking out the territory, and Québec's Public Security Minister sent in the provincial police to retake the land. A policeman was killed in the ensuing fracas – no one knows by whom – but hostilities reached a new pitch as the two sides became ever more polarized, with the Mohawks setting up barricades across the Mercier Bridge, one of Montréal's main commuter arteries. A particularly gruesome moment occurred when the natives tried to evacuate their women and children only to be pelted by stones thrown by white Québécois. The federal government offered to buy the land for the natives as long as they surrendered, but negotiations failed and the stand-off continued for 78 days, until the core group of twenty-five Mohawks was encircled by army soldiers and forced to give up. The fate of the disputed land is still being negotiated.

the shores of Lac des Deux-Montagnes and **campsites** ($30).

ST-SAUVEUR-DES-MONTS

Map 1, B2.

St-Sauveur-des-Monts, 60km north of Montréal, is the region's ritziest resort town. Its resident population of seven thousand quadruples at peak-season, and the main drag, rue Principale, boasts every type of restaurant, designer boutique and craft shop imaginable. And come nightfall, numerous flash clubs and discos fill quickly with tired skiers in trendy outfits.

Of the six separate nearby ski mountains, the best are **Mont St-Sauveur** and **Mont-Habitant**. The former has the most extensive night-skiing in the province and often has enough snow to keep the ski season going til June ($40/adults, $24/6–12 years; ☎ 450/227-4671, ⓦ *www.mont-saintsauveur.com*). The latter is a great spot for families with kids just starting out with ten gentle slopes and a good ski school ($31/adults, $20/6–12 years;   ☎ 450/227-2637, ⓦ *www.monthabitant.com*).

Information on shopping and skiing is available from the Bureau Touristique, 3rd Floor, 100 rue Guindon (Mon–Fri 9am–5pm) and at ⓦ *www.saint-sauveur.net*.

Accommodation

Auberge aux Petits Oiseaux

342 rue Principale ☎ 450/227-6116 or 1-877/227-6116.
A modern B&B with three glossy wood-panelled rooms; with private bathrooms and cable television. ❸

Le Bonnet d'Or

405 rue Principale ☎ 450/227-9669 or 1-877/277-9669, ⓦ *www.bbcanada.com/bonnetdor*.
A quaint B&B with five handsome rooms that go up in price as amenities like in-room fireplace are added; all have private bathrooms. ❸

Manoir St-Sauveur

246 chemin du Lac Millet ☎ 1-800/361-0505, ⓦ *www.manoir-saint-sauveur.com*.
A massive complex with over 200 well-appointed rooms; the best are on the top floor, nestled in the eaves. ❹

Eating and drinking

La Bohème

251 rue Principale ⓣ 450/227-6644. Moderate.
French food in a rustic ambience with specialities like frogs legs *provençale* and *bœuf bourguignon*.

Brûlerie des Monts

197 rue Principale ⓣ 450/227-6157. Inexpensive.
A trendy café specializing in finely roasted coffees and offering standard sandwiches, quiches and breakfast fare.

Papa Luigi

155 rue Principale ⓣ 450/227-5311. Moderate.
A lively restaurant in a handsome blue house with a range of tasty dishes – not surprisingly, Italian is the stronghold, but steak and fondues crop up on the menu as well. Reservations strongly recommended.

VAL-DAVID

Map 1, B1.

Some 16km further north along Hwy 117 lies artsy **Val-David**, the most laid-back of the Laurentiens' towns, chosen by artists and craftspeople as a haven from the yuppie developments elsewhere. The main street, rue de l'Église, reflects the town's cultural bent with several galleries and craft shops that make for a pleasant afternoon of browsing.

Though surrounded by three small mountains – **Mont-Alta** has the most pistes at 22 (ⓣ819/322-3206, $10/over-12, $6/under-13) – the town sets itself apart with non-ski-related attractions come summertime. The lush **Jardins de Rocailles**, 1319 rue Lavoie (mid-June to early Sept daily 10am–5.30pm; autumn and spring weekends 10am–5.30pm; $4), is a lovely hangout as hundreds of plants bloom amidst a rock garden with a soothing waterfall at its centre. Val-David is also home to the Laurentians' tackiest attraction, the **Village du Père Noel** at 987 rue Morin (early June to early Sept daily 10am–6pm; $8.50), a Santa's village whose star attraction is the Wise Goat. His wisdom stems from an ability to climb an obstacle course and feed himself from pails suspended on pulleys; it's fun for kids anyway.

Information is available at the tourist office, 2501 de l'Église (daily 9.30am–5pm), or at Ⓦ *www.valdavid.com*.

Accommodation

Le Chalet Beaumont
1451 Beaumont ☏ 819/322-1972 or 1-800/461-8585. Youth hostel in a massive chalet with roaring fires in the winter with dormitory, double and single room accommodation; call from the bus station and they'll come pick you up. $19.50/dormitory; $47/single room.

Relais de la Piste
1430 rue de l'Academie ☏ 819/322-2280, Ⓦ *www.relaisdelapiste.com*. A woodsy B&B with six comfortable rooms complete with slanted ceilings, cable television and private bath. Closed mid-Oct to mid-Dec and mid-March to mid-May. ❸

La Sapinière
1244 chemin de la Sapinière ☏ 819/322-2020 or 1-800/567-6635, Ⓦ *www.sapiniere.com*. An upscale ski lodge of log and stone offering seventy well-appointed rooms with cable television and air conditioning, some with fireplace, and a host of outdoor activities on the property. ❺

VAL-DAVID

Eating and drinking

L'Express

1337 chemin de la Sapinière

☏ 819/322-3090. Inexpensive.
A café-bistro with standard
soup and sandwiches, as well
as flavourful couscous and
good daily specials like
tourtière.

Le Grand Pa

2481 rue de l'Église

☏ 819/322-3104. Inexpensive.
A friendly restaurant serving
simple and affordable French
food that turns into a
rollicking *boîte a chanson* on
weekend evenings.

La Sapinière

1244 chemin de la Sapinière

☏ 819/322-2020
or 1-800/567-6635. Expensive.
An upmarket restaurant
serving a five-course *table
d'hôte* with a good range of
meat, fish and vegetarian
options on the menu (the
smoked salmon is made in-
house).

MONT-TREMBLANT

Situated some 130km north of Montréal, **Mont-
Tremblant** is the Laurentians' oldest and most renowned
ski area, focused on the range's highest peak (915m). In
1997, the company that developed British Columbia's
Whistler ski-resort pumped some $50 million into Mont-
Tremblant, and the resulting European-style ski village has
made it one of Canada's premier ski destinations. The acco-
lades abound for the slopes too, since Tremblant boasts 96
ski runs in all ranges, including the longest run in Québec
(6km). **Ski passes** cost $55 per day.

There are scores of places to **stay** around Mont-
Tremblant, starting with the ski village at the base of the
mountain and extending south 15km to the town of **Saint-
Jovite**, which offers more affordable accommodation. The

actual village of Mont-Tremblant located at the foot of the mountain is tiny but has some quaint B&Bs. To suss out your lodging options you're best to visit Mont-Tremblant's Web site, ⓦ*www.tremblant.com*; it lists everything in the area and includes photos, rates and ski packages.

SUMMERS ON MONT-TREMBLANT

Mont-Tremblant ski resort is but a small part of the Parc du Mont-Tremblant ($3.50; ☏819/688-2281 or 1-877/688-2289, ⓦ*www.sepaq.com*), a mammoth 1490 square-km provincial park spreading out north of the mountain and marked by undulating hills and hundreds of lakes. The park is a natural habitat for moose, white-tailed deer and beavers, and one of the best ways to spot them is by canoe, though determined landlubbers can head out on the plentiful hiking trails and bike paths that cut through the park. Camping is available (mid-May to early Oct $16.52–40), and you can rent almost everything on site (except camping gear). The park has several entry points, most of which lead off from the northern end of Hwy 117, east of the Tremblant resort.

Les Cantons-de-l'Est

Beginning 80km southeast of Montréal and extending to the US border, the scenic **Cantons-de-l'Est** (Eastern Townships) were once Québec's best-kept secret, but the nineteenth-century Loyalist villages are fast becoming popular with shoppers seeking out antiques and discounted labels at outlet stores. A growing ski industry, like that at **Mont-Orford**, is also making its mark on the land. However, the region's charm still outweighs the ever-increasing commercialization, with plenty of picture-post-card villages, their white-clapboard churches and handsome brownstones clustered around glistening lakeshores.

The region's main **information centre** is located off exit 68 on Hwy 10, west of Granby (Mon–Fri & Sun 8.30am–5pm, Sat till 6pm; ☎819/820-2020 or 1-800/355-5755, ⓦ www.tourisme-cantons.qc.ca).

The scenery of the Cantons-de-l'est alone makes trekking out of the city worthwhile as the northern range of the Appalachian Mountains cuts through the region, especially majestic come autumn. The townships start at Granby to the west and end with Sherbrooke, but it's the picturesque villages nestled in the valleys between them that brim with atmosphere. Quaint **Knowlton** exudes

Victoriana and boasts terrific antique shops, while **North Hatley**'s breathtaking collection of mansions lend the town a refined air. Between these two lies **Magog-Orford**, whose appeal is the excellent year-round activities afforded by its impressive lake and the rugged Mont-Orford.

Magog is the only town accessible by **bus** from Montréal's Station Centrale (up to 8 trips daily; 1hr 30min; call ☏ 842-2281 for schedules and fares). To stop at Knowlton and North Hatley, you'll have to rent a car (see Chapter 19, "City directory"). From Montréal, the Autoroute des Cantons-de-l'Est (Hwy 10) flies across the top of the region, but the slower Hwy 112 is more picturesque as it winds through the heart of Loyalist country.

KNOWLTON

Map 1, G6.

The peaceful township of **Lac Brome**, named for the 20km-long shimmering lake at its centre, is home to seven sleepy communities, the most handsome of which is pocket-sized **Knowlton**. Settled at the lake's southern end, the town's Loyalist flavour is still strongly felt along its two main drags – chemin Lakeside and perpendicular running chemin Knowlton – which boast an eye-catching combination of brownstones and clapboard houses. At the centre of town the small **Parc Colbrook** sits at the edge of a quaint waterfall and stream.

Lac Brome is renowned for its ducks, celebrated
during the annual Duck Festival, a jamboree of music and
gastronomy held in October (☏ 450/242-2870).

The town's only museum, the cluttered **Musée historique du comté de Brome**, 130 chemin Lakeside (mid-May to mid-Sept Mon–Sat 10am–4.30pm, Sun

11am–4.30pm; $3.50), is strongest on military artefacts; the show-stopper is an original Fokker DVII airplane, the type flown by the Red Baron. Nearby, at 367 chemin Knowlton, the **Théâtre Lac Brome** (⊕450/242-2270) offers light-hearted fare during its late-June to mid-August season; tickets are in the $20 range.

Most visitors overlook these cultural attractions in favour of shopping. **Antique shops** are clustered along chemin Knowlton, while designer **clothing outlets** selling discounted Polo Ralph Lauren and Vittadini labels, among others, are found on chemin Lakeside. The annual **antique show and sale** held at Raquettes Brome, 584 chemin Knowlton (mid-Oct; call ⊕243-6134 for information), vies for popularity with the duck Festival.

Knowlton is easily handled as an afternoon jaunt out of the city, so there's no need to stay the night. For **food**, *Bistro Cedric's Pub*, 51 chemin Lakeside (⊕450/242-2929), serves pub grub on a terrace overlooking the town stream; *Le St-Raphaël*, 281 chemin Knowlton (⊕450/243-4168), offers scrumptious scones and rich duck pizza.

MAGOG AND AROUND

Map 1, H5 & H6.

The twinned resort towns of **Magog-Orford**, about 30 minutes east of Knowlton along Hwy 10 or Hwy 112, combine some of the best swimming and cycling in the Eastern Townships. Most head for Magog, which fans out around one of the townships' largest lakes, **Lac Memphrémagog**. It's a lively spot fairly teeming with bars and restaurants along its main street, rue Principale. Magog's north–south artery, rue Merry (Hwy 141) hosts most of the town's accommodation and accesses the thrust of the area's outdoorsy activities since it crests both Parc du Mont-Orford (see overleaf) and the lake. Idyllic **boat**

MAGOG AND AROUND

cruises ply Lac Memphrémagog daily during the summer and on weekends in September and October (1hr 45min tour; $12), and a sheltered **beach** fringes its western side; a kiosk rents out water transport ranging from pedal boats to sailboats (early June to early Sept ☏819/847-3181; $10–90). **Buses** from Montréal stop on rue Sherbrooke, diagonal to Magog's main drag, rue Principale.

A tourist office is located at 55 rue Cabana, just off Hwy 112 on the way into Magog (June to mid-Oct daily 8.30am–8pm; mid-Oct to May daily 9am–5pm, Fri til 6pm; ☏1-800/267-2744, *www.tourisme-memphremagog.com*).

Parc du Mont-Orford

Map 1, H6. 3321 chemin du Parc ☏819/843-9855, Ⓦ*www.mt-orford.com*.

The large **Parc du Mont-Orford**, about ten minutes north of Magog along rue Merry (Hwy 141), actually comprises three mountain peaks of which Orford, at 853m, is the highest. In summer, the grassy slopes are a nature-lover's paradise of hiking trails, golfing and swimming. Winter, though, is when the park really comes to life, offering 52 downhill skiing runs and 10km of snowshoeing trails. The chair lifts operate year-round ($6.50 one-way, $9.50 return; daily ski-passes $36).

Abbaye St-Benoît-du-Lac

Map 1, H6. St-Benoît-du-Lac ☏819/843-4080, Ⓦ*www.st-benoit-du-lac.com*.

The Eastern Township's most unique attraction, the **Abbaye St-Benoît-du-Lac**, looms over Lac Memphrémagog 25km southwest of Magog. The granite towered Abbaye is a fantastical, castle-like building colourfully trimmed with pinks, yellows and greens. To get here, take Hwy 245 south from the western edge of Magog and follow the signs to St-Benoit-du-Lac.

Sixty Benedictine monks, renowned for their **Gregorian chants**, reside in the abbey and perform up to twice daily in the barn-like church at its western end (daily 11am plus Fri–Wed 5pm; July–Aug Tues 7pm; Sept–June Thurs 7pm). They also make some of the region's best cheese – their light Ermite blue cheese started the tradition and is sold at the on-site boutique.

Accommodation

Auberge du Centre d'Arts Orford
3165 chemin du Parc (Hwy 141) ☎819/843-8595 or 1-800/567-6155; May–Oct.
An excellent youth hostel right in the Parc du Mont-Orford with rustic chalets (July and Aug), and three large pavilions with a range of room options the rest of the summer. $15 dorm (with HI membership card); $60/single room.

La Belle Échapée
145 rue Abbott ☎819/843-8061 or 1-877/843-8061, Ⓦwww.bbcanada.com/2699.html.

A gabled 1880 house with three pretty rooms, wicker chairs on the veranda, and bicycles. Shared or private bathroom. Closed Dec–April. ❷

La Belle Victorienne
142 rue Merry N ☎819/847-0476 or 1-888/440-0476, Ⓦwww.bellevic.com.
An attractive B&B in a Victorian home with beautiful gardens, an ivy-covered terrace, and five tastefully decorated rooms. Shared or private bathroom. ❸

MAGOG AND AROUND

For accommodation price codes see p.110.

Eating and drinking

Caffuccino
219 rue Principale O
☎ 819/868-2225. Inexpensive.
A trendy café serving up affordable breakfast fare, lunch, sinfully sweet desserts and good coffee.

Le Martimbeault
341 rue Principale O
☎ 819/843-3182. Expensive.
This upmarket French restaurant is heavy on rich meats like sweetbreads and steak.

La Memphré
12 rue Merry S
☎ 819/843-3405. Inexpensive.
A pleasant bar in a charming verandaed house near the waterfront; the draw is the tasty local beer named after the sea serpent that allegedly lives in the nearby lake.

For restaurant price designations see p.135.

NORTH HATLEY

Map 1, I6.

The region east of Magog is one of the few areas in Québec where you'll encounter vestiges of the snobbish Anglophone attitudes that once pervaded the whole province. No town epitomizes this more than picturesque **North Hatley**, thirty-minutes' drive east from Magog along Hwy 108, where boutiques sell English teas and biscuits to a resident population that steadfastly refuses to change the town's name to "Hatley Nord".

Grand manors, many of which house hotels and B&Bs,

curve in a U-shape around the pleasant **Lac Massawippi** that extends south from the centre. Just about the only organized activity here is theatre, as the province's longest-running English-language playhouse, **The Piggery**, stages several quality productions throughout the summer (℡ 819/842-2431 for information and tickets). Theatre aside, North Hatley is a quiet town with little to do but hang out with a good book and absorb the scenery. There's a public **beach** on the lake's western shores, and several small **art galleries** and **antique shops** clustered along the main drag, rue Principale, that make for a pleasant afternoon of shopping.

Accommodation

Auberge Hatley

325 rue Virgin ℡ 819/842-2451 or 1-800/336-2451, Ⓦ *www.northhatley.com*.
A high-end hotel with lake views, sumptuous rooms, and an outdoor swimming pool. ❺

An elegant inn with seven spacious, well-appointed en-suite rooms; the breakfasts are excellent. ❹

Auberge La Raveaudière

11 chemin Hatley Centre ℡ 819/842-2554, Ⓦ *www.laraveaudiere.com*.

Le Cœur d'Or

85 rue School ℡ 819/842-4363, Ⓦ *www.lcdo.qc.ca*.
A kitschy and cluttered B&B with eight comfortable, frilly rooms with private bath. ❸

For accommodation price codes see p.110.

Eating and drinking

Café de Lafontaine
35 rue Principale
☏819/842-4242. Inexpensive.
A café serving standard
hamburgers and pastas, with
live musical acts in the
summer.

Café Massawippi
3050 chemin Capelton
☏819/842-4528. Expensive.
A cosy restaurant offering
original remakes of
international classics like
smoked sturgeon carpaccio.
Open for dinner only.

Manoir Hovey
575 chemin Hovey ☏819/842-
2421. Very expensive.
Award-winning, gamey
regional cuisine – duck
figures strongly and is
enhanced with delectable
flavours like ginger and
chokecherry.

For restaurant price designations see p.135.

CONTEXTS

A brief history of Montréal	297
Books	308
French language and glossary	313

A brief history
of Montréal

Beginnings

Little is known about the earliest peoples who roamed the
Montréal region – nomadic groups of **hunter-gatherers**,
living off a plentiful supply of fish, fowl, moose, deer and
caribou – but by around 1000 BC Iroquois-speaking peoples lived in the area. It took another two millennia for
these Iroquois nations to develop a sedentary lifestyle, culti-
vating crops – primarily corn, beans and squash – and making pottery in which to store food. These tribes surrounded
their villages with wooden palisades, inside of which up to
1500 people would live in communal, bark-covered long-
houses some twenty to thirty metres long.

It was such a settlement, named **Hochelaga** ("Place of the
Beaver"), situated at the base of the mountain and occupied
by the St Lawrence Iroquois, that **Jacques Cartier** stumbled
across on his second trip to North America in 1535. The
year before, he had claimed all of Canada for Francis I of
France and he then returned to uncover both gold and a

shorter trade route to Asia. While he found neither, he did manage to provide the source for Montréal's name, labelling the hill that towered over Hochelaga **Mont Royal** (although some argue he actually named it Monreale, for the bishop of that town who was one of his trip's sponsors).

The founding of Ville-Marie

It's uncertain whether warfare with other tribes or disease brought by the Europeans was at fault, but in the latter half of the sixteenth century the population of St Lawrence Iroquois plummeted. By the time French explorer **Samuel de Champlain** arrived in 1603, all traces of Hochelaga had vanished. Champlain briefly left the scene as well, travelling east to found Québec City in 1608, but he returned three years later to the Montréal area to begin the first European construction on the island at Pointe-à-Callière, titling the immediate area Place Royale. Champlain then turned his energies to the smaller island just offshore, naming it in honour of his twelve-year-old bride, Hélène – a decent thing to do given that he purchased it with her dowry.

The next few decades saw only intermittent European activity, the French settlement at Place Royale being little more than a small garrison. The Récollets (reformed Franciscans) and Jesuit missionaries from France – called the "Black Robes" by the natives who suspected them of sorcery – also maintained a small presence on the island, attempting to convert the Iroquois. The priests' task was not an easy one. The French had already aligned themselves with the Algonquin and Huron nations to gain access to their **fur-trading networks**, while those groups' traditional enemies, the Iroquois Confederacy, had themselves formed alliances with the Dutch and subsequently the British. Periodic bouts between the factions over control of the industry would continue over the next half-century.

Meanwhile, a group of French aristocrats and merchants soon obtained a title from Louis XIII to colonize Canada for commercial gain, and Paul de Chomedey, **Sieur de Maisonneuve**, was chosen to lead the mission. After wintering over in Québec City, he established the colony of Ville-Marie on the site of Champlain's Place Royale along with some fifty settlers on either May 16 or 17 in 1642. That winter the settlement – which would before too long be known as Montréal – seemed destined to disappear as quickly as it came with rising floods threatening to wipe it out. The fervent de Maisonneuve's prayers were answered on Christmas Day when the waters receded, and in gratitude, he planted a **cross** near the mountain's summit, commemorated by the present-day landmark. Floods, though, were only the beginning of de Maisonneuve's problems, as native attacks plagued the colony; even after the Frenchman bested an Iroquois chief in single combat in 1644, settlers risked ambushes for the next two decades.

New France

Ville-Marie's survival remained tenuous until Louis XIV made Québec a royal province in 1663. This allowed for the dispatch of a thousand French troops, a shipment that tilted even further the already unbalanced gender gap. In order to rectify this imbalance, unmarried women, the so-called *filles du roi*, were shipped over by the boatload throughout the next decade (see p.103). Still, even with the much stronger (and now happier) military presence, periodic skirmishes between the French and English and their native allies continued to be a destabilizing factor, stunting the growth of the colony. In the early part of the eighteenth century, **treaties** between both the First Nations and the British were signed, allowing the fur trade to flourish, greatly increasing the town's fortunes.

It wasn't until mid-century that further serious conflict broke out, with the British and French again at odds in the **Seven Years War**. Although the early years of fighting were concentrated in the Atlantic colonies, the turning point took place in 1759 when, after a summer of punishing bombardment of Québec City, General James Wolfe defeated the French under the Marquis de Montcalm in the twenty-minute **Battle of the Plains of Abraham**. When Québec City fell, Montréal briefly served as the capital of New France, until the Marquis de Vaudreuil surrendered to the Brits a year later, without a shot being fired.

British control and the birth of a city

Except for the fleeing of a few upper-class merchants, the transfer to **British rule** saw little change in the life of most Québécois. But when an attempt was made in 1763 to impose British administrative structures that left the status of the powerful Catholic clergy in doubt, grumbles rose from the largely Francophone and rural population. Worried that unrest similar to that occurring in the American colonies might be played out here, the British enacted the 1774 **Quebec Act**, a stopgap measure that allowed the French to maintain their language, civil code, seigneurial system and religion.

The British occupation suffered a brief hiccup in the mid-1770s when **Americans**, led by General Richard Montgomery took over the city, and the likes of **Benjamin Franklin** tried to convince a sceptical populace to join the American struggle against the British. The Americans were soon defeated in Québec City, but after they won independence from Britain in their own land, a flood of British Loyalists fled across the Canadian border, settling primarily in the Eastern Townships and present-day Ontario. The new Anglophone residents, as well as the Francophone bourgeoisie, were chafing under the terms of the Quebec Act, and both wanted an elected assembly. The British response was the 1791 **Constitutional Act**, which divided the territory into Lower and Upper Canada (present-day Québec and Ontario), giving both a legislative assembly. The act emphasized the inequalities between Anglophones and Francophones, however, as real power lay with the **Château Clique** – the council composed mainly of members of the wealthy establishment and answerable to a British governor and council appointed in London.

The town by now was well on its way to becoming Canada's commercial centre, a fact confirmed with the establishment of the **Bank of Montreal** in 1817. From around 1815, waves of British and Irish immigrants swelled the population enough that by the 1820s Montréal's total passed that of Québec City and in 1831 Anglophones formed the majority of Montréal's residents.

Resentment, however, was brewing just under the surface as the Château Clique vetoed bills passed in the Francophone-dominated assembly and in 1837 French **Patriotes** led by Louis-Joseph Papineau rose up against the British. Their failed insurgency led to an investigation by the British-appointed governor general, Lord Durham, who concluded that English and French relations were akin to two nations warring within the bosom of a single state. His prescription for peace was immersing French-Canadians in the English culture of North America; the subsequent establishment of the **Province of Canada** with the 1840 Act of Union can be seen as a deliberate attempt to marginalize Francophone opinion within an English-speaking state.

Industrialization and expansion

The mid-nineteenth century was a time for **industrialization** in Montréal – much as it was in urban areas across

Canada and the US. Vast tracts of factories sprouted up along the Lachine Canal and in east-end towns like Hochelaga, refining grain and sugar, producing shoes and other leather goods, textiles and heavy machinery for the rail and ship industries. In conjunction, massive blocks of substandard row houses were built to accommodate, in part, the mass migration of Francophones who fled the country-side to work in the factories – by 1866 Montréal's language scale had tipped, leaving **Francophones in the majority** for good.

The city's hold on the national economy was further strengthened by the completion of the coast-to-coast **Canadian Pacific Railway** in the 1880s, and the city continued to jump its boundaries, absorbing 22 adjacent municipalities between 1883 and 1918. Pogroms in Eastern Europe sent thousands of Jews fleeing to Montréal and with a continued exodus from the rural areas the city's popula-tion reached half a million in 1911, doubling in the next two decades with an influx of émigrés from war-torn Europe.

Morality and the early 1900s

For the first half of the twentieth century, Montréal's liber-ated mores stood out against the staid Puritanism of other Canadian cities, earning it a reputation as Canada's "**sin city**". US Prohibition in the 1920s allowed Québec to become the continent's main **alcohol supplier** – the Molsons (brewers), Bronfmans (owners of Seagram dis-tillers) and their ilk made their fortunes here – and prostitu-tion and gambling thrived under the protection of city and police officials.

Even the Great Depression couldn't dampen the carous-ing, in part because **Camillien Houde**, the off-and-on mayor of Montréal between 1928 and 1954, mitigated much of its effects with massive **public works projects** (like the construction of the Jardin Botanique). His magnanimity bankrupted the city, though, and it was forced into trusteeship by the province in 1940. Yet despite this, and the jail term he served for urging citizens to resist conscription for World War II, Houde's popularity did not cease, and he returned to power for another decade. With the war, the economy picked up again and by this time Montréal had forty nightclubs and lounge bars, whose lavish floor shows, big bands and visiting entertainers – including Harlem jazz acts at the famous Rockhead's Paradise – pulled in crowds until dawn.

The pace only let up when Pacifique "Pax" Plante became head of the **Morality Squad** in 1946. Whereas his predecessors had pretty much gone along with the times, organizing sham raids and scaring no one, Plante surprised everyone by shutting down the gambling joints and whorehouses virtually overnight. But rather than receive praise, he was ousted eighteen months later by the new chief of police, and the city roared back to life. It wasn't until 1950 that outraged citizens finally sparked a four-year-long judicial inquiry into corruption and other matters, and on the strength of its damning report, prosecuting lawyer **Jean Drapeau** won a landslide victory in the October 1954 race for mayor with his promise to clean up Canada's wide-open city.

The Drapeau years and the Quiet Revolution

Drapeau's reforming zeal did not sit well with the premier of Québec, **Maurice Duplessis**, who used his organizational might to fix the 1957 election against him. It was hardly a stretch for Duplessis, who had the support of both the Anglophone business elite and the clergy. Rural Québec at this time was almost a feudal state, held under the thrall of both the clergy and the State, and despite their demographic strength Francophones continued to be ill-paid and badly housed in comparison to their Anglo counterparts. Frustrated by this disparity, a French-speaking middle class began articulating the workforce's grievances, leading to the so-called **Quiet Revolution** that began in 1960. Spurred on by the provincial government under the leadership of **Jean Lesage** and his Liberal Party of Québec, the local government took control of welfare, health and education from the Church and, under the slogan "*Maîtres chez-nous*" (Masters of our own house), established state-owned industries that kick-stared the development of a **Francophone business class**.

In 1960, Drapeau returned to power as well, and set about attending to his legacy: in large part, changing Montréal's physical appearance during his next 26 years as mayor. He, like Camillien Houde before him, is remembered for the megaprojects bestowed on the city, and on his watch Place Ville Marie, the Underground City, Place des Arts and the **Métro system** were all created. The first underground trains began running in 1966, just in time for the hugely successful 1967 Universal Exposition – better known as **Expo '67** – a world fair that attracted 50 million guests and catapulted the city to international status.

It was during this event that Charles de Gaulle made his famous **"Vive le Québec libre!"** speech from the balcony of the Hôtel de Ville, echoing the sentiments of nationalists who, woken by the social and cultural possibilities of the Quiet Revolution, were intent on making political results as well. Despite inroads into the corridors of real power, many still felt that it was Montréal's Anglophones who were benefiting from the prosperity of the boom that accompanied the Expo and the city's rapid expansion, and beneath the smooth surface Francophone frustrations were reaching dangerous levels.

The crisis peaked in October 1970, when the radical **Front de Libération du Québec** (FLQ) kidnapped the British trade commissioner, James Cross, and then a Québec cabinet minister, Pierre Laporte. As ransom, the FLQ demanded the publication of the FLQ manifesto, the transportation to Cuba of 25 FLQ prisoners awaiting trial for acts of violence, and $500,000 in gold bullion. Prime Minister **Pierre Trudeau** responded with the War Measures Act, suspending civil liberties and putting troops on the streets of Montréal. The following day, Laporte's body was found in the trunk of a car. By December, the so-called October Crisis was over: Cross had been released, and his captors and Laporte's murderers arrested. But the reverberations shook the nation.

At last recognizing the need to redress the country's social imbalances, the federal government poured money into countrywide schemes to promote French-Canadian culture, while in Montréal, Drapeau funnelled money into the last of his grand projects – hosting the **1976 Summer Olympics**.

The ongoing threat of Separatism

Francophone discontent was alleviated by the provincial election of **René Lévesque** and his Parti Québécois in 1976 and the consequent language law – the Charte de la langue française, better known as **Bill 101** – enacted the following year. It established French as the province's official language, making it a compulsory part of the school curriculum and banning English-only signs on business premises; any signs had to be bilingual, with the French printed twice as large as the English. Anglophones promptly began an **exodus** in the tens of thousands from Montréal. The shift westward to Toronto included over a hundred companies, several head offices and a massive amount of capital, and provoked a steep decline in housing prices, a halt on construction work and the withdrawal of investment.

For Québec to shape its own future, many nationalists felt the province needed control over laws and taxes, although they wanted to maintain an economic association with Canada. In 1980, a **referendum on sovereignty association** was held, but still reeling from the terrorist activities of the FLQ and scared that separatism would leave Québec economically adrift, the 6.5-million population voted 60/40 against. Canadian Prime Minister Trudeau then set about repatriating the country's **Constitution** in the autumn of 1981. Québec was prepared to contest the agreement with the support of other provincial leaders, but was spectacularly denied the opportunity to do so when Trudeau called a late-night meeting on the issue and did not invite Lévesque to the table. "The night of the long knives", as the event became known, wound up imposing a Constitution on the province that placed its language rights in jeopardy and removed its veto power over constitutional amendments. Accordingly, the provincial government refused to sign it – and still hasn't to this day.

In October 1993, Québec's displeasure with federalism was evident in the election of Lucien Bouchard's Bloc Québécois to the vastly ironic status of Her Majesty's Loyal Opposition in Ottawa. The cause received added support in 1994 when the Parti Québécois was returned to provincial power after vowing to hold a **provincewide referendum** on separation from Canada. The referendum was held a year later and the vote was so close – the province opted to remain a part of Canada by a margin of less than one per-cent – that calls immediately arose for a third referendum (prompting pundits to refer to the process as the "neverendum").

Contemporary Montréal

Political uncertainty and continuing tensions, combined with a Canada-wide economic recession, had Montréal on shaky ground in the mid-1990s. After the 1995 referendum, however, a tacit truce was made on the issue of separation. The communal bonds between Québécois were further strengthened by the shared adversity of the **ice storm** of 1998, which plunged pockets of the province into darkness for days after torrents of icy rain downed power lines and left 1.4 million without electricity – some for weeks on end. The ice storm's impact on Montréal's green spaces was enormous, and most pronounced on the mountain, where some 80,000 trees were damaged.

The city's physical appearance has changed in other ways in the past few years, with a good deal of rejuvenation on the city's commercial streets. Boarded-up shops that lined rue Ste-Catherine, for example, in the mid-1990s have been re-opened and do bustling business nowadays. As well, derelict pockets on the edges of downtown and Vieux-Montréal have been renovated to house the growing multimedia industry, just one element of the city's transition to a new economy. This restored economic confidence, along with a more stable political climate – seemingly more amity than enmity between Francophones increasingly confident with their lot and Anglophones who have remained and adjusted to the turbulence and change – is leading Montréal's resurgence in the twenty-first century.

Books

The listings below represent a highly selective reading list on Montréal, with a couple of broader Québec-specific books thrown in. Wherever possible, they've been listed by their most recent edition and most accessible publisher; many should be readily available in Canada, the US and the UK. If they can't be found in bookstores, try to order through the publisher, or online from Montréal bookstores (see p.196). Out-of-print titles are indicated by o/p.

History, society and politics

Lucien Bouchard, *On the Record* (Stoddart, Canada). A recording of the sovereignty movement's *raison d'être*, written by one of its most charismatic leaders; so persuasive you may wish to join up – that is, until you read Lawrence Martin's *The Antagonist* (see opposite).

Edgar Andrew Collard, *Montreal Yesterdays* (Longmans, Canada, o/p). Collard's light-hearted tomes often blend momentous stories with quirky anecdotes, and this volume, which combines a chapter on Mark Twain's visit to the *Windsor Hotel* with tales of haunted houses and reclusive hermits, is no exception.

John A. Dickinson and Brian Young, *A Short History of*

Quebec (McGill-Queen's University Press, Canada). Though not especially short, this book is nonetheless a readable trawl through the province's social, economic, governmental, cultural and religious aspects with loads of suggestions for further reading.

John Gilmore, *Who's Who of Jazz in Montreal* (Vehicule Press, Canada). A handbook for jazz aficionados with hundreds of biographies of musicians that worked in the city from the dawn of the jazz era to 1970, including home-grown talents like Oscar Peterson and Americans like Louis Metcalfe and Slap Rags White.

Lawrence Martin, *The Antagonist* (Viking, Canada). Martin's excellent biographies of influential Canadian politicians generally hinge on a controversial hypothesis; here he psychoanalyses Separatist leader Lucien Bouchard as having "esthetic character disorder" – pyschobabble for highly unstable.

Jennifer Robinson (ed), *Montreal's Century* (Éditions du Trécarré, Canada). A good potted history of twentieth-century Montréal with essays on city life, politics and sports supplemented by scads of colour photographs from both the *Montreal Gazette* and *Journal de Montréal*'s archives.

William Weintraub, *City Unique* (McClelland and Stewart, Canada). This riveting narrative of the city in the 1940s and 1950s is full of salacious stories of corruption, sex and boozing, with an especially juicy section on the stripteaser Lili St-Cyr.

Architecture and photography

Sandra Cohen-Rose, *Northern Deco – Art Deco Architecture in Montreal* (Corona, Canada). This glossy pictorial study beautifully captures the city's finest Art Deco buildings, including the interior of the private Maison Cormier (see p.61).

Isabelle Gournay and France Vanlaethem, *Montréal Metropolis* (Stoddart, Canada). The definitive analysis of Montréal's architectural evolution from 1880 to 1930, complete with a studied collection of black-and-white photographs and layout plans.

Phyllis Lambert & Alan Stewart, *Opening the Gates of Eighteenth Century Montreal* (Canadian Centre for Architecture, Canada). A thorough, if academic, volume documenting the impact of Vieux-Montréal's fortifications on urban planning.

Jean-Claude Marsan, *Montreal in Evolution* (McGill-Queen's University Press, Canada). This analysis of Montréal's architectural trends and urban planning motifs spans three centuries and culminates with an exhaustive look at the orchestration of Expo '67.

Jean–Eudes Schurr and Louise Larivière (eds), *Montréal Métropole* (Aux Yeux du Monde, Canada). A coffee-table book showcasing evocative photographs of the city taken by thirty photojournalists during a three-day blitz in the autumn of 1999.

Impressions, travel and specific guides

Nick Auf der Maur, *Nick: A Life* (Vehicule Press, Canada). This regaling collection of works by the *Montreal Gazette*'s most illustrious columnist is as much about the late Auf der Maur's boisterous life as it is about Montréal.

Joe Fiorito, *Tango on the Main* (Nuage Editions, Canada). Winner of the 1996 National Newspaper Award, Fiorito's columns about the city's people, places and things make great, if sentimental, reading.

Kirk Johnson and David Widgington, *Montréal Up Close* (Cumulus Press, Canada). Two great walking tours through the city that give the low-down on every gargoyle, frieze and bas-relief carving throughout Vieux-Montréal and downtown; comes with a handy fold-out map.

Leif R. Montin, *Get Outta Town* (No Fixed Address Publications, Canada). A terrific day-trip guide to 52 attractions within driving distance of Montréal.

John Symon, *The Lobster Kids' Guide to Exploring Montréal* (Lobster Press, Canada). A comprehensive guide to kids' activities around and outside the city with listings of child-friendly restaurants, playlands, and the like.

Fiction

Yves Beauchemin, *The Alley Cat* (McClelland and Stewart, Canada). An engaging story centred on the *Binerie* restaurant (see p.132) and owner Florent Boissonneault's struggles to keep the place and his personal life afloat while one sinister Egon Ratablavasky strives to bring him down.

Roch Carrier, *The Hockey Sweater* (Tundra Books, Canada). Every kid in Québec has read this story about a boy who longs for a Montréal Canadiens hockey jersey but gets a Toronto Maple Leafs instead, much to the scorn of his fellow shinny players. A must if you have children in tow.

Leonard Cohen, *The Favourite Game* (McClelland and Stewart, Canada). Songwriter Cohen's debut novel chronicles the escapades of the irresistible Lawrence Beavman through the streets, sheets and bars of Montréal and New York City, in punchy and lyrical prose.

John Farrow, *City of Ice* (HarperCollins, Canada). A tense thriller about the city's biker gangs with all the criminal activity you'd expect – CIA plants, crooked cops, dodgy lawyers and the like – set during a bone-chilling Montréal winter.

Charles Foran, *Butterfly Lovers* (HarperCollins, Canada). Ailing and embittered David LeClair's meandering narrative of self-discovery starts and ends in a Mile End Bar called Remys, but spends a good chunk in China, where his relationship with a married woman prompts a profound metamorphosis.

Hugh McLellan *Two Solitudes* (McClelland and Stewart, Canada). The story of Canada's French–English relations is mapped onto the equally epic but more poignant narrative of Paul Tallard's struggles as the son of a French-Canadian father and Irish mother; an even-handed and enlightening read.

Kathy Reich *Déjà Dead* (Pocket Books, US). A chilling forensic crime novel about one woman's attempts to track down a serial killer fond of dismembering women's bodies and stashing them about town; a serious page-turner.

Mordechai Richler, *Barney's Version* (Alfred A. Knopf, Canada/Washington Square Press, US/Random House, UK); *The Apprenticeship of Duddy Kravitz* (McClelland and Stewart, Canada/Washington Square Press, US). Richler's latest novel, *Barney's Version*, is as much about himself as it is Barney Panofsky, his affable protagonist whose passions, hockey and Anglophone rights in Montréal, often get side-tracked by his fondness for women. His debut, *The Apprenticeship of Duddy Kravitz*, introduced Canadian Lit's greatest scoundrel, whose capers are told here in witty style.

Gabrielle Roy, *The Tin Flute* (McClelland and Stewart, Canada). The houses crammed together on rue St-Augustin with their backs to the railway tracks (see p.104) inspired this touching novel about an impoverished family's struggles during World War II.

Michel Tremblay, *The Fat Woman Next Door is Pregnant* (Talonbooks, Canada). A great title for a wonderful book chronicling the events of one day, May 2, 1942, in the life of a Plateau family; no one captures the ethos of working-class Francophone Montréal better.

French language and glossary

No amount of French training will prepare you for the vagaries of the Québécois dialect – even the French have difficulty understanding the slurring drawl that's spoken at lightning speed. Don't be embarrassed to ask people to repeat themselves more slowly (*s'il vous plaît, répétez plus lentement*), or just ask if they speak English (*parlez-vous anglais?*); most in Montréal do and they won't be offended at your asking. With **pronunciation** there's little point trying to mimic the local dialect – just stick to the classic French rules. Consonants at the ends of words are usually silent and at other times are much like English, except that **ch** is always sh, **ç** is s, **h** is silent, **th** is the same as t, **ll** is like the y in yes and **r** is growled. Vowelwise, **é** resembles a long a, **è** is eh and **a** is ah. If you plan on spending much time in the province, consider the pocket-size **Rough Guide to French** (Penguin, UK/US), in a handy A–Z format.

FRENCH LANGUAGE

Basics

Good morning/Hello	*Bonjour*
Good evening	*Bonsoir*
Good night	*Bonne nuit*
Goodbye	*Au revoir*
Yes	*Oui*
No	*Non*
Please	*S'il vous/te plaît*
Thank you	*Merci*
You're welcome	*Bienvenu/de rien*
OK	*D'accord*
How are you?	*Comment allez-vous?/Ça va?*
Fine, thanks	*Très bien, merci*
Do you speak English?	*Parlez-vous anglais?*
I don't speak French	*Je ne parle pas français*
I don't understand	*Je ne comprends pas*
Excuse me	*Je m'excuse*
Sorry	*Pardon/désolé(e)*
Today	*Aujourd'hui*
Tomorrow	*Demain*
Yesterday	*Hier*
Morning	*Dans le matin*
Afternoon	*Dans l'après-midi*
Evening	*Dans le soir*
Here/there	*Ici/là*
With/without	*Avec/sans*
Near/far	*Près (pas loin)/loin*
More/less	*Plus/moins*

Questions

Where?	*Où?*
When?	*Quand?*

What? (what is it?)	*Quoi? (qu'est-ce que c'est?)*
How much/many?	*Combien?*
Why?	*Pourquoi?*
What time is it?	*Quelle heure est-il?*
What time does it open?	*À quelle heure ça ouvre?*
How much does it cost?	*Combien cela coûte-t-il?*

Numbers

1	*un/une*	14	*quatorze*
2	*deux*	15	*quinze*
3	*trois*	16	*seize*
4	*quatre*	17	*dix-sept*
5	*cinq*	18	*dix-huit*
6	*six*	19	*dix-neuf*
7	*sept*	20	*vingt*
8	*huit*	21	*vingt-et-un*
9	*neuf*	100	*cent*
10	*dix*	110	*cent-dix*
11	*onze*	500	*cinq cents*
12	*douze*	1000	*mille*
13	*treize*	2000	*deux milles*

Accommodation and transport

room with a double bed	*chambre avec un lit double*
with a shower/bath	*avec douche/salle de bain*
for one/two/three nights	*pour une/deux/trois nuit(s)*
for one/two weeks	*pour une/deux semaine(s)*
How much is it?	*C'est combien?*
Can I see it?	*Est-ce que je peux la voir?*
Do you have anything cheaper?	*Avez-vous quelque chose de moins cher?*
Is breakfast included?	*Est-ce que le petit-déjeuner est compris?*

Continues over

Aeroplane	*Avion*
Bus	*Autobus*
Train	*Train*
Car	*Voiture*
Taxi	*Taxi*
Bicycle	*Vélo*
Ferry	*Traversier*
Bus station	*Terminus d'autobus/gare des autobuses*
Railway station	*Gare centrale*
Ferry terminal	*Le quai du traversier*
I'd like a ticket to . . .	*J'aimerais un billet pour . . .*
One-way/return	*Aller simple/aller-retour*

Eating and drinking

Do you have an English menu?	*Avez-vous un menu en anglais?*
Breakfast	*Petit déjeuner/déjeuner*
Lunch	*Déjeuner/dîner*
Dinner	*Dîner/souper*
Appetizer	*Entrée*
Main course	*Plat principal*
Dessert	*Dessert*
Set menu	*Table d'hôte*
Sugar	*Sucre*
Milk	*Lait*
Butter	*Beurre*
Salt	*Sel*
Pepper	*Poivre*

Bread	*Pain*
Coffee	*Café*
Tea	*Thé*
Eggs	*Oeufs*
Sausages	*Saucissons*
Bacon	*Bacon*
Meat pie	*Tourtière*
Baked beans	*Fèves au lard*
Shrimp	*Crevettes*
Mussels	*Moules*
Fish	*Poisson*
Chicken	*Poulet*
Duck	*Canard*
Pork	*Porc*
Ham	*Jambon*
Beef	*Bœuf*
Veal	*Veau*
Pasta	*Pâtes*
Potato	*Patate*
Fries	*Frites*
Apple	*Pomme*
Lemon	*Citron*
Salad	*Salade*
Lettuce	*Laitue*
Beer	*Bière*
White wine	*Vin blanc*
Red wine	*Vin rouge*
Check, please	*L'addition s'il vous plaît*

Index

A

Abbaye Cistercienne d'Oka 280
Abbaye St-Benoît-du-Lac......290–291
Accommodation 109–124
  bed and breakfasts 119–121
  gay and lesbian 216–218
  hostels 122–124
  hotels 109–119
  price codes 110
  university residences 122–124
airlines 242
airports...6–7
Aldred Building.................................21
antique shops.................104, 195–196
area codes 242
Arrival 6–9
Atwater Market.............103–104, 208
Automatistes, Les.............49–50, 63
autoroutes 8–9
avenue du Mont-Royal 69
avenue du Parc 73
avenue Duluth 70
avenue Fairmount...........................73
avenue Laurier 73
avenue McGill College 44–45

B

B&Bs 119–121
La Baie.............................46–47, 204
banks..242

Banque de Montréal 20–21, 301
Bars.......................................156–168
  downtown/
    Golden Square Mile 159–162
  gay and lesbian 218–220
  Mile End/Outremont 167–168
  Plateau Mont-Royal 163–167
  Quartier Latin 162–163
  Vieux-Montréal 158–159
baseball 82, 222–223
Basilique Notre-Dame................21–23
Basilique-Cathédrale
    Marie-Reine-du-Monde 39–40
Bassin Bonsecours 34
Bay, The 46–47, 204
Beaver Lake 74
Bessette, Frère André...............77–79
Bibliothèque Nationale 53
biking 15, 226
Biodôme de Montréal.....................83
Biosphère................................93–94
boat cruises 36, 228
Books on Montréal............308–312
bookshops 196–199
Borduas, Paul-Émile 49–50, 63
Botanical Garden 83–88
boulevard St-Laurent 50, 71–72
Bourgeoys, Marguerite 31, 102–103
boxing 224
bus station 8
buses 16–17

C

Cafés 127–135
  downtown/Golden
    Square Mile 129–130
  Internet cafés 244
  Mile End/Outremont 134–135
  Plateau Mont-Royal 131–134
  Quartier Latin/The Village 130–131
  Vieux-Montréal 128–129
Canadian football 223
Cantons-de-l'Est 287–294
car rental 97
Centre de Design de l'UQAM 52
Centre Canadien
  d'Architecture 65–66
Centre d'Histoire de Montréal 33
Centre Eaton 45, 205
Centre iSci 35–36
Centre Molson 41, 179, 222
Champ de Mars 25–26
Chapelle de Notre-Dame-de-Bon-
  Secours 30–31
Château Dufresne 89–90
Château Ramezay, Musée du ... 27–28
chemin Olmsted 74–75
Children's attractions 229–234
Chinatown 51–52
Christ Church Cathedral 45–46
Cimetière Mont-Royal 75–76
Cimetière Notre-Dame-des-Neiges .. 76
cinemas 191–193
Circuit Gilles-Villeneuve 96, 237
Cirque du Soleil 188
City directory 242–246
classical music 183–185
clothing shops 199–204
Clubs 169–180
  clubs 169–180
  after hours 174
  comedy 174–175
  dance clubs 171–174
  gay and lesbian 218–220
  live music 176–180
  strip clubs 175
Complexe Desjardins 48–49

consulates 243
Cours Mont-Royal 42, 206
cross (Parc du Mont-Royal) 75, 299
cross-country skiing 224
Cuban Consulate 61
currency exchange 243
cycling 15, 226

D

dance 186–187
dentists 243
department stores 204–205
Directory 242–246
Dorval airport 6–7
Downtown Montréal 37–54
drinking .... see "bars"
driving 8–9

E

Eastern Townships 287–294
Eating .... see "cafés" and "restaurants"
Eaton Centre 45, 205
Écomusée du Fier Monde 53
Édifice Ernest-Cormier 24
Édifice Sun Life 39
Église St-Léon 99
Église St-Pierre-Apôtre 53–54
emergencies 243
ex-Centris 72, 192

F

Festivals 235–241
film 191–193
football 223
Fort de l'Île Ste-Hélène 94
Frère André 77–79

G

Galerie de l'UQAM 52
galleries 209
Gare Centrale 8
Gare Windsor 41
Gay and lesbian Montréal .. 214–220
  accommodation 216–218
  information and resources 214–215

INDEX

nightlife 218–220
saunas..................................217
Village, the 53–54, 214
getting around 13–17
glossary of French terms 314–317
Golden Square Mile 55–66
Grace Church..............................101
Grand Prix 96, 237
guided tours 14–15

H

Henry Birks and Sons 46
History of Montréal.............297–307
hockey 41, 222
holidays, public 245
hospitals.....................................244
hostels 122–124
Hôtel de Ville (Westmount) 100
Hôtel de Ville
   (Vieux-Montréal) 27
Hotels 109–119
   downtown 113–115
   Golden Square Mile 113–115
   Plateau Mont-Royal 117–119
   Quartier Latin 116–117
   Vieux-Montréal 110–112
   Village, The.................216–218

I

ice-hockey 41, 222
ice-skating 225
Île Notre-Dame 96–97
Île Ste-Hélène 92–96
Illuminated Crowd, The................44
iInformation..........................9–12
in-line skating 226–227
Insectarium................................87–88
Internet..........................10–11, 244

J

Jardin Botanique de
   Montréal........................83–88
Jardins des Floralies 97
jazz.....................176–178, 238
jet-boating 227

K

Kids' Montréal 229–234
Knowlton 288–289

L

Lac aux Castors 74
Lac Brome 288
Lachine 104–106
Lachine Canal 98, 302
Lachine Rapids 105
Laser Quest 231
Latin Quarter ....see "Quartier Latin"
laundry.....................................244
Laurentides (Laurentians)....278–286
left luggage 244
Lieu historique national du
   Commerce-de-la-
   Fourrure-à-Lachine 105–106
Lieu Historique Sir-
   George-Étienne-Cartier 28–29
Little Italy 154
Live music 176–180

M

Magog...........................289–292
mail 244
Main, The 71–72
Maison Cormier 61
Maison du Calvet 29–30, 112
Maison St-Gabriel................102–103
Maison Smith 75
Maisonneuve 88
malls.............................205–206
Marché Atwater 103–104, 208
Marché Bonsecours 30
Marché Jean-Talon 154, 208–209
McGill University 57–58
Métaforia Centre........................231
Métro 15–16
Mile End 72–73
Mirabel airport 7
Molson Centre 41, 179, 222
money exchange 243
Mont-Alta 283

Mont-Orford 290
Mont Royal 73–76
Mont St-Sauveur 282
Mont-Tremblant 285–286
Montréal Tower 82–83
Mount Royal Cemetery 75–76
Musée d'Archéologie et d'Histoire de
    Montréal 31–33
Musée d'Art Contemporain de
    Montréal 49–50
Musée des Arts Décoratifs 61
Musée des Beaux-Arts............60–64
Musée Marc-Aurèle Fortin 33
Musée McCord d'Histoire
    Canadienne.......................56–57
Musée Redpath 58–59
Musée Stewart 94–95
Museum of Fine Arts 60–64
music, classical 183–185
Music, live............................176–180

N

Nelson Monument 25
newspapers 12
Nightlife................................169–180
North Hatley 292–294
Notre Dame Basilica................21–23

O

Oka 280–281
Old Courthouse 24
Old Customs House................32–33
Old Montréal 18–33
Old Port..................................33–36
Olympic Stadium 81–83, 180, 223
opera 183–185
Oratoire St-Joseph..................76–79
Outdoor activities 221–228
Outremont 73

P

Palais de Justice 24
Palais des Congrès 49
Parc d'Oka............................280–281
Parc des Écluses 34

Parc du Mont-Orford 290
Parc du Mont-Royal 73–75
Parc Jean-Drapeau 91–97
Parc Lafontaine 70
Parc Olympique 81–83
Performing arts....................181–190
pharmacies 244
Piggery, The 293
Place d'Armes 20
Place d'Youville 33
Place des Arts 48–49, 182
Place du Canada 40–41
Place Émilie-Gamelin 53
Place Jacques-Cartier 24–25
Place Vauquelin 25
Place Ville Marie 42–44
Planétarium de Montréal...............231
Plateau Mont-Royal 67–72
Pointe St-Charles 101–103
Pointe-à-Callière........................31–33
police 243, 244
post offices 244
Public transport 13–17

Q

Quai de l'Horloge 36
Quai King-Edward 35
Quartier Latin 52–53
Québec City 249–277
    accommodation...................253–256
    arrival 251–252
    bars 275–277
    Basilique Notre-Dame
        de Québec 263–264
    Batterie Royal 262
    Breakneck Stairs 260, 263
    cafés 272–274
    Château Frontenac 254, 258
    Citadelle.............................268
    clubs 275–277
    Couvent des Ursulines 266
    Église Notre-Dame-des-Victoires 261
    escalier casse-cou 260,263
    festivals 276
    funicular 260, 263
    getting around 253

Grande-Allée 269
history 250–251
hostels 255–256
Hôtel du Parlement 269
hotels 253–255
information.................................252
Maison Jacquet 266
Maison Kent 267
Martello Tower 269
Musée d'Art Inuit Brousseau 267
Musée de l'Amérique Française ..265
Musée de la Civilisation 262
Musée du Québec 270–271
National Assembly 269
National Battlefields Park 268–269
Parc de l'Esplanade 267
Parc des Champs-de-Bataille..268–269
Parc Montmorency 260
Parliament Buildings...................269
Place d'Armes 258–259
Place de Paris 262
Place Royale 260–261
Plaines d'Abraham 268–269, 300
Porte St-Louis 267
Quartier du Petit-Champlain ..262–263
restaurants 272–274
rue du Petit-Champlain 263
rue St-Louis 266–267
Séminaire de Québec..................264
Ursuline Convent 266
Vieux-Port de Québec 262

Quartier Latin/The Village 144–146
Vieux-Montréal......................138–139
ridesharing 245
Riopelle, Jean-Paul..................50, 63
rollerblading 226–227
La Ronde 95–96
rue le Royer 24
rue Peel 42
rue Prince-Arthur 71
rue St-Denis 52–53, 70
rue St-Paul 29–30
rue St-Sulpice...........................23–24
rue St-Viateur 73
rue Ste-Catherine 38
rue Sherbrooke 59
Russian Consulate 61

R

radio..12
rape crisis...................................245
Ravenscrag..................................60
Redpath Museum.....................58–59
Restaurants 135–155
by cuisine....................136–137
Chinatown 143–144
downtown/
  Golden Square Mile 139–143
Little Italy 154
Mile End/Outremont 153–155
Plateau Mont-Royal 146–153
price codes 135

S

St-Eustache 279–280
St George's Anglican Church 41
St-Henri 103–104
St James United Church 47
St Joseph's Oratory 76–79
St-Jovite.............................285–286
St Patrick's Basilica 47–48
St-Sauveur-des-Monts 281–283
Schwartz's 72, 133–134
Séminaire de St-Sulpice 23
Shaughnessy House 66
Shopping 194–213
antiques 195–196
books..........................196–199
clothing 199–204
department stores 204–205
food and drink 206–209
galleries 209
kids' 232–233
malls 205–206
markets 208–209
music 210–211
specialty shops 211–212
sporting goods 212–213
twentieth-century design 195–196
Sir George-Étienne
  Cartier monument 74
skateboarding 226–227

skating rinks 225
skiing, cross-country 224
skiing, downhill 279,
.........................282–283, 285, 290
snowshoeing 224
sporting-goods shops 212–213
Sports 221–228
Square Dorchester 39
Square Phillips 46–47
Square St-Louis 71
Stade Olympique 81–83, 180, 223
STCUM 13
Stewart Museum 94–95
strip clubs 175
subway...................................15–16
Summit Park 101

T

Tam Tams......................................74
tax 245
taxis 17
telephones 245
television 12
theatre.................187–190, 289, 293
Théâtre de Verdure................70, 182
tickets 245–246

tipping 246
Todd, Frederick G. 77, 93, 269
Tour de l'Horloge 36
Tour de Montréal 82–83
tourist offices 9–12
tours...14–15
train station 8
Transport, public 13–17
travel agents.................................246

U

Underground City............................43
Université du Québec à Montréal 52
university residences 122–124

V

Val-David 283–285
Vieux-Montréal 18–33
Vieux-Port..............................33–36
Village, the 53–54, 214

W

Westmount 99–101
Westmount Square 99

Stay in touch with us!

ROUGH NEWS

THE ROUGH GUIDES

The view from Johannesburg
ARE WE IN AFRICA YET?

COLONIAL HONG KONG

RAINFOREST TOURISM

ROUGHNEWS is Rough Guides'
free newsletter.
In three issues a year we give you
news, travel issues, music reviews,
readers' letters and the latest
dispatches from authors on the road.

I would like to receive ROUGHNEWS: please put me on your free mailing list.

NAME ....

ADDRESS ....

Please clip or photocopy and send to: Rough Guides, 62-70 Shorts Gardens,
London WC2H 9AH, England

or Rough Guides, 375 Hudson Street, New York, NY 10014, USA.

ROUGH GUIDES: Travel

Amsterdam
Andalucia
Australia
Austria
Bali & Lombok
Barcelona
Belgium & Luxembourg
Belize
Berlin
Brazil
Britain
Brittany & Normandy
Bulgaria
California
Canada
Central America
Chile
China
Corfu & the Ionian Islands
Corsica
Costa Rica
Crete
Cyprus
Czech & Slovak Republics
Dodecanese
Dominican Republic
Egypt
England
Europe
Florida
France
French Hotels & Restaurants 1999
Germany
Goa
Greece

Greek Islands
Guatemala
Hawaii
Holland
Hong Kong & Macau
Hungary
India
Indonesia
Ireland
Israel & the Palestinian Territories
Italy
Jamaica
Japan
Jordan
Kenya
Laos
London
London Restaurants
Los Angeles
Malaysia, Singapore & Brunei
Mallorca & Menorca
Maya World
Mexico
Morocco
Moscow
Nepal
New England
New York
New Zealand
Norway
Pacific Northwest
Paris
Peru
Poland
Portugal
Prague

Provence & the Côte d'Azur
The Pyrenees
Romania
St Petersburg
San Francisco
Scandinavia
Scotland
Sicily
Singapore
South Africa
Southern India
Southwest USA
Spain
Sweden
Syria
Thailand
Trinidad & Tobago
Tunisia
Turkey
Tuscany & Umbria
USA
Venice
Vienna
Vietnam
Wales
Washington DC
West Africa
Zimbabwe & Botswana

THE ROUGH GUIDE TO

Canada

ROUGH GUIDES: Mini Guides, Travel Specials and Phrasebooks

MINI GUIDES
Antigua
Bangkok
Barbados
Big Island of Hawaii
Boston
Brussels
Budapest
Dublin
Edinburgh
Florence
Honolulu
Lisbon
London Restaurants
Madrid
Maui
Melbourne
New Orleans
St Lucia

Seattle
Sydney
Tokyo
Toronto

TRAVEL SPECIALS
First-Time Asia
First-Time Europe
More Women Travel

PHRASEBOOKS
Czech
Dutch
Egyptian Arabic
European
French

German
Greek
Hindi & Urdu
Hungarian
Indonesian
Italian
Japanese
Mandarin
  Chinese
Mexican
  Spanish
Polish
Portuguese
Russian
Spanish
Swahili
Thai
Turkish
Vietnamese

AVAILABLE AT ALL GOOD BOOKSHOPS

ROUGH GUIDES:
Reference and Music CDs

REFERENCE
Classical Music
Classical:
  100 Essential CDs
Drum'n'bass
House Music

World Music:
  100 Essential CDs
English Football
European Football
Internet
Millennium

ROUGH GUIDE
  MUSIC CDs
Music of the Andes
Australian
  Aboriginal
Brazilian Music
Cajun & Zydeco
Classic Jazz
Music of Colombia
Cuban Music
Eastern Europe
Music of Egypt
English Roots
  Music
Flamenco
India & Pakistan
Irish Music
Music of Japan
Kenya & Tanzania
Native American
North African
Music of Portugal

Jazz
Music USA
Opera
Opera:
  100 Essential CDs
Reggae
Rock
Rock:
  100 Essential CDs
Techno
World Music

Reggae
Salsa
Scottish Music
South African
  Music
Music of Spain
Tango
Tex-Mex
West African Music
World Music
World Music Vol 2
Music of Zimbabwe

AVAILABLE AT ALL GOOD BOOKSHOPS

Sorted

100 Essential CDs

Eight titles, one name

ROUGH GUIDES

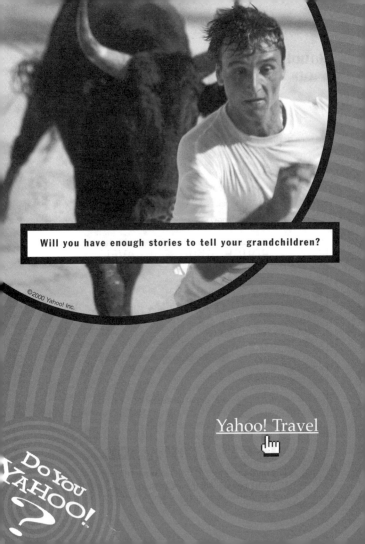

Will you have enough stories to tell your grandchildren?

©2000 Yahoo! Inc.

Yahoo! Travel

Do You
YAHOO!

Rough Guides
on the Web

www.travel.roughguides.com

We keep getting bigger and better! The Rough Guide to Travel Online
now covers more than 14,000 searchable locations. You're just a click
away from access to the most in-depth travel content, weekly
destination features, online reservation services, and an outspoken
community of fellow travelers. Whether you're looking for ideas for
your next holiday or you know exactly where you're going, join us online.

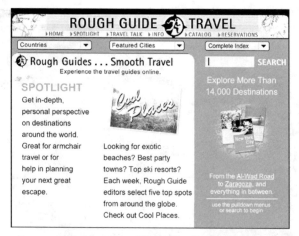

You can also find us on Yahoo!® Travel (http://travel.yahoo.com) and
Microsoft Expedia® UK (http://www.expediauk.com).

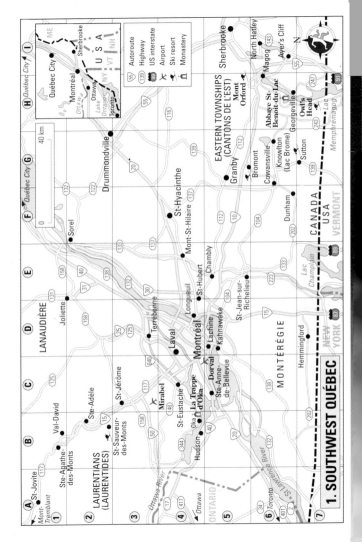

1. SOUTHWEST QUÉBEC

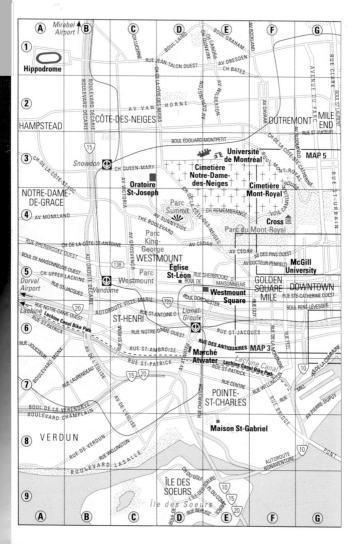

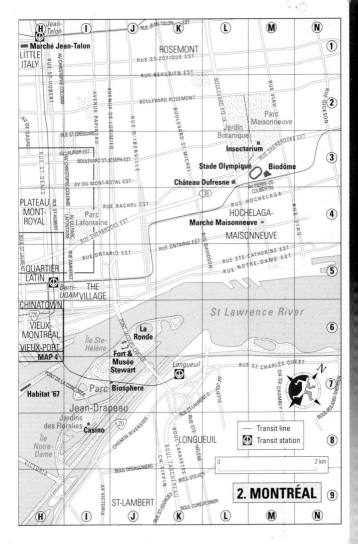

2. MONTRÉAL

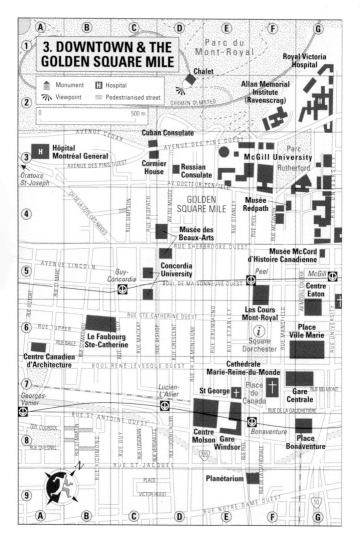

3. DOWNTOWN & THE GOLDEN SQUARE MILE

Monument ☖   **Hospital** Ⓗ
Viewpoint 🕉   **Pedestrianised street** ▬

0 ———————— 500 m

Parc du Mont-Royal

Chalet

Royal Victoria Hospital

Allan Memorial Institute (Ravenscrag)

CHEMIN OLMSTED

AVENUE CEDAR

Cuban Consulate

AVENUE DES PINS OUEST

Hôpital Montréal General

Cormier House

Russian Consulate

McGill University

Parc Rutherford

AVENUE DES PINS OUEST

Oratoire St-Joseph

CH DE LA CÔTE DES NEIGES

AV DOCTEUR PENFIELD

GOLDEN SQUARE MILE

Musée Redpath

RUE SIMPSON

RUE REDPATH

AV DU MUSÉE

RUE STANLEY

RUE PEEL

RUE McTAVISH

RUE UNIVERSITY

Musée des Beaux-Arts

RUE SHERBROOKE OUEST

Musée McCord d'Histoire Canadienne

AVENUE LINCOLN

Concordia University

Guy-Concordia

Peel

McGill

RUE ST-MARC

BOUL DE MAISONNEUVE OUEST

McGILL COLLEGE

Centre Eaton

RUE GUY

RUE STE-CATHERINE OUEST

Les Cours Mont-Royal

Place Ville Marie

RUE UNIVERSITY

RUE TUPPER

RUE MACKAY

RUE BISHOP

RUE CRESCENT

RUE DE LA MONTAGNE

RUE DRUMMOND

RUE STANLEY

RUE MANSFIELD

RUE BAILE

Le Faubourg Ste-Catherine

ⓘ Square Dorchester

Centre Canadien d'Architecture

BOUL RENÉ-LÉVESQUE OUEST

Cathédrale Marie-Reine-du-Monde

Gare Centrale

RUE BELMONT

Georges-Vanier

Lucien-L'Allier

St George ✝

Place du Canada

✝

Gare Centrale

RUE ST-ANTOINE OUEST

Bonaventure

RUE DE LA GAUCHETIÈRE

TER COURSOL

RUE ST-MARTIN

RUE RICHMOND

RUE LUSIGNAN

RUE VERSAILLES

RUE LUCIEN-L'ALLIER

Centre Molson

Gare Windsor

Bonaventure

RUE PEEL

RUE DE LA CATHÉDRALE

Place Bonaventure

RUE QUESNEL

720

RUE ST-JACQUES

Planétarium

PLACE VICTOR-HUGO

10

RUE NOTRE-DAME OUEST

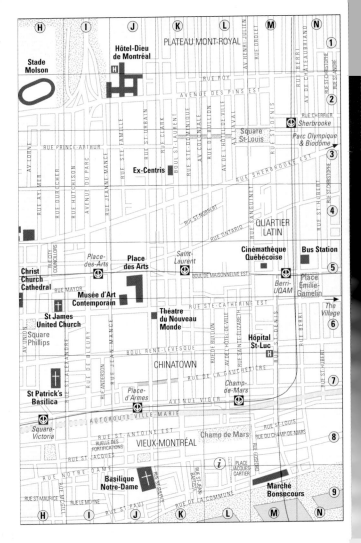

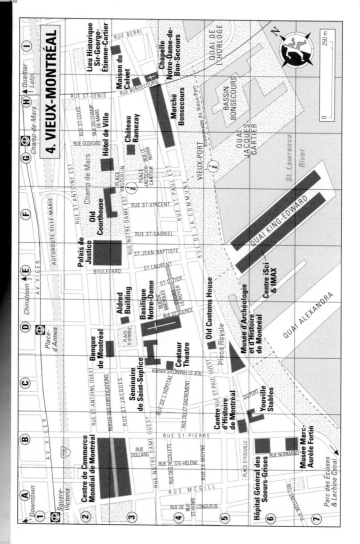